EVERYDAY
BREADS

Publications International, Ltd.

Copyright © 2024 Publications International, Ltd.

All rights reserved. This publication may not be reproduced or quoted in whole or in part by any means whatsoever without written permission from:

Louis Weber, CEO
Publications International, Ltd.
8140 Lehigh Ave
Morton Grove, IL 60053

Permission is never granted for commercial purposes.

Photographs on front cover and pages 124, 151 and 173 copyright © Shutterstock.com.

Pictured on the front cover: Quick Honey Butter Rolls *(page 125)*.

Pictured on the back cover *(clockwise from top left):* Blueberry Muffins *(page 64),* Zucchini Bread *(page 24),* Barbecue Chicken Flatbread *(page 146)* and Quick Casserole Bread *(page 108).*

ISBN: 978-1-63938-550-8

Manufactured in China.

8 7 6 5 4 3 2 1

Microwave Cooking: Microwave ovens vary in wattage. Use the cooking times as guidelines and check for doneness before adding more time.

WARNING: Food preparation, baking and cooking involve inherent dangers: misuse of electric products, sharp electric tools, boiling water, hot stoves, allergic reactions, foodborne illnesses and the like, pose numerous potential risks. Publications International, Ltd. (PIL) assumes no responsibility or liability for any damages you may experience as a result of following recipes, instructions, tips or advice in this publication.

While we hope this publication helps you find new ways to eat delicious foods, you may not always achieve the results desired due to variations in ingredients, cooking temperatures, typos, errors, omissions or individual cooking abilities.

Let's get social!
@Publications_International
@PublicationsInternational
www.pilbooks.com

TABLE OF CONTENTS

Quick Breads — 4

Biscuits — 34

Muffins — 54

Scones — 84

Yeast Breads — 98

Rolls & Buns — 124

Pizzas & Flatbreads — 142

Shortcut Breads — 174

Index — 188

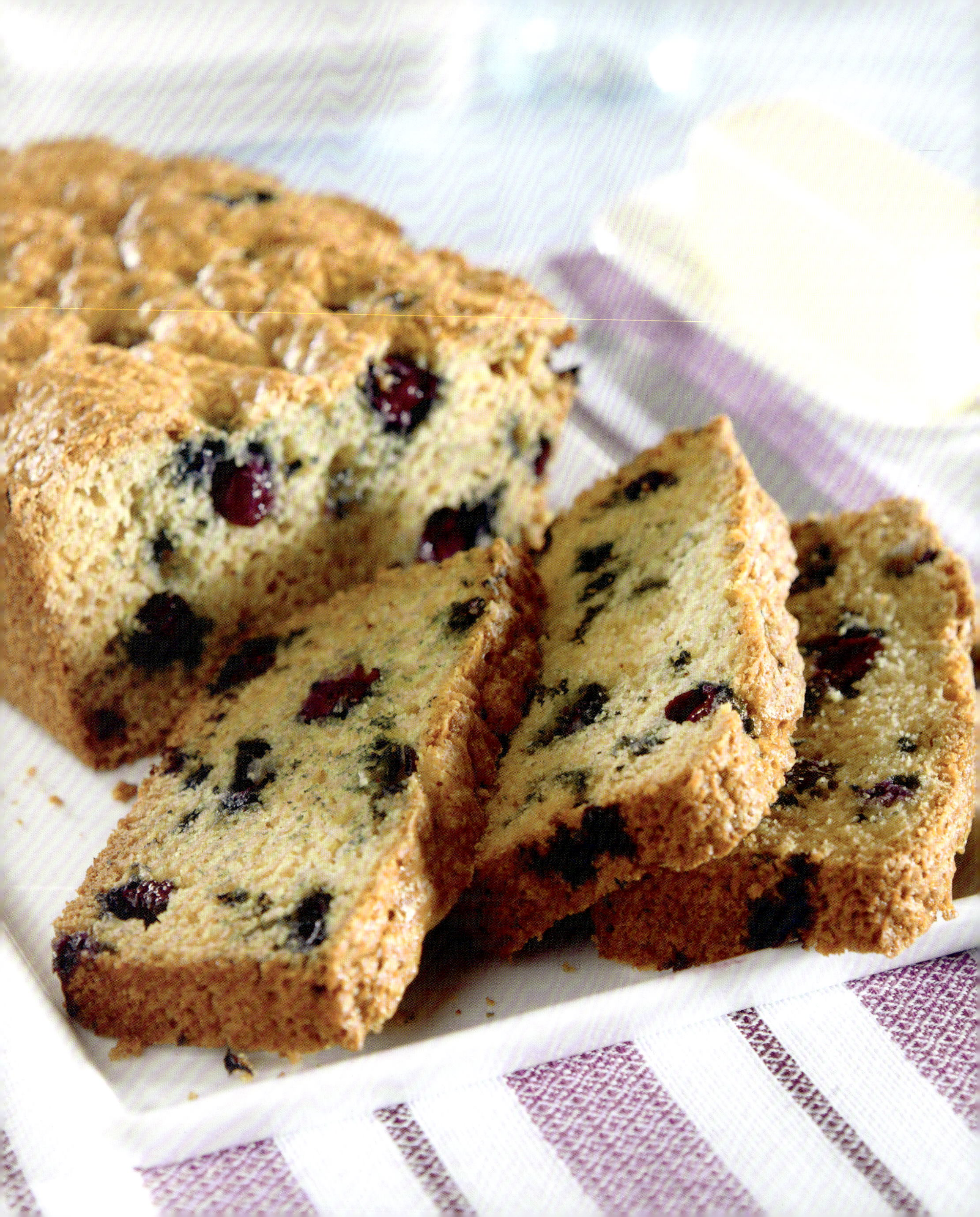

QUICK BREADS

Blueberry Hill Bread
MAKES 1 LOAF

- 2 cups all-purpose flour
- ¾ cup packed brown sugar
- 2 teaspoons baking powder
- 1 teaspoon baking soda
- 1 teaspoon salt
- ½ teaspoon ground nutmeg
- ¾ cup buttermilk
- 1 egg
- ¼ cup vegetable oil or melted butter
- 1 cup fresh or thawed frozen blueberries

1. Preheat oven to 350°F. Spray 8×4-inch loaf pan with nonstick cooking spray.

2. Combine flour, brown sugar, baking powder, baking soda, salt and nutmeg in food processor; process 5 seconds to blend. Whisk buttermilk, egg and oil in medium bowl until blended. Pour over flour mixture; process 5 to 10 seconds or just until dry ingredients are moistened. (Do not overprocess; batter should be lumpy.)

3. Sprinkle blueberries over batter; pulse several times just to incorporate blueberries into batter. (Batter will be stiff.) Pour batter into prepared pan.

4. Bake 50 to 60 minutes or until toothpick inserted in center comes out clean. Cool in pan 15 minutes; remove to wire rack to cool completely.

Simple Golden Corn Bread

MAKES 9 TO 12 SERVINGS

1¼ cups all-purpose flour
¾ cup yellow cornmeal
⅓ cup sugar
2 teaspoons baking powder
1 teaspoon salt
1¼ cups whole milk
¼ cup (½ stick) butter, melted
1 egg
Honey Butter (recipe follows, optional)

1. Preheat oven to 400°F. Spray 8-inch square baking pan with nonstick cooking spray.

2. Combine flour, cornmeal, sugar, baking powder and salt in large bowl; mix well. Whisk milk, butter and egg in medium bowl until well blended. Add to flour mixture; stir just until dry ingredients are moistened. Pour batter into prepared pan.

3. Bake 25 minutes or until golden brown and toothpick inserted into center comes out clean.

4. Prepare Honey Butter, if desired. Serve with corn bread.

HONEY BUTTER Beat 6 tablespoons (¾ stick) softened butter and ¼ cup honey in medium bowl with electric mixer at medium-high speed until light and creamy.

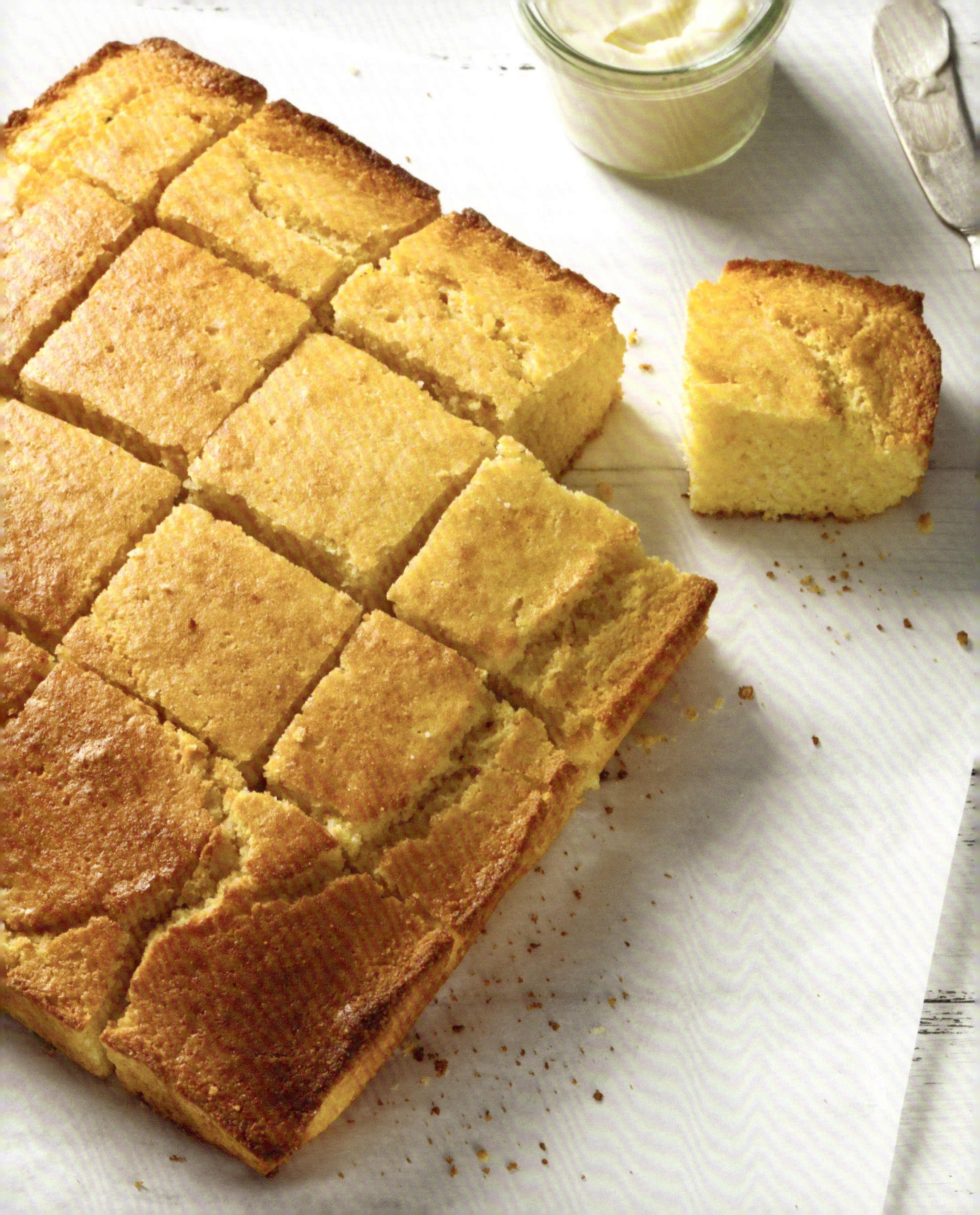

Peanut Butter Chocolate Chip Bread

MAKES 1 LOAF

- 1½ cups all-purpose flour
- 2 teaspoons baking powder
- ¼ teaspoon salt
- ¼ teaspoon ground cinnamon
- ¼ teaspoon ground nutmeg
- ⅔ cup milk
- 1 teaspoon vanilla
- ¾ cup packed dark brown sugar
- ½ cup vegetable oil
- ½ cup creamy peanut butter
- 2 eggs
- 1 cup finely chopped roasted salted peanuts
- 1 cup mini semisweet chocolate chips

1. Preheat oven to 350°F. Spray 9×5-inch loaf pan with nonstick cooking spray or line with parchment paper.

2. Combine flour, baking powder, salt, cinnamon and nutmeg in medium bowl; mix well. Combine milk and vanilla in small bowl.

3. Beat brown sugar, oil and peanut butter in large bowl until well blended. Add eggs, one at a time; beat until blended. Alternately add flour mixture and milk mixture in two additions, stirring just until blended. Stir in peanuts and chocolate chips. Pour batter into prepared pan.

4. Bake about 1 hour or until toothpick inserted into center comes out clean. Cool in pan 15 minutes; remove to wire rack to cool completely.

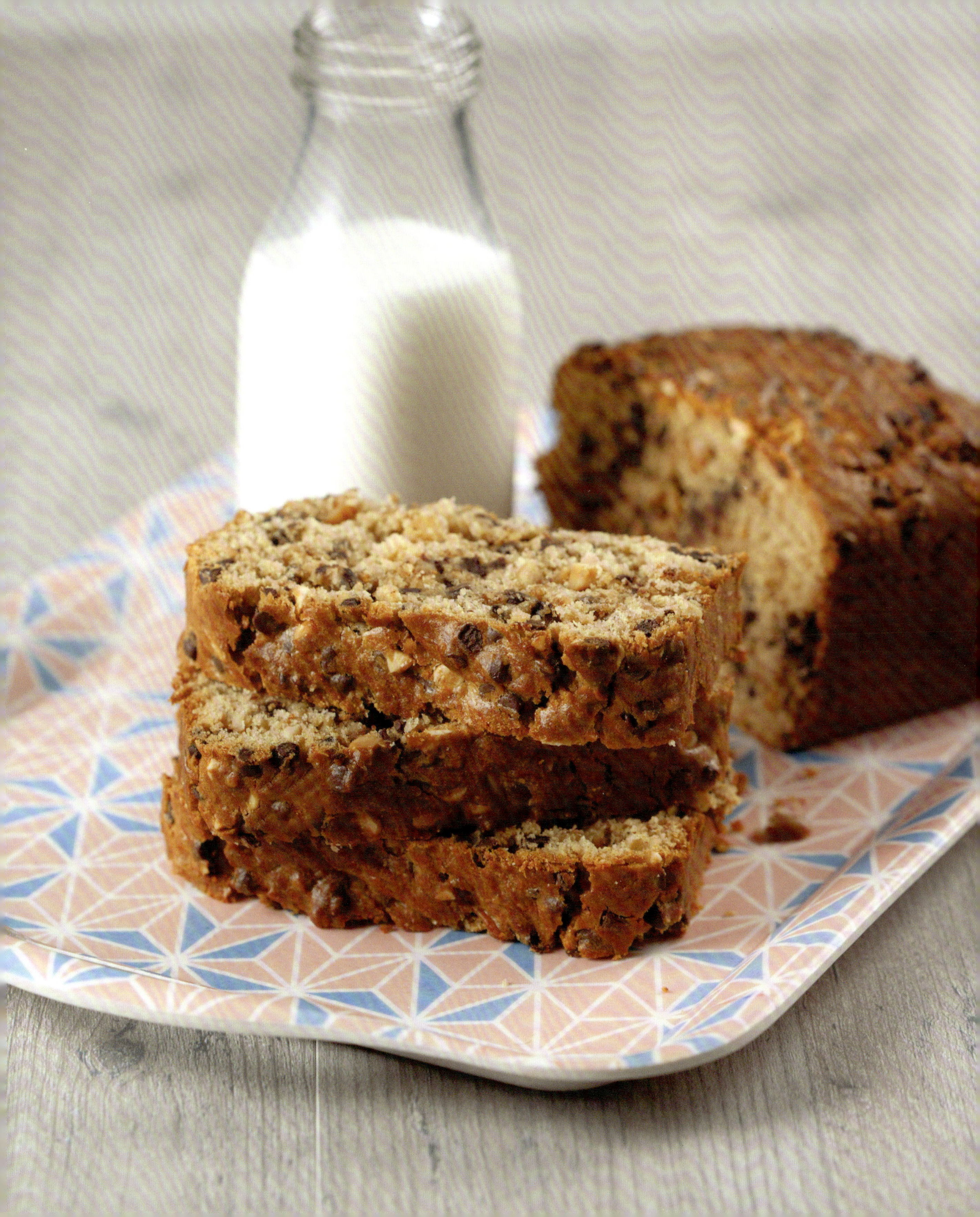

Brown Soda Bread

MAKES 1 LOAF

- 2 cups all-purpose flour
- 1 cup whole wheat flour
- 1 teaspoon baking soda
- ½ teaspoon salt
- ½ teaspoon ground ginger
- 1¼ to 1½ cups buttermilk
- 3 tablespoons dark molasses (preferably blackstrap)

1. Preheat oven to 375°F. Line baking sheet with parchment paper.

2. Combine 2 cups all-purpose flour, whole wheat flour, baking soda, salt and ginger in large bowl; mix well. Whisk 1¼ cups buttermilk and molasses in medium bowl until well blended. Stir into flour mixture until blended. Add additional buttermilk, 1 tablespoon at a time, if needed to make dry, rough dough.

3. Turn out dough onto floured surface; knead 8 to 10 times or just until smooth. (Do not overknead.) Shape dough into round loaf about 1½ inches thick. Place on prepared baking sheet.

4. Use floured knife to cut halfway through dough, scoring into quarters. Sprinkle top of dough with additional all-purpose flour, if desired.

5. Bake about 35 minutes or until bread sounds hollow when tapped. Remove to wire rack to cool slightly. Serve warm.

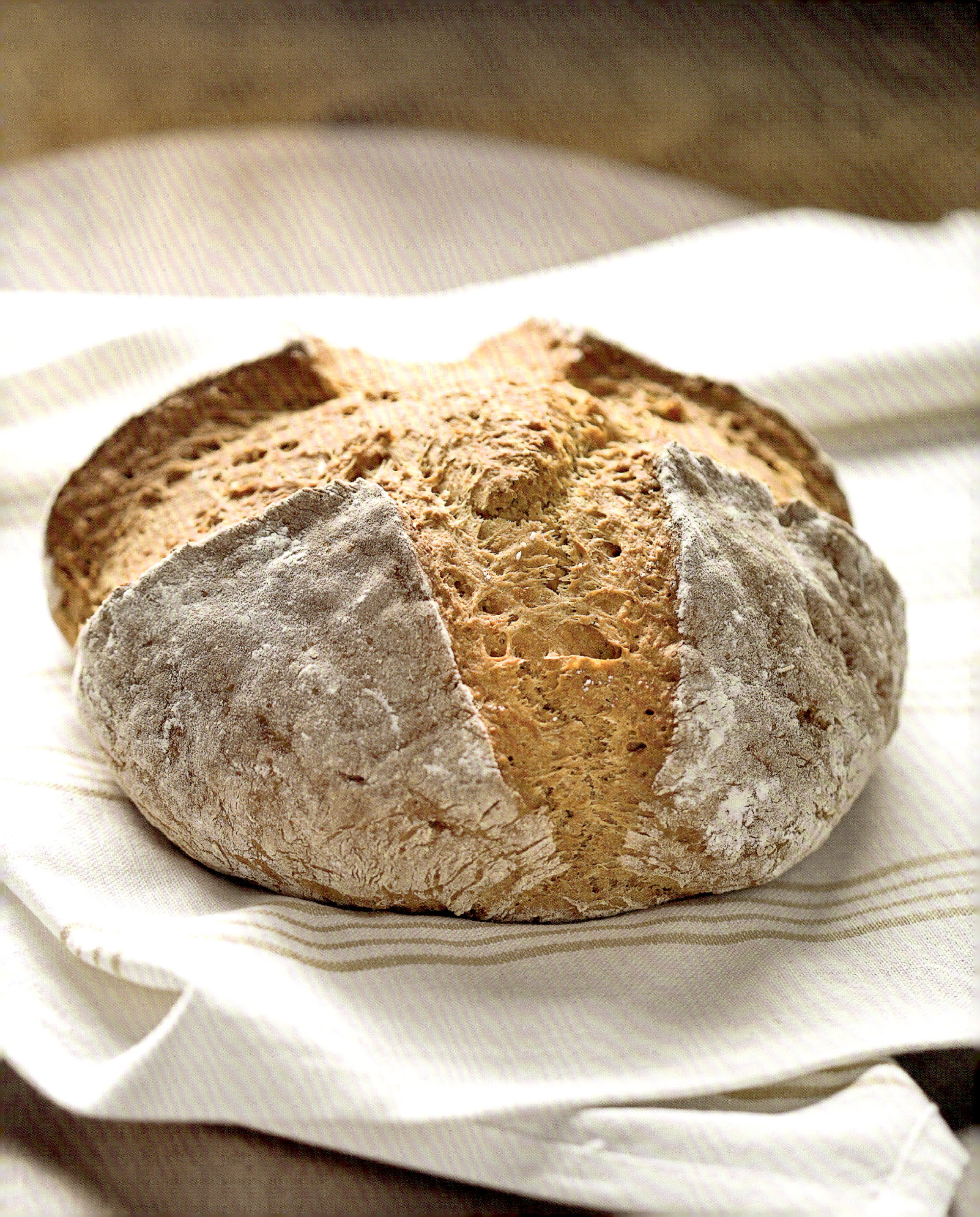

Date Nut Bread

MAKES 1 LOAF

- 2 cups all-purpose flour
- ½ cup packed brown sugar
- 1 tablespoon baking powder
- ½ teaspoon salt
- ¼ cup (½ stick) cold butter, cut into small pieces
- 1 cup chopped walnuts, toasted*
- 1 cup chopped dates
- 1¼ cups milk
- 1 egg
- ½ teaspoon grated lemon peel

*To toast walnuts, spread on ungreased baking sheet. Bake in preheated 350°F oven 6 to 8 minutes or until lightly browned, stirring occasionally.

1. Preheat oven to 375°F. Spray 9×5-inch loaf pan with nonstick cooking spray.

2. Combine flour, brown sugar, baking powder and salt in large bowl; mix well. Cut in butter with pastry blender or two knives until mixture resembles fine crumbs. Add walnuts and dates; stir until coated.

3. Whisk milk, egg and lemon peel in small bowl until blended. Add to flour mixture; stir just until dry ingredients are moistened. Pour batter into prepared pan.

4. Bake 45 to 50 minutes or until toothpick inserted into center comes out clean. Cool in pan 10 minutes; remove to wire rack to cool completely.

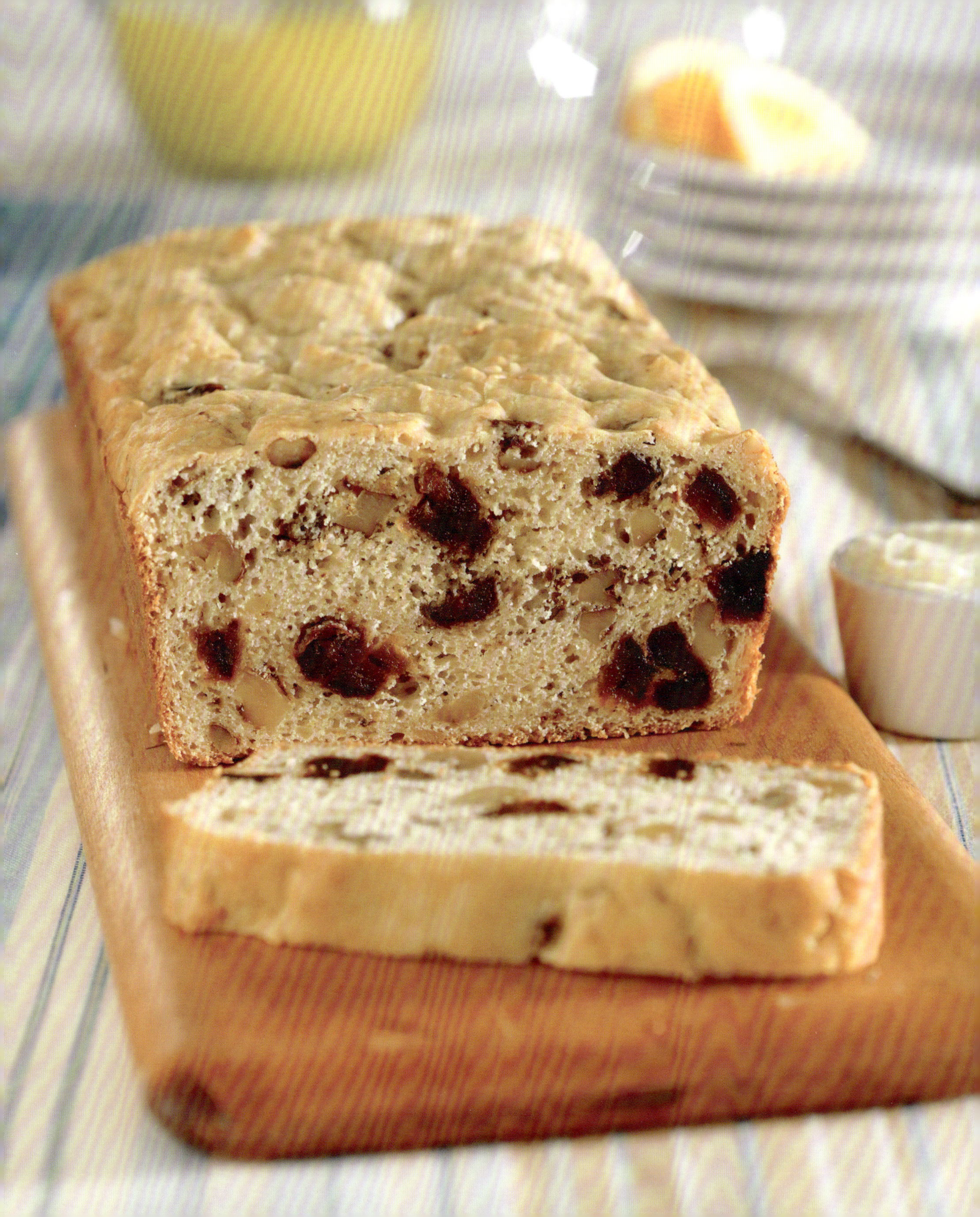

Applesauce Spice Bread

MAKES 9 SERVINGS

1½ cups all-purpose flour
1 cup unsweetened applesauce
¾ cup packed brown sugar
¼ cup shortening
1 egg
1 teaspoon vanilla
¾ teaspoon baking soda
¾ teaspoon ground cinnamon
¼ teaspoon baking powder
¼ teaspoon salt
¼ teaspoon ground nutmeg
½ cup toasted chopped walnuts
½ cup raisins (optional)
Powdered sugar

1. Preheat oven to 350°F. Spray 9-inch square baking pan with nonstick cooking spray.

2. Combine flour, applesauce, brown sugar, shortening, egg, vanilla, baking soda, cinnamon, baking powder, salt and nutmeg in large bowl; beat with electric mixer at low speed 30 seconds. Beat at high speed 3 minutes. Stir in walnuts and raisins, if desired. Pour batter into prepared pan.

3. Bake 30 minutes or until toothpick inserted into center comes out clean. Cool completely in pan on wire rack. Sprinkle with powdered sugar before serving.

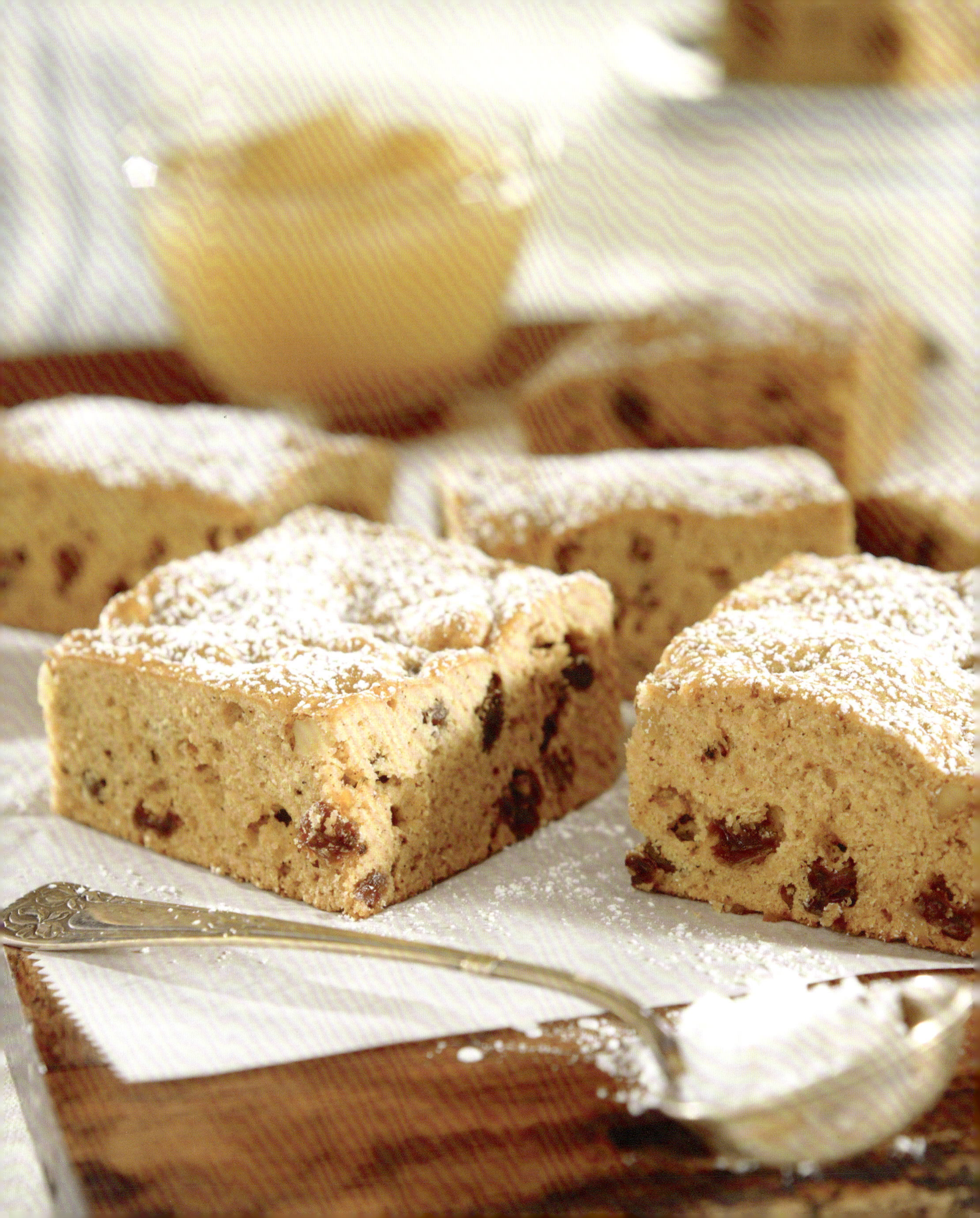

Boston Black Coffee Bread

MAKES 1 LOAF

½ cup rye flour
½ cup cornmeal
½ cup whole wheat flour
1 teaspoon baking soda
½ teaspoon salt
¾ cup strong brewed coffee, room temperature or cold
⅓ cup molasses
¼ cup canola oil
¾ cup raisins

1. Preheat oven to 325°F. Grease and flour 9×5-inch loaf pan.

2. Combine rye flour, cornmeal, whole wheat flour, baking soda and salt in medium bowl; mix well. Add coffee, molasses and oil; stir until mixture forms thick batter. Fold in raisins. Pour batter into prepared pan.

3. Bake 50 minutes or until toothpick inserted into center comes out clean. Cool completely in pan on wire rack.

TIP To cool hot coffee, pour it over two ice cubes in a measuring cup to measure ¾ cup total. Let stand 10 minutes to cool.

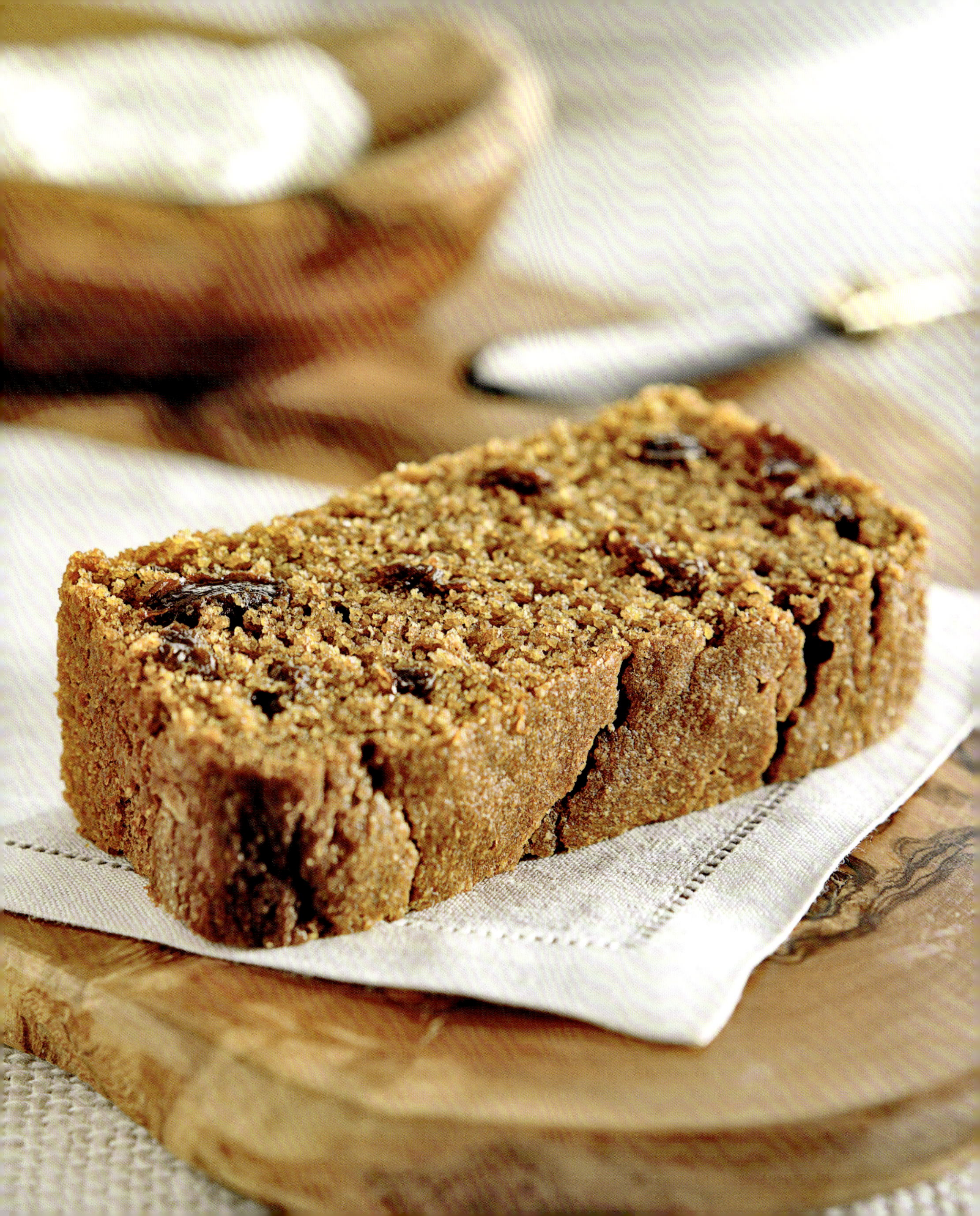

Fruit and Nut Oat Bread

MAKES 1 LOAF

- 2 cups all-purpose flour
- 1 cup old-fashioned oats
- ½ cup granulated sugar
- ¼ cup packed brown sugar
- 2½ teaspoons baking powder
- ½ teaspoon baking soda
- 1 teaspoon salt
- 1 egg
- 1 cup buttermilk
- ⅓ cup vegetable oil
- 1 teaspoon vanilla
- 1 cup coarsely chopped dried plums
- ½ cup chopped walnuts

1. Preheat oven to 350°F. Grease and flour 9×5-inch loaf pan.

2. Combine flour, oats, granulated sugar, brown sugar, baking powder, baking soda and salt in large bowl; mix well.

3. Beat egg in medium bowl. Whisk in buttermilk, oil and vanilla until blended. Add to flour mixture; stir just until dry ingredients are moistened. Stir in dried plums and walnuts. Pour batter into prepared pan.

4. Bake 50 to 55 minutes or until toothpick inserted into center comes out clean. Cool in pan 20 minutes; remove to wire rack to cool completely.

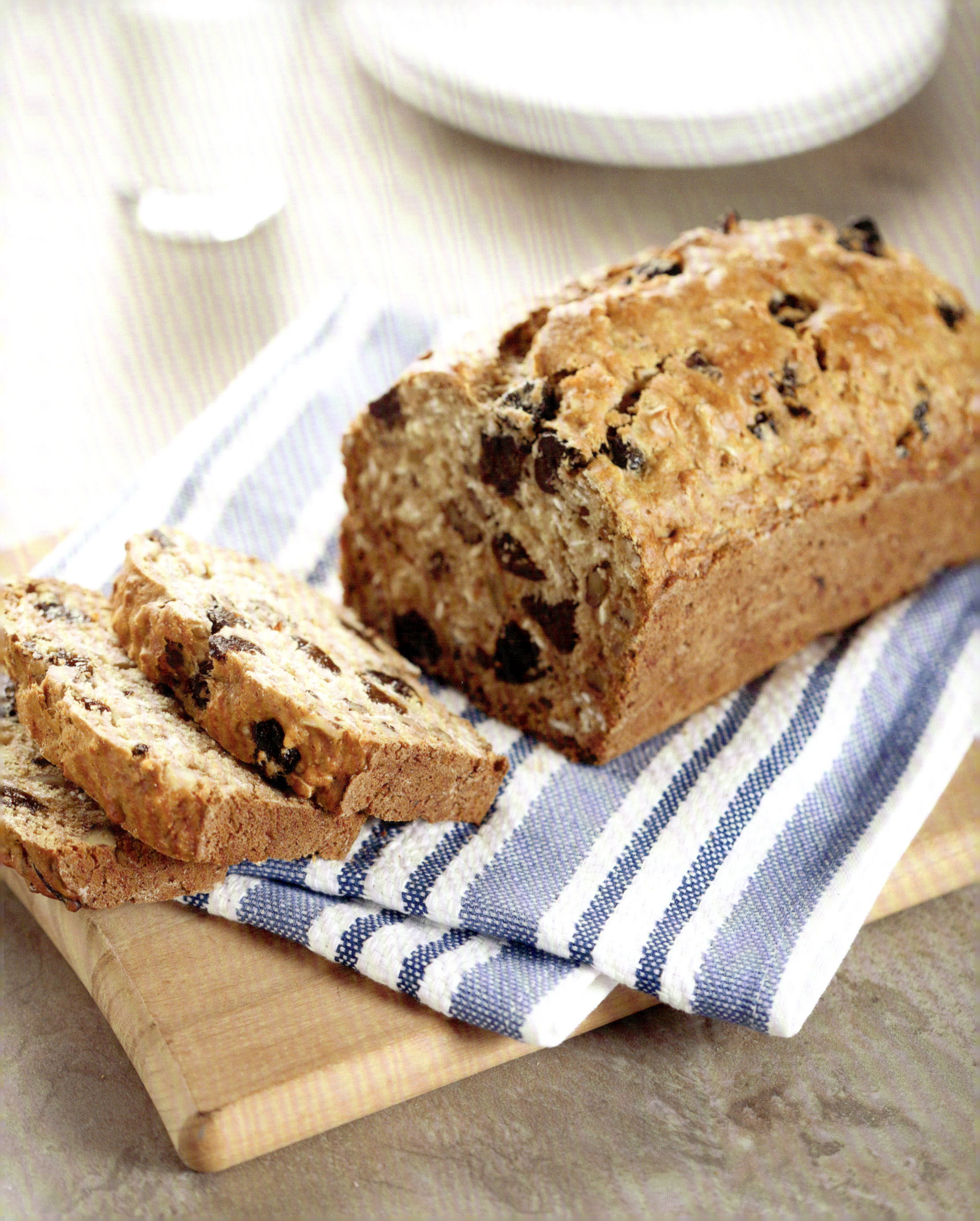

Pumpkin Bread

MAKES 2 LOAVES

2¼ cups all-purpose flour
1 tablespoon pumpkin pie spice
1 teaspoon baking powder
1 teaspoon baking soda
¾ teaspoon salt
3 eggs
1 can (15 ounces) pure pumpkin
1 cup granulated sugar
1 cup packed brown sugar
⅔ cup vegetable oil
1 teaspoon vanilla
¼ cup roasted salted pumpkin seeds, coarsely chopped or crushed

1. Preheat oven to 350°F. Spray two 8×4-inch loaf pans with nonstick cooking spray.

2. Combine flour, pumpkin pie spice, baking powder, baking soda and salt in medium bowl; mix well.

3. Beat eggs in large bowl. Add pumpkin, granulated sugar, brown sugar, oil and vanilla; whisk until well blended. Add flour mixture; stir just until dry ingredients are moistened. Pour batter into prepared pans; smooth tops. Sprinkle with pumpkin seeds; pat seeds gently into batter to adhere.

4. Bake about 50 minutes or until toothpick inserted into centers comes out mostly clean with just a few moist crumbs. Cool in pans 10 minutes; remove to wire racks to cool completely.

> **NOTE** The recipe can be made in one 9×5-inch loaf pan instead of two 8×4-inch pans. Bake about 1 hour 20 minutes or until toothpick inserted into center comes out with just a few moist crumbs. Check bread after 50 minutes; cover loosely with foil if top is browning too quickly.

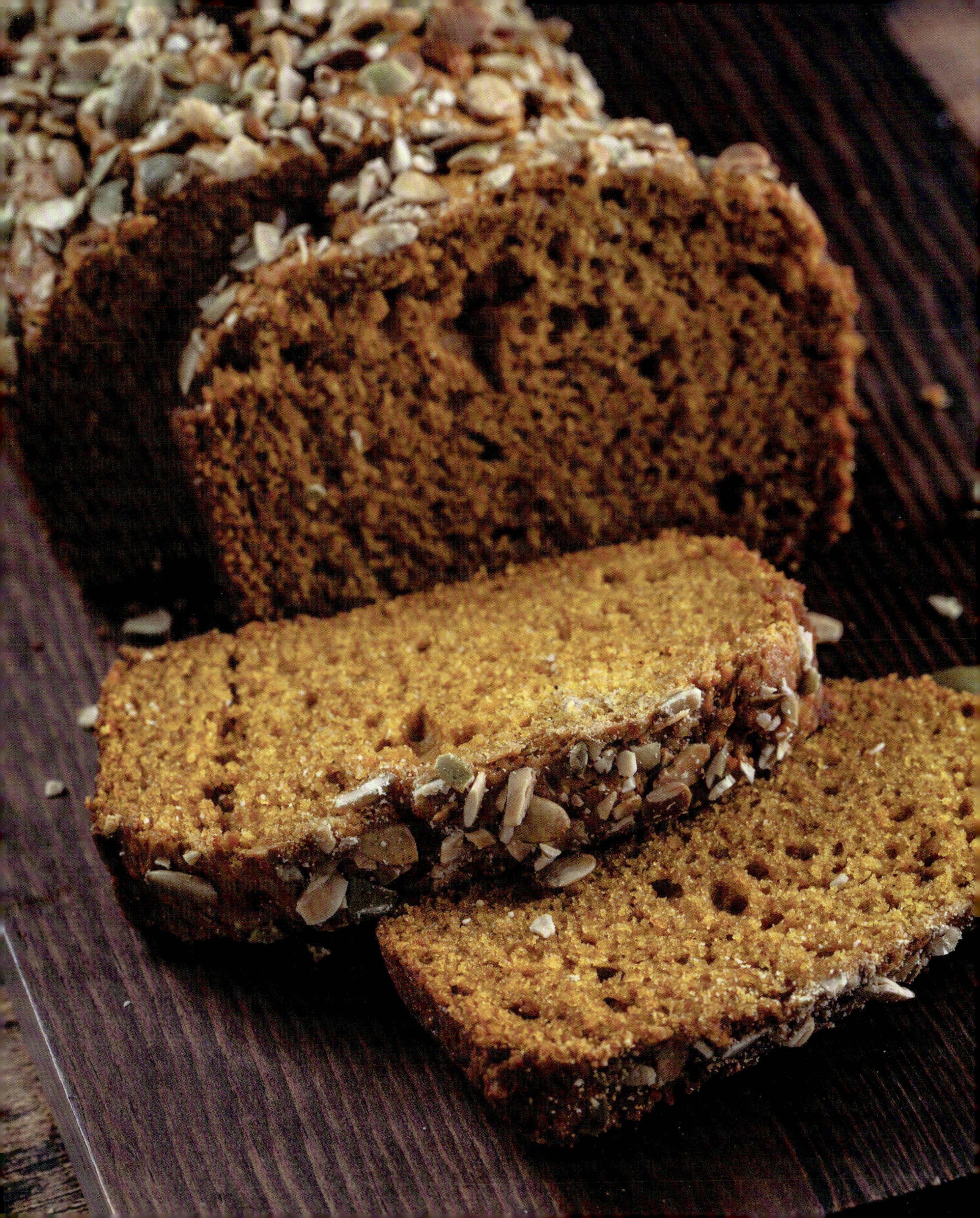

Orange Walnut Bread

MAKES 1 LOAF

- 1¾ cups all-purpose flour
- ½ cup plus 1 tablespoon sugar, divided
- 1 tablespoon grated orange peel
- 1½ teaspoons baking powder
- ¼ teaspoon baking soda
- ¼ teaspoon salt
- 1 egg
- ¾ cup buttermilk
- ⅓ cup plus 2 tablespoons orange juice, divided
- ¼ cup vegetable oil
- ½ cup chopped walnuts

1. Preheat oven to 350°F. Spray 8×4-inch loaf pan with nonstick cooking spray.

2. Combine flour, ½ cup sugar, orange peel, baking powder, baking soda and salt in medium bowl; mix well. Whisk egg, buttermilk, ⅓ cup orange juice and oil in small bowl until well blended. Add to flour mixture; stir just until dry ingredients are moistened. Fold in walnuts. Pour batter into prepared pan.

3. Bake 50 to 55 minutes or until toothpick inserted into center comes out clean.

4. Whisk remaining 2 tablespoons orange juice and 1 tablespoon sugar in small bowl until well blended and sugar is dissolved; brush over warm bread. Cool in pan on wire rack 10 minutes. Remove to wire rack; serve warm or cool completely.

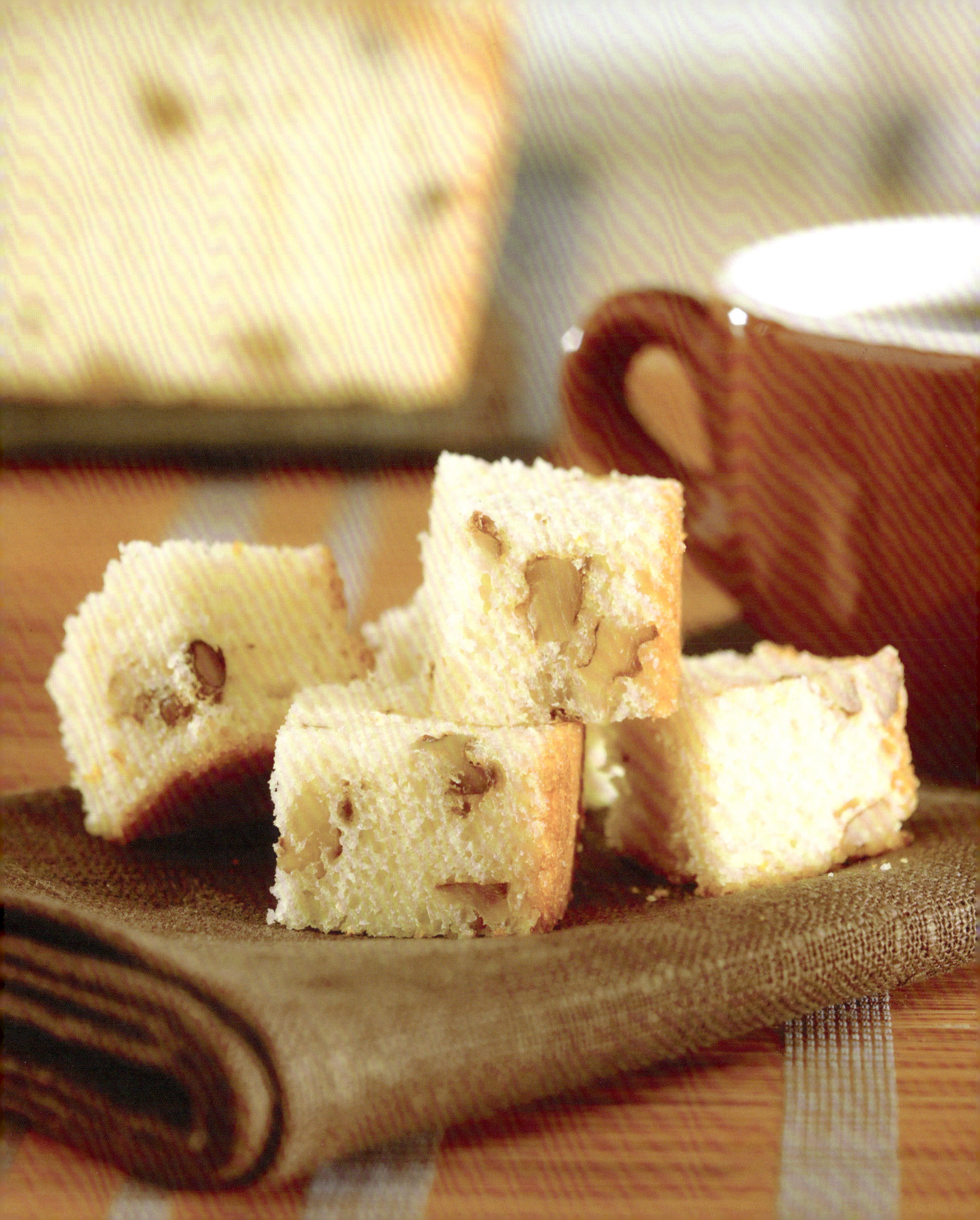

Zucchini Bread
MAKES 1 LOAF

- 2 cups all-purpose flour
- 1 teaspoon salt
- 1 teaspoon ground cinnamon
- ¾ teaspoon baking powder
- ¾ teaspoon baking soda
- ¼ teaspoon ground nutmeg
- ½ cup vegetable oil
- 2 eggs
- ½ cup granulated sugar
- ½ cup packed brown sugar
- 1 teaspoon vanilla
- 2 cups packed grated zucchini (2 to 3 medium)

1. Preheat oven to 350°F. Spray 9×5-inch loaf pan with nonstick cooking spray or line with parchment paper.

2. Combine flour, salt, cinnamon, baking powder, baking soda and nutmeg in medium bowl; mix well. Whisk oil, eggs, granulated sugar, brown sugar and vanilla in large bowl until well blended. Add flour mixture; stir just until dry ingredients are moistened. Stir in zucchini. Pour batter into prepared pan.

3. Bake 55 to 60 minutes or until toothpick inserted into center comes out clean. Cool in pan 20 minutes; remove to wire rack to cool completely.

Irish Soda Bread
MAKES 1 LOAF

2½ cups all-purpose flour
1¼ cups whole wheat flour
1 cup currants
¼ cup sugar
4 teaspoons baking powder
2 teaspoons caraway seeds (optional)
1 teaspoon salt
½ teaspoon baking soda
½ cup (1 stick) butter, cut into small pieces
1⅓ to 1½ cups buttermilk

1. Preheat oven to 350°F. Line baking sheet with parchment paper or spray with nonstick cooking spray.

2. Combine all-purpose flour, whole wheat flour, currants, sugar, baking powder, caraway seeds, if desired, salt and baking soda in large bowl; mix well.

3. Cut in butter with pastry blender or two knives until mixture resembles coarse crumbs. Add buttermilk; stir until slightly sticky dough forms. Transfer dough to prepared baking sheet; shape into 8-inch round.

4. Bake 50 to 60 minutes or until bread is golden brown and crust is firm. Cool on baking sheet 10 minutes; remove to wire rack to cool completely.

QUICK BREADS | 25

Cheddar Quick Bread

MAKES 1 LOAF

- 2 cups all-purpose flour
- 4 teaspoons baking powder
- 1 tablespoon sugar
- ½ teaspoon salt
- ½ teaspoon onion powder
- ½ teaspoon dry mustard
- 1½ cups (6 ounces) grated Cheddar cheese
- 1 cup milk
- 1 egg
- 2 tablespoons butter, melted

1. Preheat oven to 350°F. Spray 8×4-inch loaf pan with nonstick cooking spray.

2. Combine flour, baking powder, sugar, salt, onion powder and mustard in large bowl; mix well. Stir in cheese until well blended.

3. Whisk milk, egg and butter in medium bowl until well blended. Add to flour mixture; stir just until dry ingredients are moistened. Pour batter into prepared pan.

4. Bake 40 to 45 minutes or until toothpick inserted into center comes out clean. Cool in pan 10 minutes; remove to wire rack. Serve warm or cool completely.

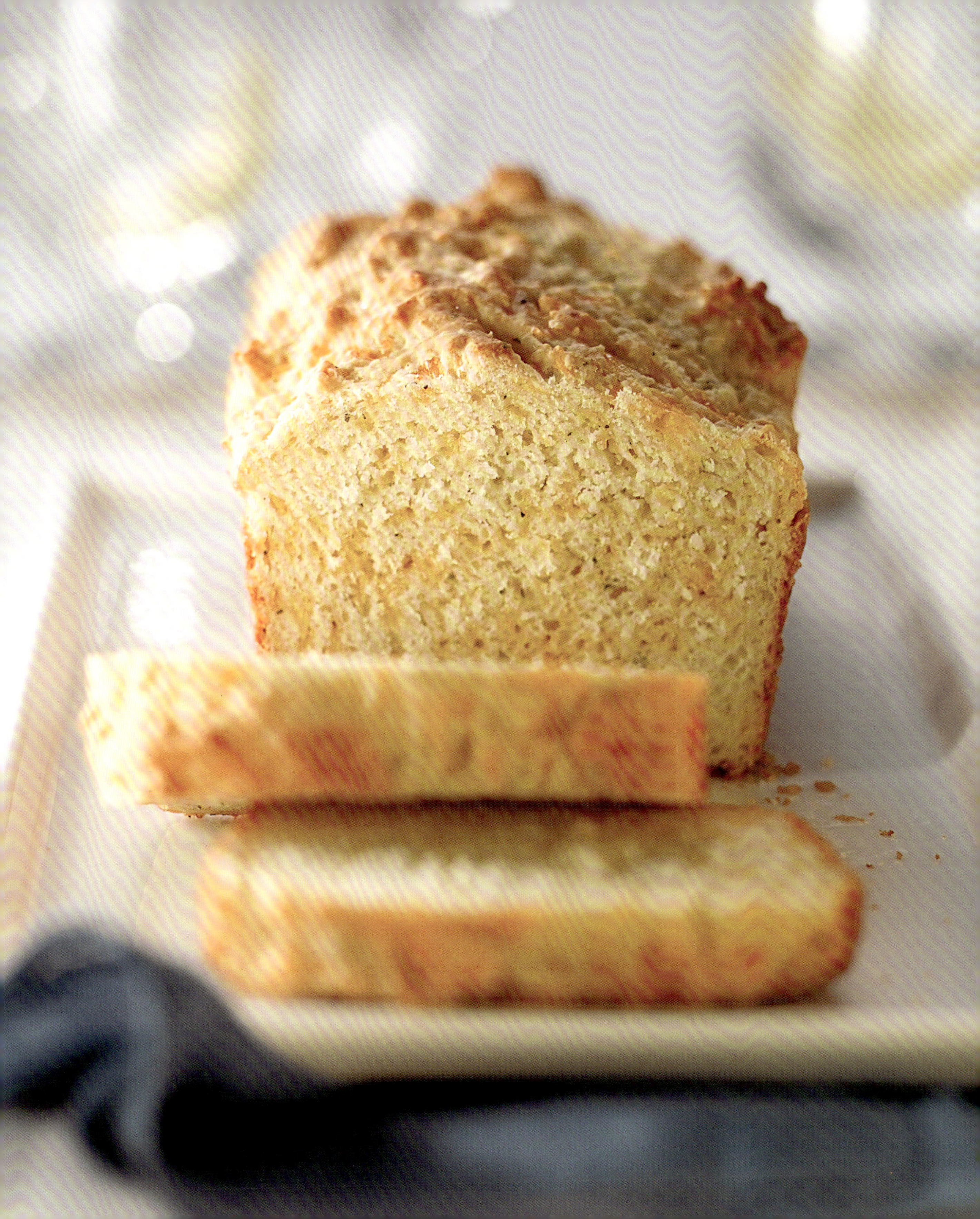

Loaded Banana Bread

MAKES 1 LOAF

- 1½ cups all-purpose flour
- 2½ teaspoons baking powder
- ¼ teaspoon salt
- 6 tablespoons (¾ stick) butter, softened
- ⅓ cup granulated sugar
- ⅓ cup packed brown sugar
- 2 eggs
- 3 ripe bananas, mashed
- ½ teaspoon vanilla
- 1 can (8 ounces) crushed pineapple, drained
- ⅓ cup flaked coconut
- ¼ cup mini chocolate chips
- ⅓ cup chopped walnuts (optional)

1. Preheat oven to 350°F. Spray 9×5-inch loaf pan with nonstick cooking spray.

2. Combine flour, baking powder and salt in small bowl; mix well. Beat butter, granulated sugar and brown sugar in large bowl with electric mixer at medium speed about 3 minutes or until light and fluffy. Beat in eggs, one at a time, scraping down bowl after each addition. Add bananas and vanilla; beat until blended.

3. Slowly add flour mixture; beat at low speed just until blended. Fold in pineapple, coconut and chocolate chips. Pour batter into prepared pan; sprinkle with walnuts, if desired.

4. Bake 50 minutes or until toothpick inserted into center comes out with a few moist crumbs. Cool in pan 1 hour; remove to wire rack to cool completely.

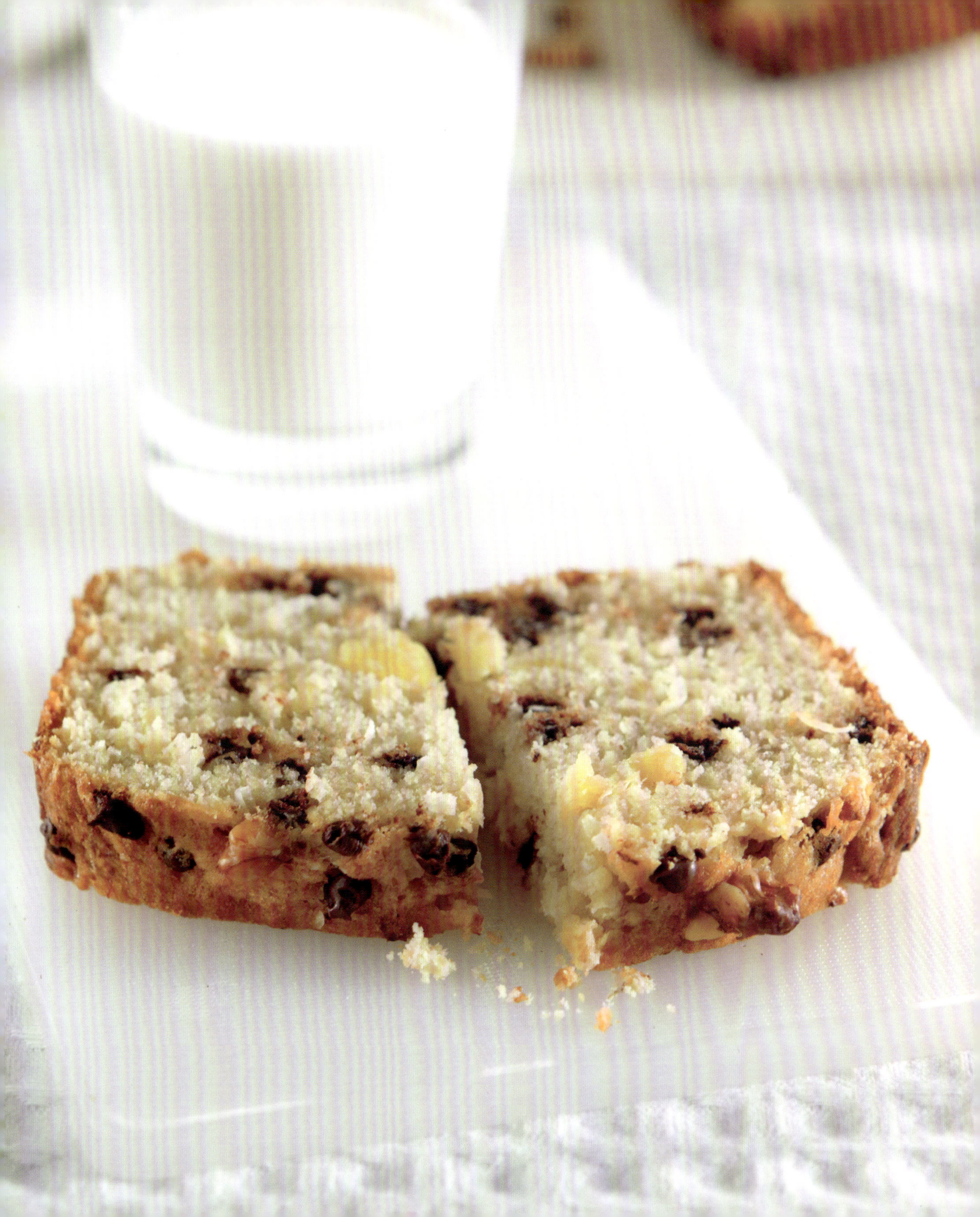

Fiesta Bread

MAKES 8 SERVINGS

- 8 ounces uncooked Mexican chorizo sausage, casings removed
- ½ cup chopped onion
- 1¼ cups all-purpose flour
- 1 cup cornmeal
- 1½ teaspoons baking soda
- 1 teaspoon ground cumin
- ½ teaspoon salt
- 1 cup Mexican beer
- 1 cup (4 ounces) shredded Cheddar cheese
- 1 can (4 ounces) diced green chiles, drained
- 1 egg, beaten

1. Preheat oven to 375°F. Spray 9-inch round or 8-inch square baking pan with nonstick cooking spray.

2. Cook sausage and onion in medium skillet over medium-high heat about 6 minutes or until browned, stirring to break up meat. Drain fat.

3. Combine flour, cornmeal, baking soda, cumin and salt in large bowl; mix well. Whisk beer, cheese, chiles and egg in medium bowl until blended. Add to flour mixture; stir just until dry ingredients are moistened. Stir in chorizo mixture. Pour batter into prepared pan.

4. Bake 20 minutes or until toothpick inserted into center comes out clean. Cool in pan 10 minutes; serve warm. Refrigerate any leftover bread.

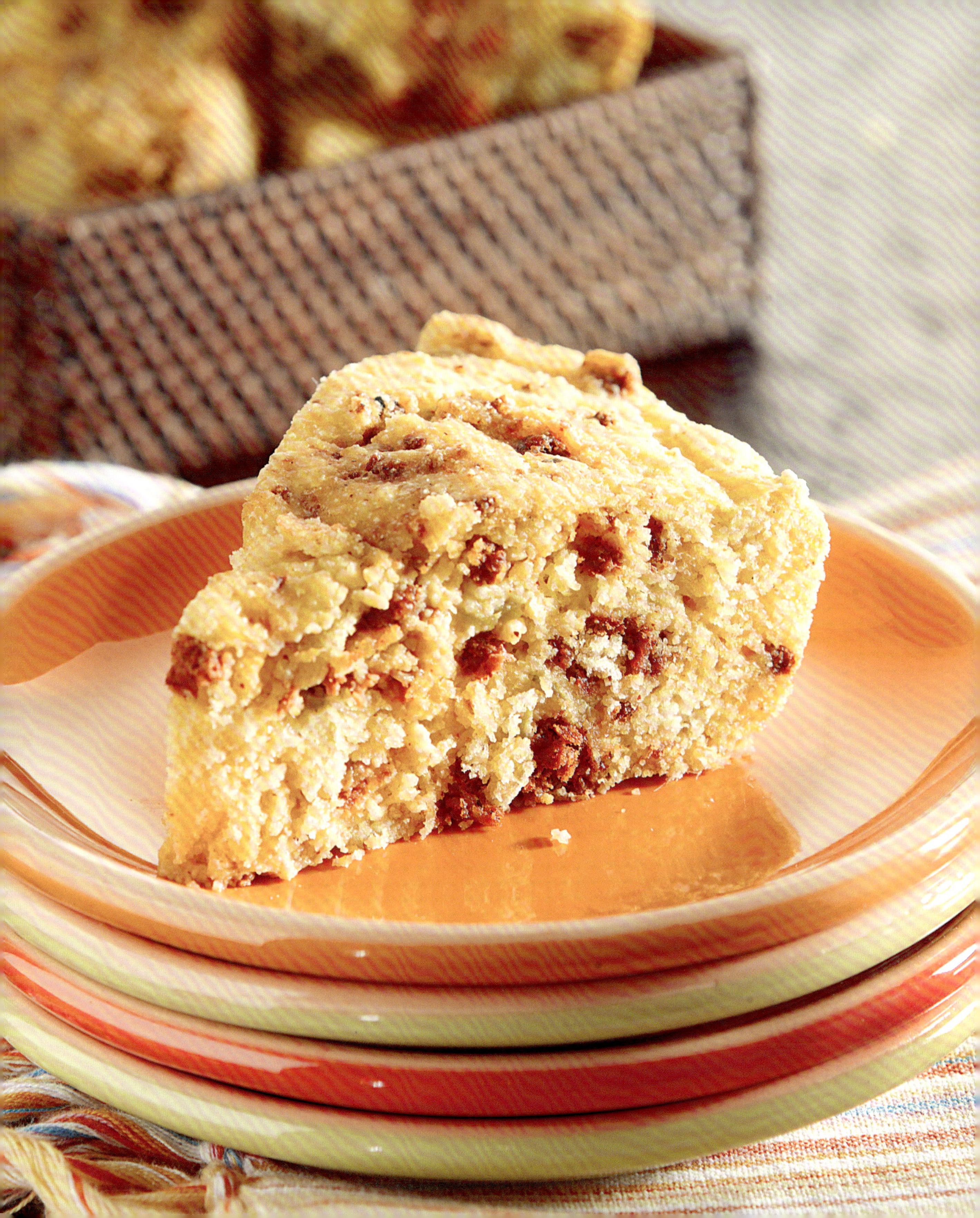

Harvest Quick Bread

MAKES 1 LOAF

1 cup all-purpose flour
1 cup whole wheat flour
½ cup packed brown sugar
¼ cup granulated sugar
1½ teaspoons baking powder
½ teaspoon baking soda
½ teaspoon ground cinnamon
½ teaspoon salt
1 egg
1 cup milk
¼ cup (½ stick) butter, melted
¾ cup dried cranberries
½ cup chopped walnuts

1. Preheat oven to 350°F. Spray 9×5-inch loaf pan with nonstick cooking spray.

2. Combine all-purpose flour, whole wheat flour, brown sugar, granulated sugar, baking powder, baking soda, cinnamon and salt in medium bowl; mix well.

3. Beat egg in large bowl. Whisk in milk and butter until blended. Gradually add flour mixture; stir just until dry ingredients are moistened. Stir in cranberries and walnuts. Pour batter into prepared pan.

4. Bake 45 to 50 minutes or until toothpick inserted into center comes out clean. Cool in pan 10 minutes; remove to wire rack to cool completely.

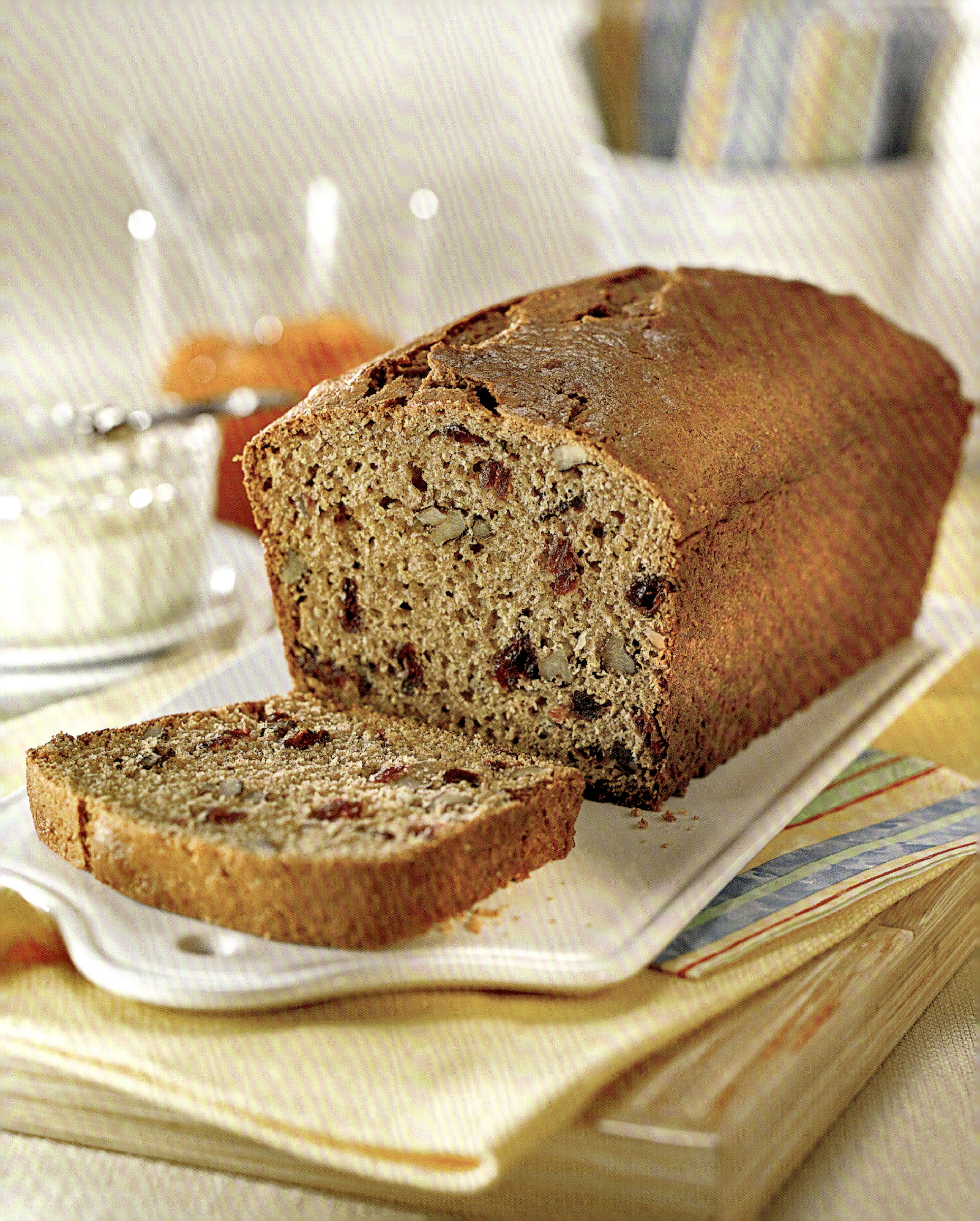

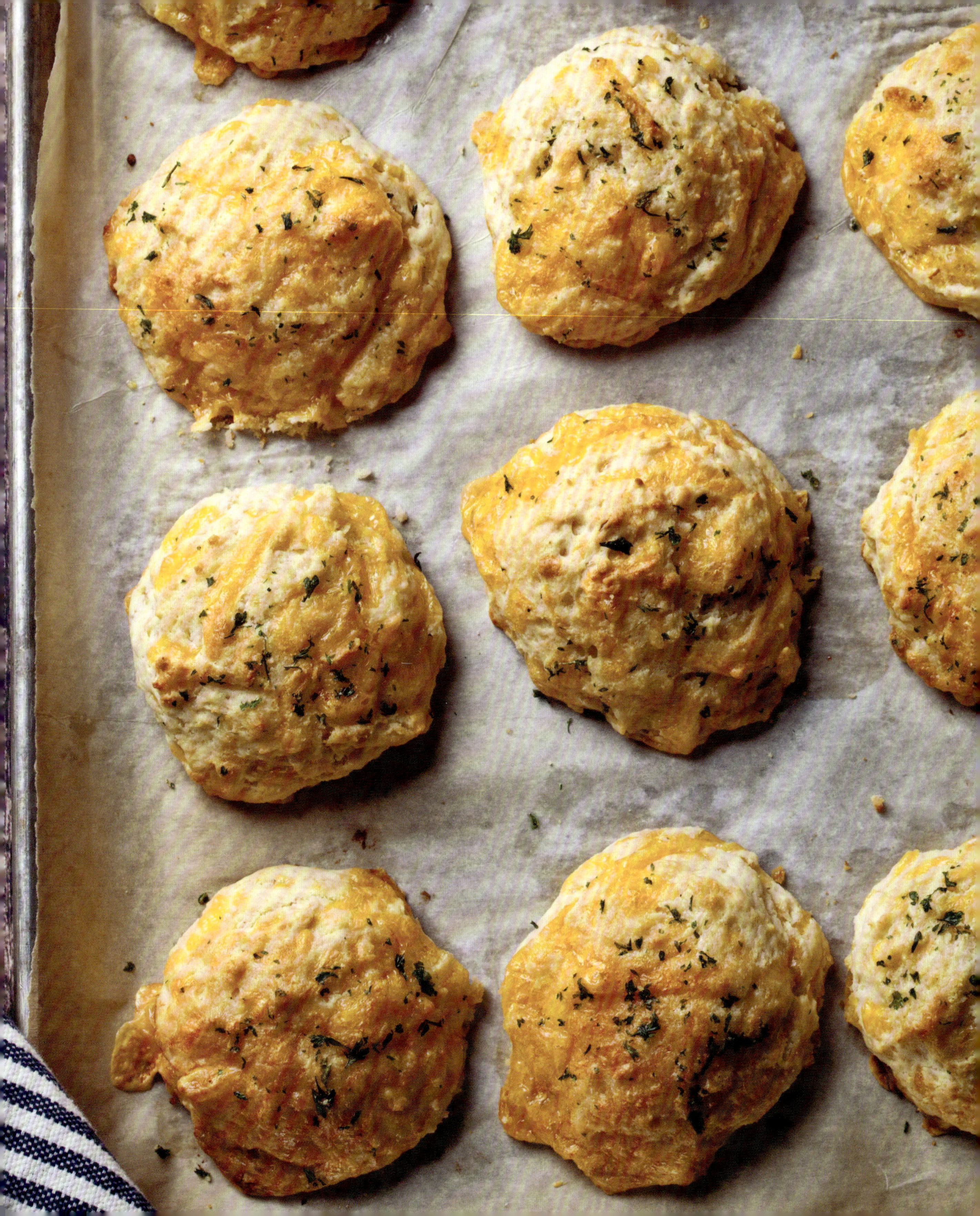

BISCUITS

Cheddar Biscuits
MAKES 15 BISCUITS

- 2 cups all-purpose flour
- 1 tablespoon sugar
- 1 tablespoon baking powder
- 2¼ teaspoons garlic powder, divided
- ¾ teaspoon plus pinch of salt, divided
- 1 cup whole milk
- ½ cup (1 stick) plus 3 tablespoons butter, melted, divided
- 2 cups (8 ounces) shredded Cheddar cheese
- ½ teaspoon dried parsley flakes

1. Preheat oven to 450°F. Line baking sheet with parchment paper.
2. Combine flour, sugar, baking powder, 2 teaspoons garlic powder and ¾ teaspoon salt in large bowl; mix well. Add milk and ½ cup melted butter; stir just until dry ingredients are moistened. Stir in cheese just until blended.
3. Drop scant ¼ cupfuls of dough 1½ inches apart onto prepared baking sheet.
4. Bake 10 to 12 minutes or until golden brown.
5. Meanwhile, combine remaining 3 tablespoons melted butter, ¼ teaspoon garlic powder, pinch of salt and parsley flakes in small bowl; brush over biscuits immediately after removing from oven. Serve warm.

Country Buttermilk Biscuits

MAKES ABOUT 9 BISCUITS

- 2 cups all-purpose flour
- 1 tablespoon baking powder
- 2 teaspoons sugar
- ½ teaspoon salt
- ½ teaspoon baking soda
- ⅓ cup cold shortening, cut into small pieces
- ⅔ cup buttermilk*

*Or combine 2½ teaspoons lemon juice plus enough milk to equal ⅔ cup. Stir; let stand 5 minutes before using.

1. Preheat oven to 450°F.
2. Combine flour, baking powder, sugar, salt and baking soda in medium bowl; mix well. Cut in shortening with pastry blender or two knives until mixture resembles coarse crumbs. Make well in center of dry ingredients. Add buttermilk; stir until mixture forms soft dough that clings together and forms a ball.
3. Turn out dough onto well-floured surface; knead gently 10 to 12 times. Roll or pat dough to ½-inch thickness. Cut out biscuits with floured 2½-inch round cutter. Place 2 inches apart on ungreased baking sheet.
4. Bake 8 to 10 minutes or until golden brown. Serve warm.

DROP BISCUITS Prepare Country Buttermilk Biscuits as directed in step 2, increasing buttermilk to 1 cup. Stir batter with wooden spoon about 15 strokes. (Do not knead.) Drop dough by heaping tablespoonfuls 1 inch apart onto greased baking sheets. Bake as directed in step 4. Makes about 18 biscuits.

SOUR CREAM DILL BISCUITS Prepare Country Buttermilk Biscuits as directed in step 2, omitting buttermilk. Combine ½ cup sour cream, ⅓ cup milk and 1 tablespoon chopped fresh dill *or* 1 teaspoon dried dill weed in small bowl until well blended. Add to flour mixture; continue as directed.

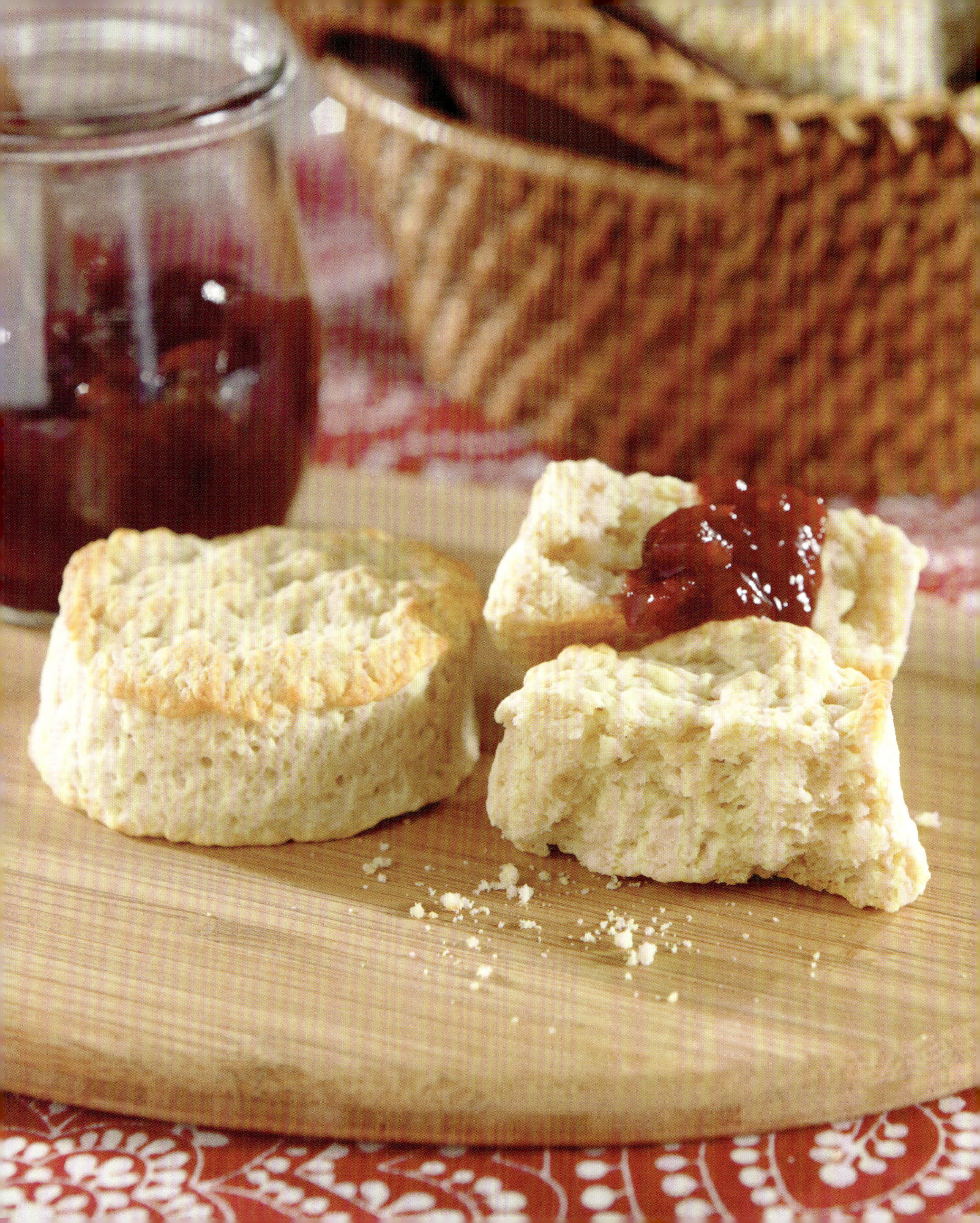

Corn and Sunflower Seed Biscuits

MAKES 12 BISCUITS

- 2 cups all-purpose flour
- 4 teaspoons baking powder
- 1 tablespoon sugar
- ½ teaspoon salt
- ½ teaspoon dried thyme
- 5 tablespoons cold butter, cut into thin slices
- 1 cup milk
- 1 cup corn*
- ⅓ cup plus 5 teaspoons salted roasted sunflower seeds, divided

*Use fresh or thawed frozen corn; do not use supersweet corn.

1. Preheat oven to 400°F. Line baking sheet with parchment paper or spray with nonstick cooking spray.

2. Combine flour, baking powder, sugar, salt and thyme in large bowl; mix well. Cut in butter with pastry blender or two knives until mixture resembles coarse crumbs. Add milk; stir gently to form soft, sticky dough. Stir in corn and ⅓ cup sunflower seeds.

3. Drop dough by ¼ cupfuls 1½ inches apart onto prepared baking sheet. Sprinkle scant ½ teaspoon sunflower seeds on each biscuit.

4. Bake 18 to 20 minutes or until golden brown. Remove to wire rack to cool slightly. Serve warm.

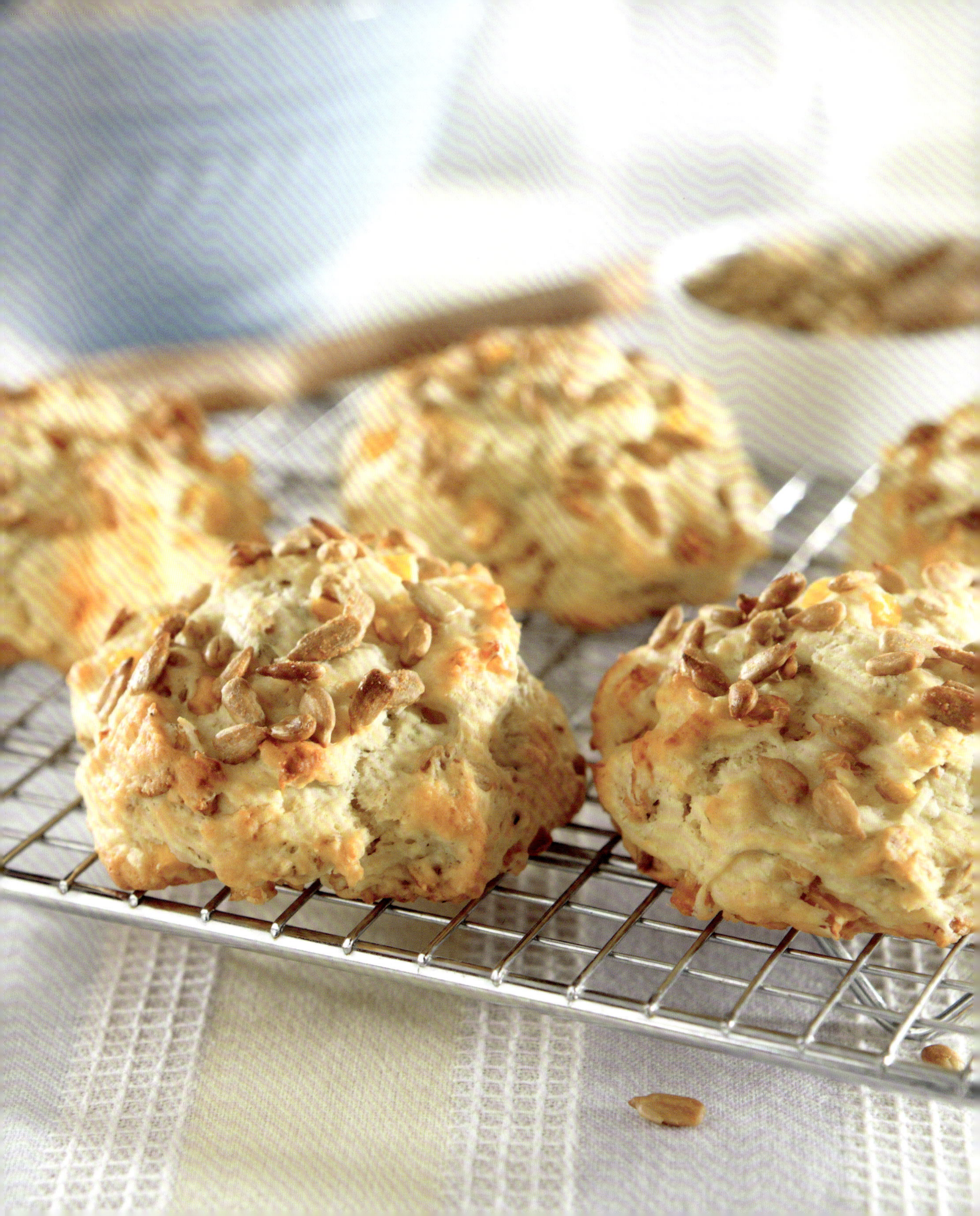

Sweet Potato Biscuits

MAKES ABOUT 12 BISCUITS

2½ cups all-purpose flour
¼ cup packed brown sugar
1 tablespoon baking powder
¾ teaspoon salt
¾ teaspoon ground cinnamon
¼ teaspoon ground ginger
¼ teaspoon ground allspice
½ cup cold shortening
½ cup chopped pecans
¾ cup mashed cooked sweet potatoes
½ cup milk

1. Preheat oven to 425°F.
2. Combine flour, brown sugar, baking powder, salt, cinnamon, ginger and allspice in large bowl; mix well. Cut in shortening with pastry blender or two knives until mixture resembles coarse crumbs. Stir in pecans.
3. Whisk sweet potatoes and milk in small bowl until well blended and smooth. Add to flour mixture; stir until soft dough forms.
4. Turn out dough onto lightly floured surface; knead lightly. Roll or pat dough to ½-inch thickness. Cut out biscuits with floured 2½-inch round cutter. Place on ungreased baking sheet.
5. Bake 12 to 14 minutes or until golden brown. Serve warm.

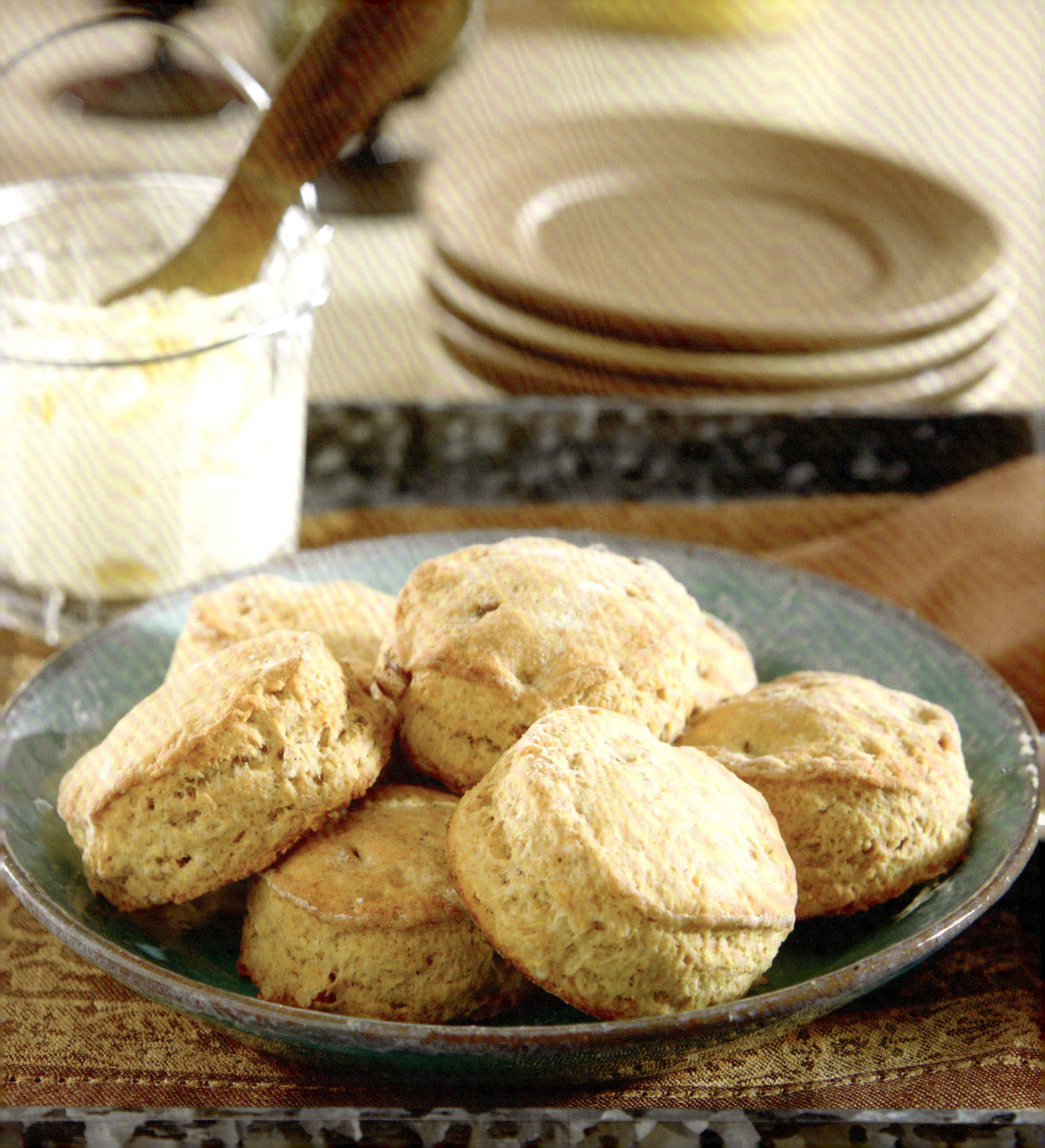

Ham and Swiss Cheese Biscuits

MAKES ABOUT 18 BISCUITS

- 2 cups all-purpose flour
- 2 teaspoons baking powder
- ½ teaspoon baking soda
- ¼ teaspoon salt
- ½ cup (1 stick) cold butter, cut into small pieces
- ⅔ cup buttermilk
- ½ cup (2 ounces) shredded Swiss cheese
- 2 ounces ham, finely chopped

1. Preheat oven to 450°F. Line baking sheet with parchment paper or spray with nonstick cooking spray.

2. Combine flour, baking powder, baking soda and salt in medium bowl; mix well. Cut in butter with pastry blender or two knives until mixture resembles coarse crumbs. Stir in buttermilk, 1 tablespoon at a time, until slightly sticky dough forms. Stir in cheese and ham.

3. Turn out dough onto lightly floured surface; knead lightly. Roll out dough to ½-inch thickness. Cut out biscuits with 2-inch round cutter. Place on prepared baking sheet.

4. Bake 10 minutes or until browned. Serve warm.

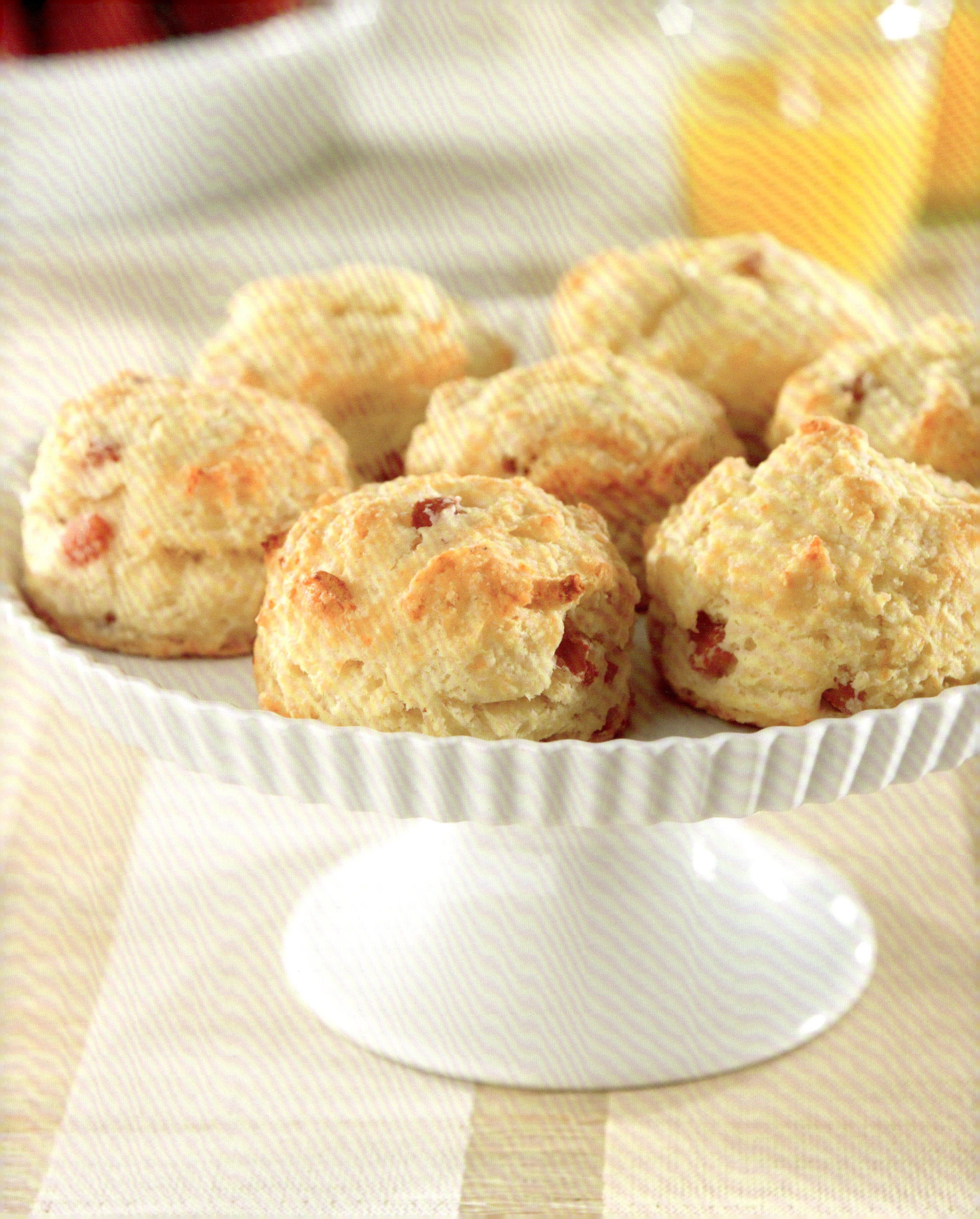

Wheaty Cranberry Buttermilk Biscuits

MAKES 8 BISCUITS

- 1 cup all-purpose flour
- 1 cup whole wheat flour
- 3 tablespoons sugar
- 2½ teaspoons baking powder
- ½ teaspoon salt
- ½ teaspoon baking soda
- ½ cup (1 stick) cold butter, cut into small pieces
- ¾ cup buttermilk
- ½ cup dried cranberries
- ⅓ cup all-bran cereal

1. Preheat oven to 425°F. Line baking sheet with parchment paper or spray with nonstick cooking spray.

2. Combine all-purpose flour, whole wheat flour, sugar, baking powder, salt and baking soda in large bowl; mix well. Cut in butter with pastry blender or two knives until mixture resembles coarse crumbs. Stir in buttermilk until soft, slightly sticky dough forms. Stir in cranberries and cereal.

3. Turn out dough onto lightly floured surface. Pat or roll dough to ¾-inch thickness. Cut out biscuits with 2½-inch round cutter. Place on prepared baking sheet.

4. Bake 15 minutes or until golden brown. Serve warm.

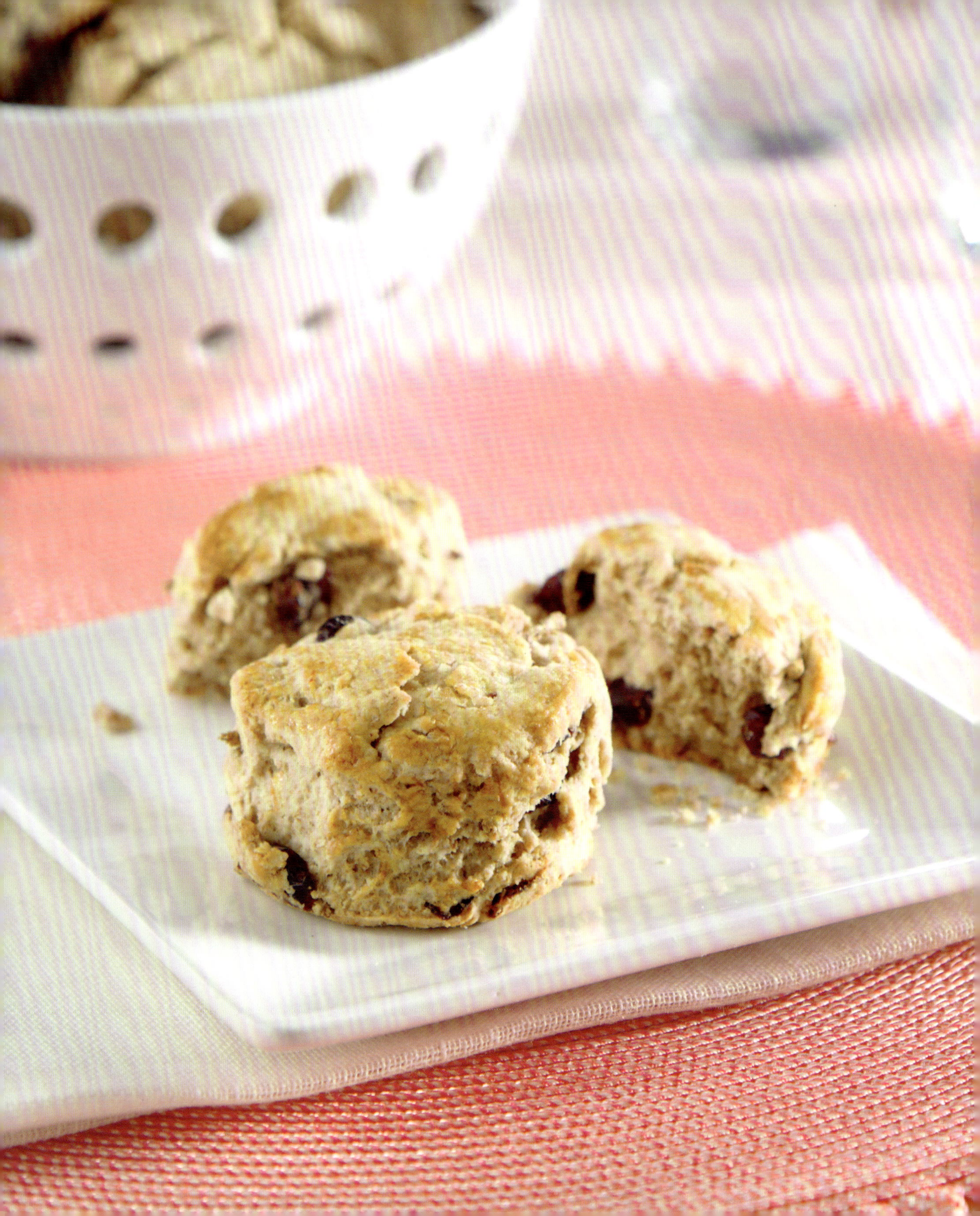

Yogurt Chive Biscuits

MAKES 12 BISCUITS

- 2 cups all-purpose flour
- 1 tablespoon sugar
- 2 teaspoons baking powder
- ½ teaspoon baking soda
- ½ teaspoon salt
- ¼ teaspoon dried oregano
- ¼ cup (½ stick) cold butter, cut into small pieces
- ⅔ cup plain Greek yogurt
- ½ cup milk
- ¼ cup sour cream
- ½ cup finely chopped fresh chives

1. Preheat oven to 400°F. Line baking sheet with parchment paper or spray with nonstick cooking spray.

2. Combine flour, sugar, baking powder, baking soda, salt and oregano in large bowl; mix well. Cut in butter with pastry blender or two knives until mixture resembles coarse crumbs. Add yogurt, milk and sour cream; stir gently to form soft, sticky dough. Stir in chives.

3. Drop dough by ¼ cupfuls 1½ inches apart onto prepared baking sheet.

4. Bake 15 to 16 minutes or until light golden brown. Remove to wire rack to cool slightly. Serve warm.

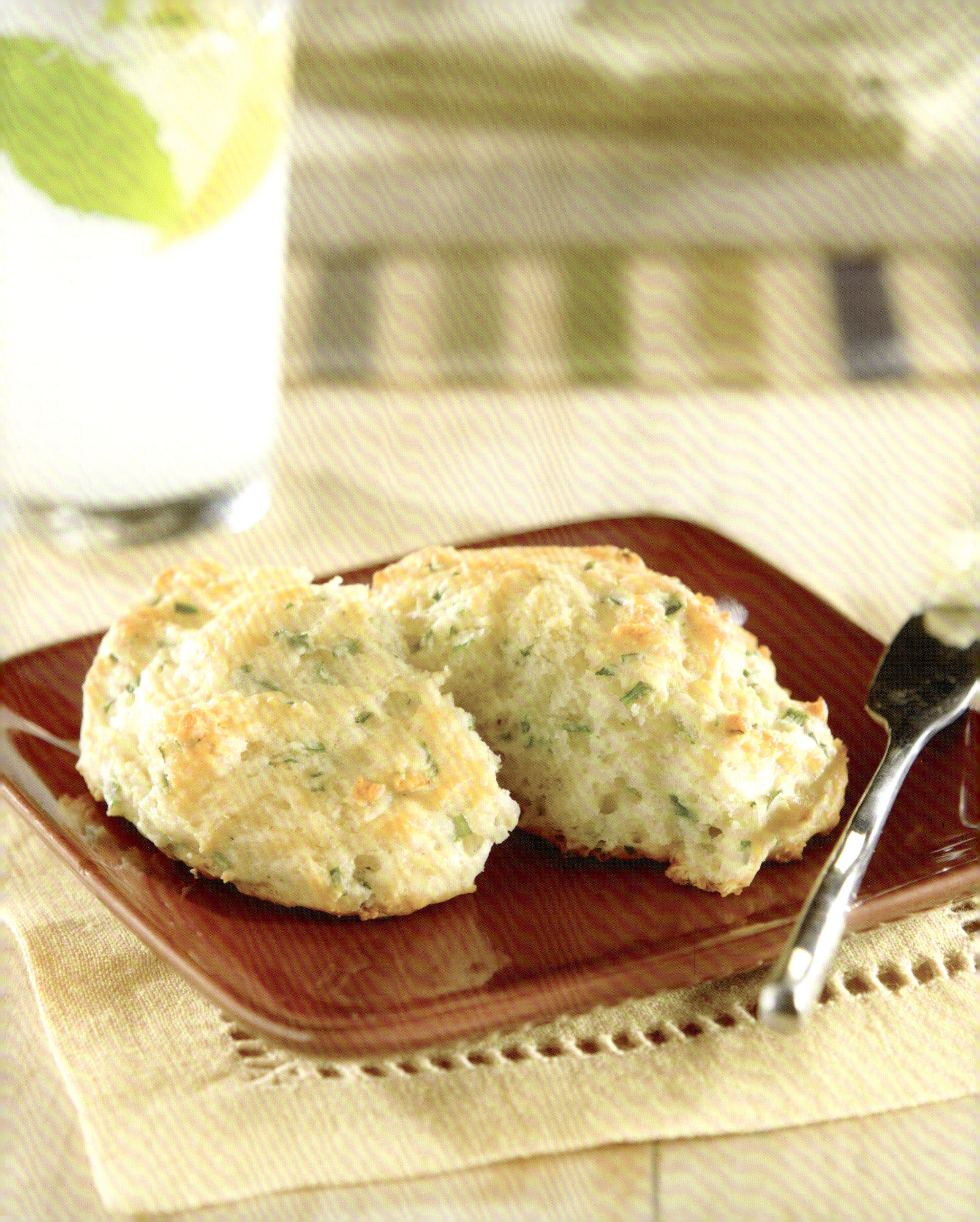

Sweet Cherry Biscuits

MAKES ABOUT 10 BISCUITS

- 2 cups all-purpose flour
- ¼ cup sugar
- 4 teaspoons baking powder
- ½ teaspoon salt
- ½ teaspoon dried rosemary (optional)
- ½ cup (1 stick) cold butter, cut into small pieces
- ¾ cup milk
- ½ cup dried sweetened cherries, chopped

1. Preheat oven to 425°F.
2. Combine flour, sugar, baking powder, salt and rosemary, if desired, in large bowl; mix well. Cut in butter with pastry blender or two knives until mixture forms small crumbs. Stir in milk to form sticky batter. Stir in cherries.
3. Pat dough to 1-inch thickness on floured surface. Cut out biscuits with 3-inch round cutter. Place 1 inch apart on ungreased baking sheet.
4. Bake about 15 minutes or until golden brown. Cool on wire rack 5 minutes. Serve warm.

Mustard Pepper Biscuits
MAKES 14 BISCUITS

- 2 cups all-purpose flour
- 1 tablespoon baking powder
- 1 teaspoon sugar
- ¾ teaspoon black pepper
- ½ teaspoon salt
- ⅛ teaspoon garlic powder
- ¼ cup cold butter, cut into small pieces
- ¾ cup milk
- 2 tablespoons Dijon mustard

1. Preheat oven to 450°F. Line baking sheet with parchment paper or spray with nonstick cooking spray.
2. Combine flour, baking powder, sugar, pepper, salt and garlic powder in medium bowl; mix well. Cut in butter with pastry blender or two knives until mixture resembles coarse crumbs.
3. Whisk milk and mustard in small bowl until blended. Add to flour mixture; stir just until dry ingredients are moistened. Drop dough by rounded tablespoonfuls 1 inch apart onto prepared baking sheet.
4. Bake about 10 minutes or until golden brown. Serve warm.

Oatmeal Drop Biscuits

MAKES ABOUT 16 BISCUITS

1½ cups all-purpose flour
½ cup quick oats
1 tablespoon baking powder
2 teaspoons sugar
½ teaspoon salt
½ teaspoon grated orange peel
6 tablespoons (¾ stick) cold butter, cut into small pieces
¾ cup milk

1. Preheat oven to 450°F.
2. Combine flour, oats, baking powder, sugar, salt and orange peel in large bowl; mix well. Cut in butter with pastry blender or two knives until mixture resembles coarse crumbs.
3. Slowly stir in ¼ cup milk, then continue adding milk, 1 tablespoon at a time, until slightly sticky dough forms. Drop dough by rounded tablespoonfuls 2 inches apart onto ungreased baking sheets.
4. Bake 10 to 12 minutes until bottoms are golden brown. Serve warm.

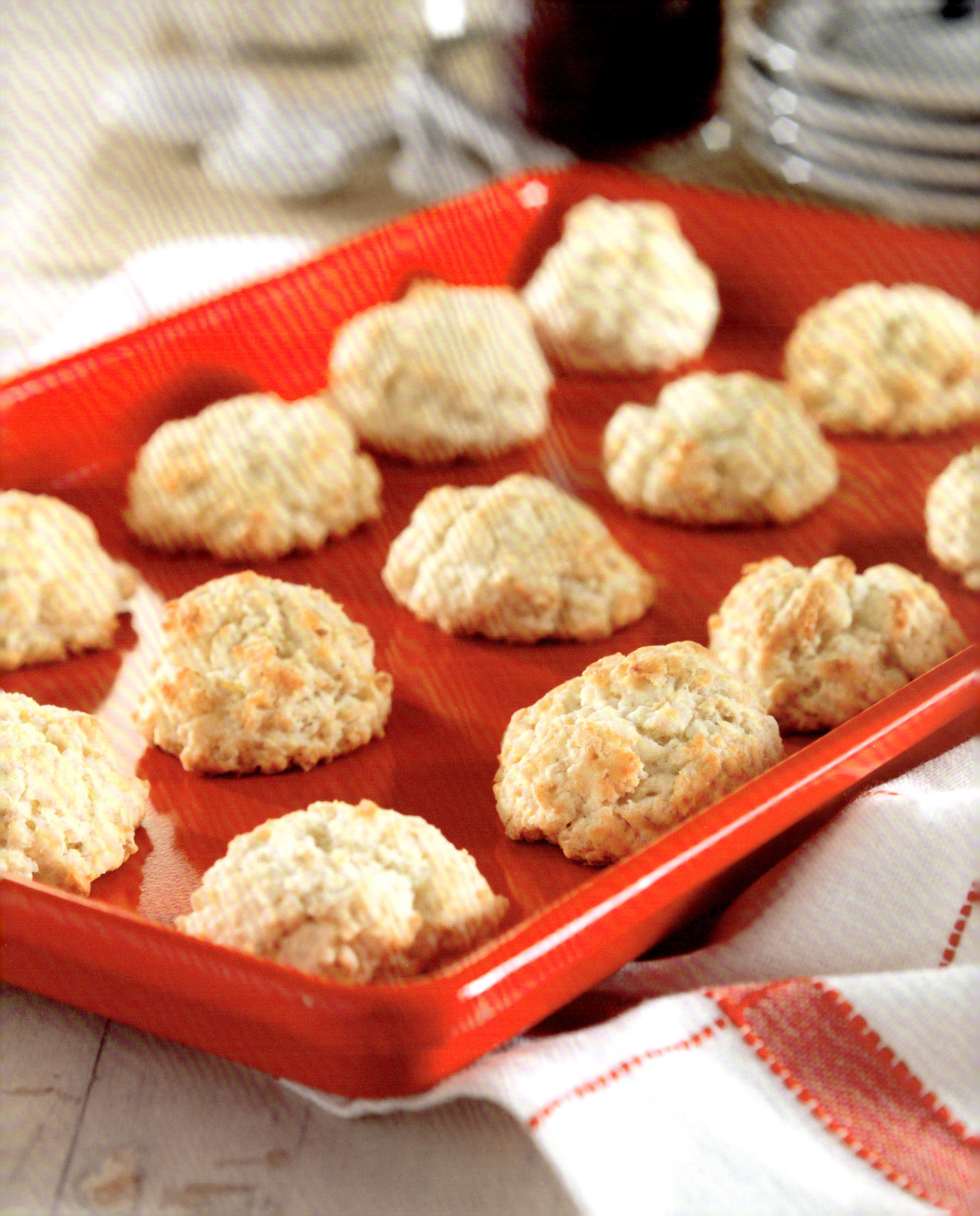

Easy Cheese Biscuits

MAKES 9 BISCUITS

1 cup all-purpose flour
2 teaspoons baking powder
1 teaspoon sugar
½ teaspoon salt
¼ cup (½) stick butter, cut into small pieces
1 cup (4 ounces) grated sharp Cheddar cheese
½ cup milk

1. Preheat oven to 425°F. Line baking sheet with parchment paper.

2. Combine flour, baking powder, sugar and salt in medium bowl; mix well. Cut in butter with pastry blender or two knives until mixture resembles coarse crumbs. Add cheese; stir until blended. Add milk; stir until soft dough forms.

3. Turn out dough onto lightly floured surface; knead several times until smooth, sprinkling with additional flour as necessary. Pat dough into 6-inch square; cut into nine (2-inch) squares. Place 2 inches apart on prepared baking sheet.

4. Bake 10 to 12 minutes or until golden brown. Cool on baking sheet 2 minutes; serve warm.

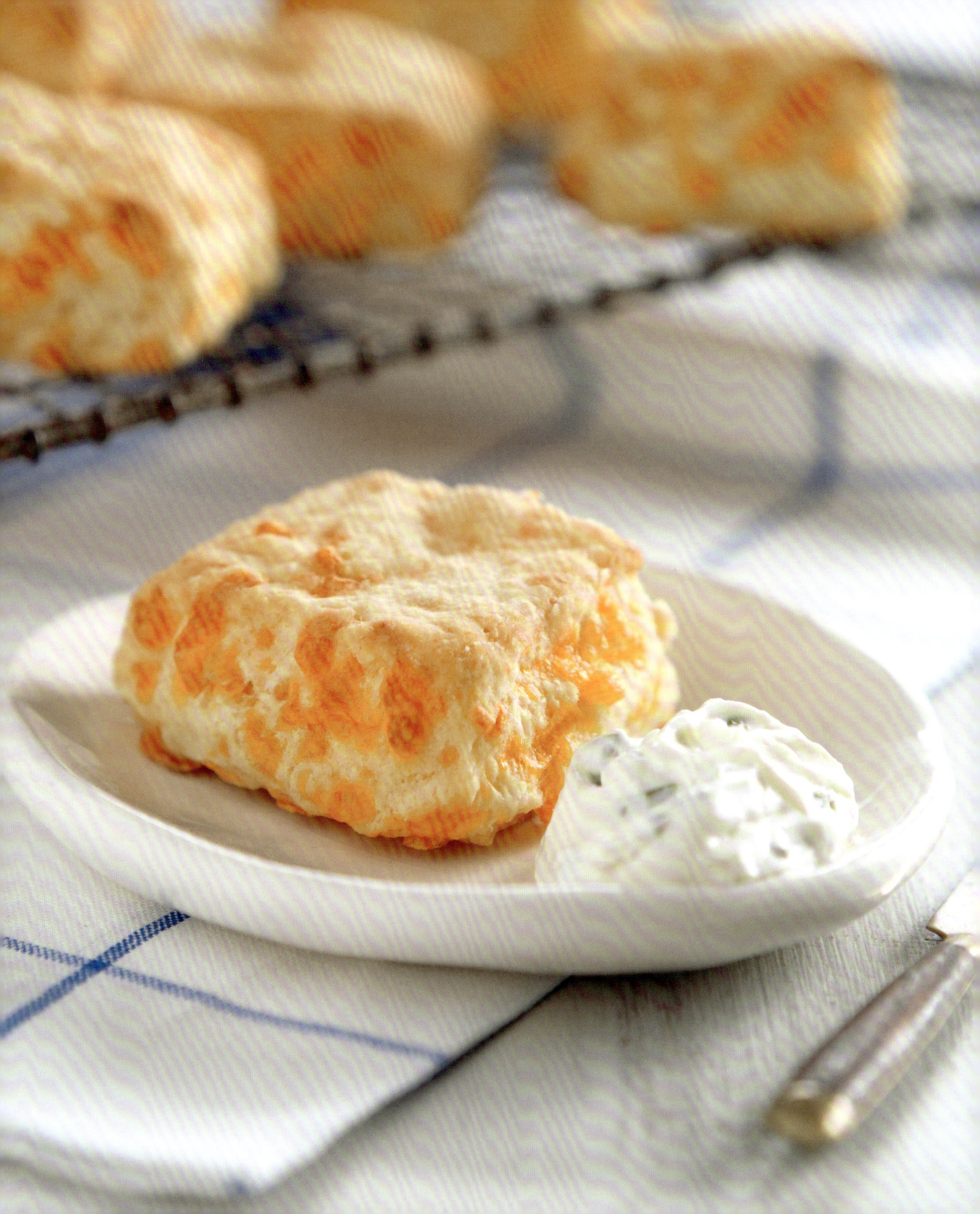

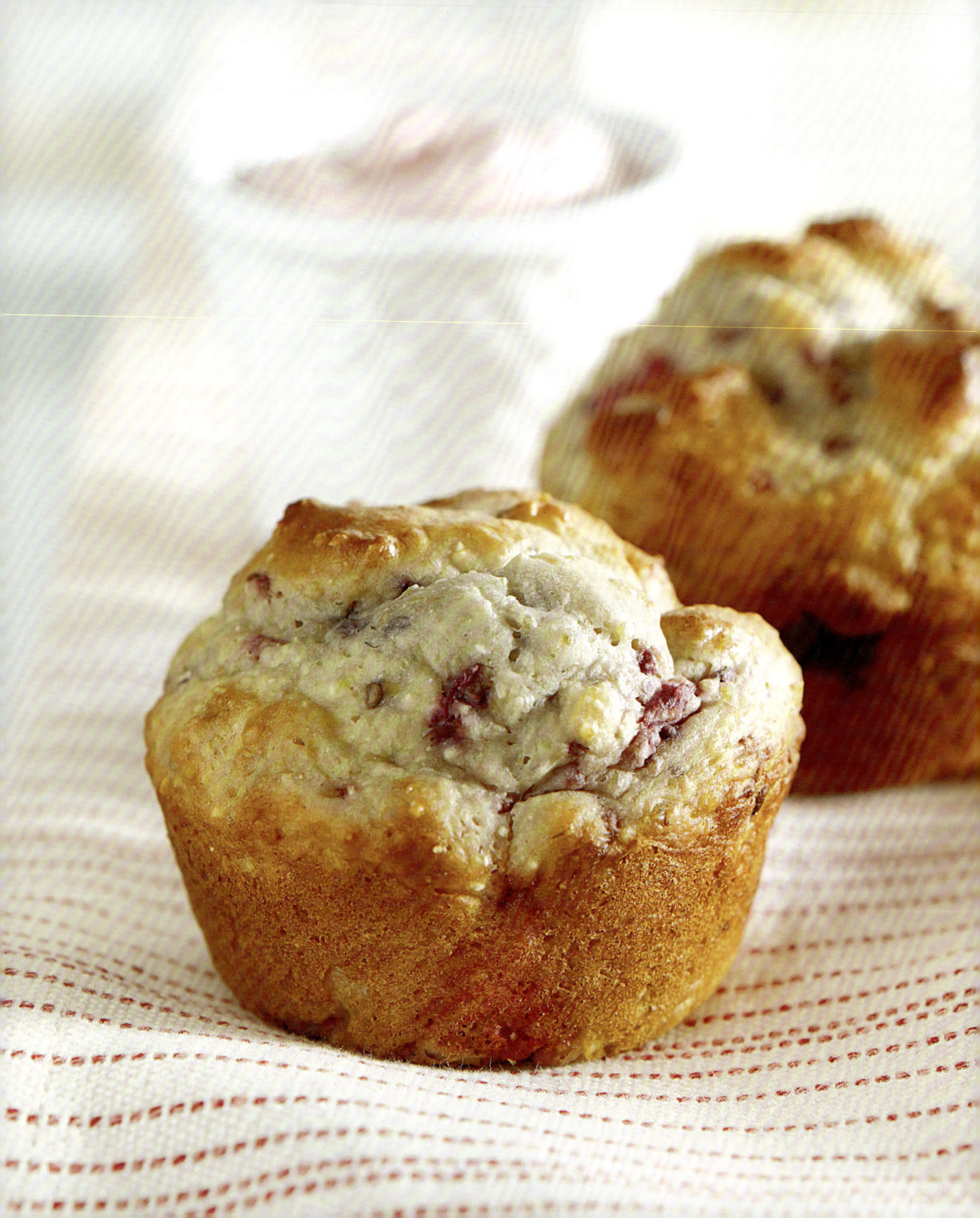

MUFFINS

Raspberry Corn Muffins
MAKES 12 MUFFINS

- 1 cup all-purpose flour
- ¾ cup yellow cornmeal
- ½ cup sugar
- 2 teaspoons baking powder
- ½ teaspoon baking soda
- ½ teaspoon salt
- ⅔ cup plain Greek yogurt
- ⅓ cup milk
- ¼ cup (½ stick) butter, melted
- 1 egg
- 1¼ cups fresh or frozen raspberries

1. Preheat oven to 400°F. Spray 12 standard (2½-inch) muffin cups with nonstick cooking spray or line with paper baking cups.

2. Combine flour, cornmeal, sugar, baking powder, baking soda and salt in large bowl; mix well.

3. Whisk yogurt, milk, butter and egg in medium bowl until well blended. Add to flour mixture; stir just until combined. Gently fold in raspberries. Spoon batter evenly into prepared muffin cups.

4. Bake 16 to 18 minutes or until toothpick inserted into centers comes out clean. Cool in pan 5 minutes; remove to wire rack to cool completely.

Apple Butter Spice Muffins

MAKES 12 MUFFINS

½ cup sugar
1 teaspoon ground cinnamon
¼ teaspoon ground nutmeg
⅛ teaspoon ground allspice
½ cup chopped pecans or walnuts
2 cups all-purpose flour
2 teaspoons baking powder
¼ teaspoon salt
1 cup milk
¼ cup vegetable oil
1 egg
¼ cup apple butter

1. Preheat oven to 400°F. Line 12 standard (2½-inch) muffin cups with paper baking cups or spray with nonstick cooking spray.

2. Combine sugar, cinnamon, nutmeg and allspice in large bowl; mix well. Remove 2 tablespoons sugar mixture to small bowl; toss with pecans until coated. Add flour, baking powder and salt to remaining sugar mixture.

3. Whisk milk, oil and egg in medium bowl until well blended. Add to flour mixture; stir just until dry ingredients are moistened. Spoon 1 tablespoon batter into each prepared muffin cup. Top with 1 teaspoon apple butter; spoon remaining batter evenly over apple butter. Sprinkle with pecan mixture.

4. Bake 20 to 25 minutes or until golden brown and toothpick inserted into centers comes out clean. Remove to wire rack to cool 10 minutes. Serve warm or cool completely.

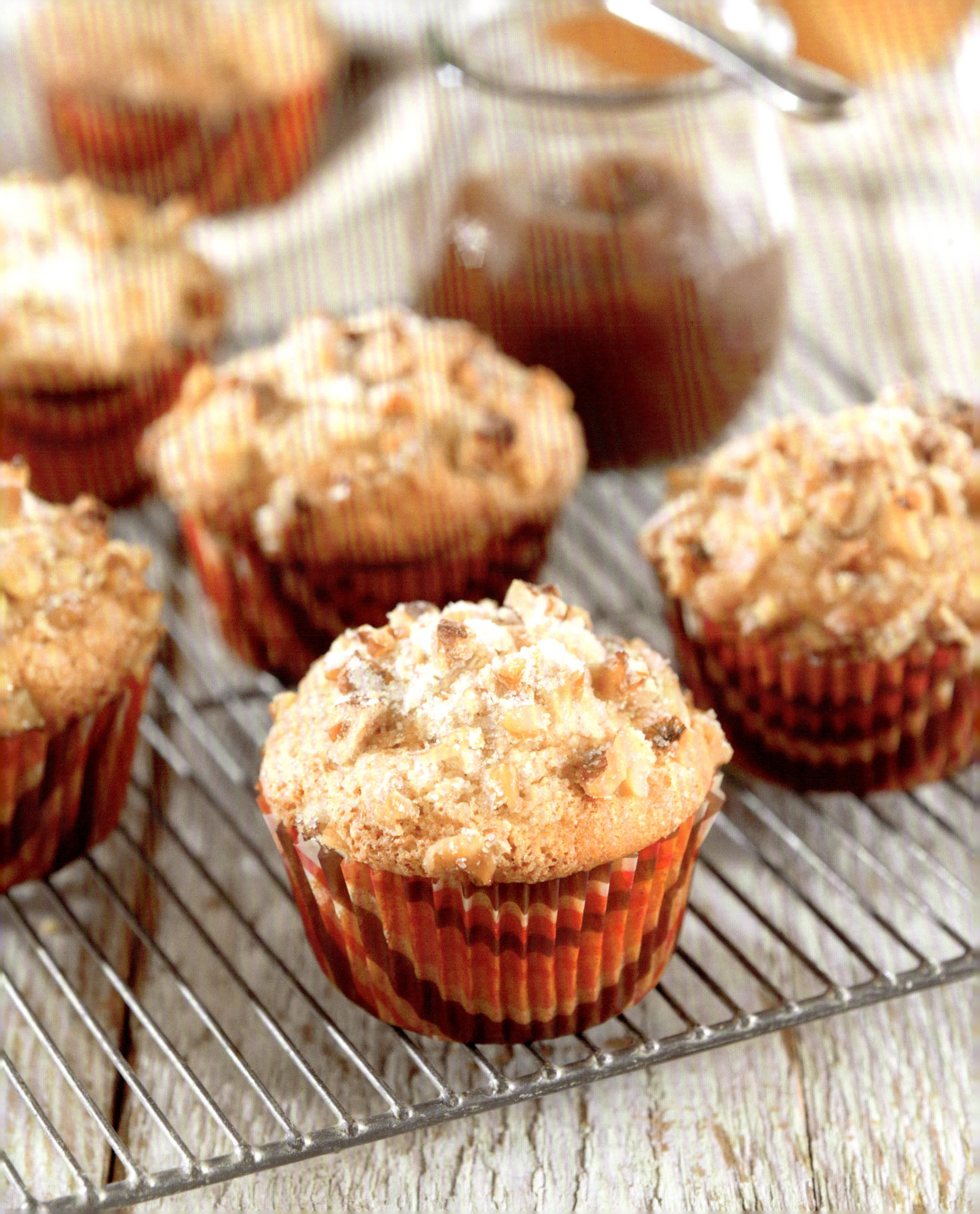

Cherry Lemon Poppy Seed Muffins

MAKES 12 MUFFINS

- 2 cups all-purpose flour
- 1 cup sugar
- 1 tablespoon baking powder
- 1 teaspoon salt
- ¾ cup buttermilk
- ¼ cup vegetable oil
- ¼ cup (½ stick) butter, melted
- 2 eggs, lightly beaten
- Grated peel of 1 lemon
- 1 tablespoon lemon juice
- 1 teaspoon vanilla
- ½ cup dried sweet cherries, chopped
- ½ cup chopped pecans
- 2 tablespoons poppy seeds

1. Preheat oven to 350°F. Spray 12 standard (2½-inch) muffin cups with nonstick cooking spray or line with paper baking cups.

2. Combine flour, sugar, baking powder and salt in large bowl; mix well.

3. Whisk buttermilk, oil, butter, eggs, lemon peel, lemon juice and vanilla in medium bowl until well blended. Add to flour mixture; stir just until blended. Stir in cherries, pecans and poppy seeds. Spoon batter evenly into prepared muffin cups.

4. Bake 20 to 24 minutes or until golden brown and toothpick inserted into centers comes out clean. Cool in pan 5 minutes; remove to wire rack to cool completely.

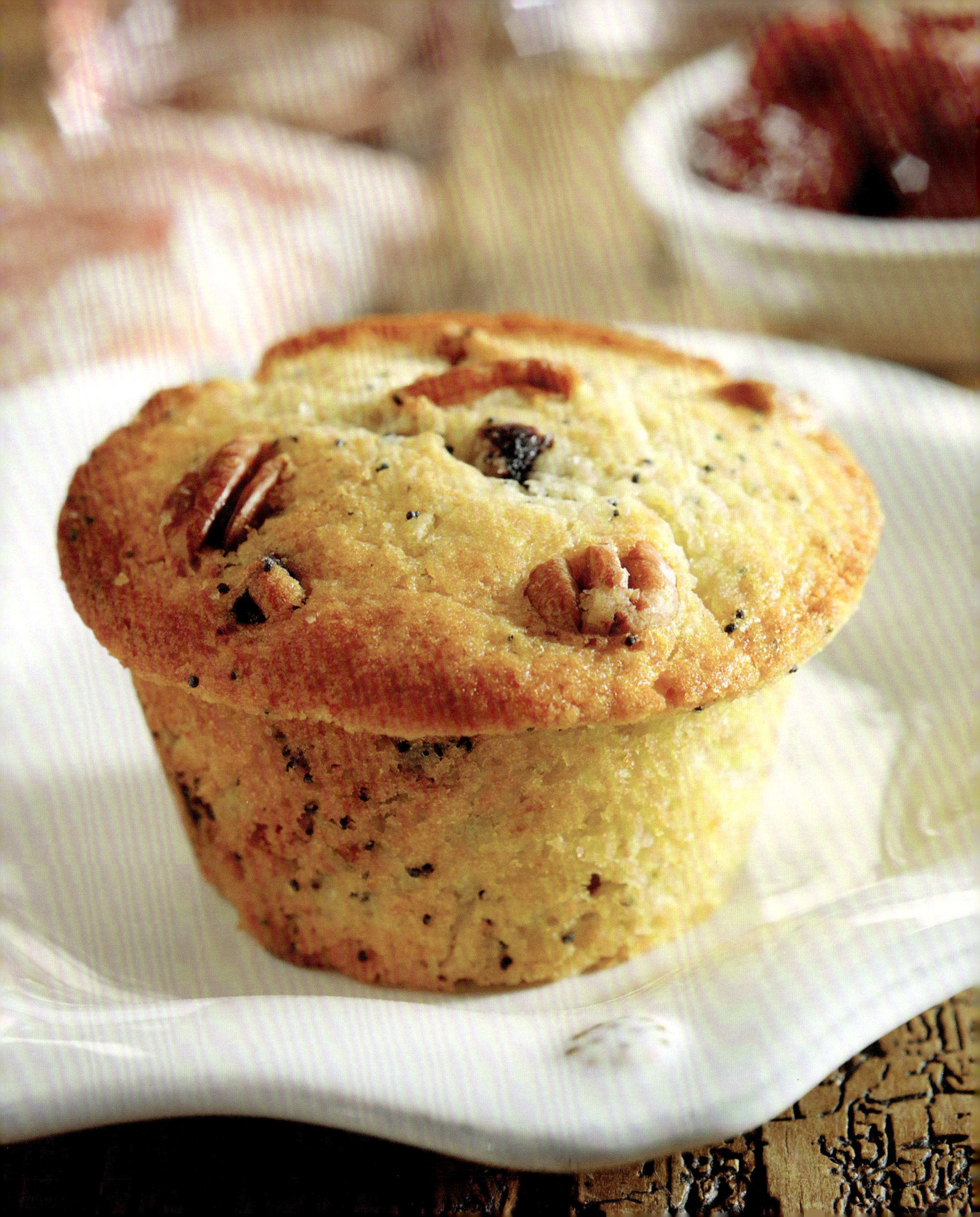

Carrot Oat Muffins

MAKES 12 MUFFINS

- ¾ cup plus 2 tablespoons old-fashioned oats
- ¾ cup all-purpose flour
- ¾ cup whole wheat flour
- ⅓ cup sugar
- 1½ teaspoons baking powder
- 1 teaspoon ground cinnamon
- ½ teaspoon baking soda
- ¼ teaspoon salt
- ½ cup milk
- ½ cup unsweetened applesauce
- 2 eggs
- 2 tablespoons vegetable or canola oil
- ½ cup shredded carrot (1 medium to large carrot)
- ¼ cup finely chopped walnuts (optional)

1. Preheat oven to 350°F. Spray 12 standard (2½-inch) muffin cups with nonstick cooking spray or line with paper baking cups.
2. Combine oats, all-purpose flour, whole wheat flour, sugar, baking powder, cinnamon, baking soda and salt in medium bowl; mix well.
3. Whisk milk, applesauce, eggs and oil in large bowl until blended. Stir in carrot. Add flour mixture; stir just until dry ingredients are moistened.
4. Spoon batter into prepared muffin cups, filling two-thirds to three-fourths full. Sprinkle each muffin with 1 teaspoon walnuts, if desired.
5. Bake 20 to 22 minutes or until golden brown. Cool in pan 5 minutes; remove to wire rack to cool completely.

> **NOTE** These muffins are best eaten the same day.

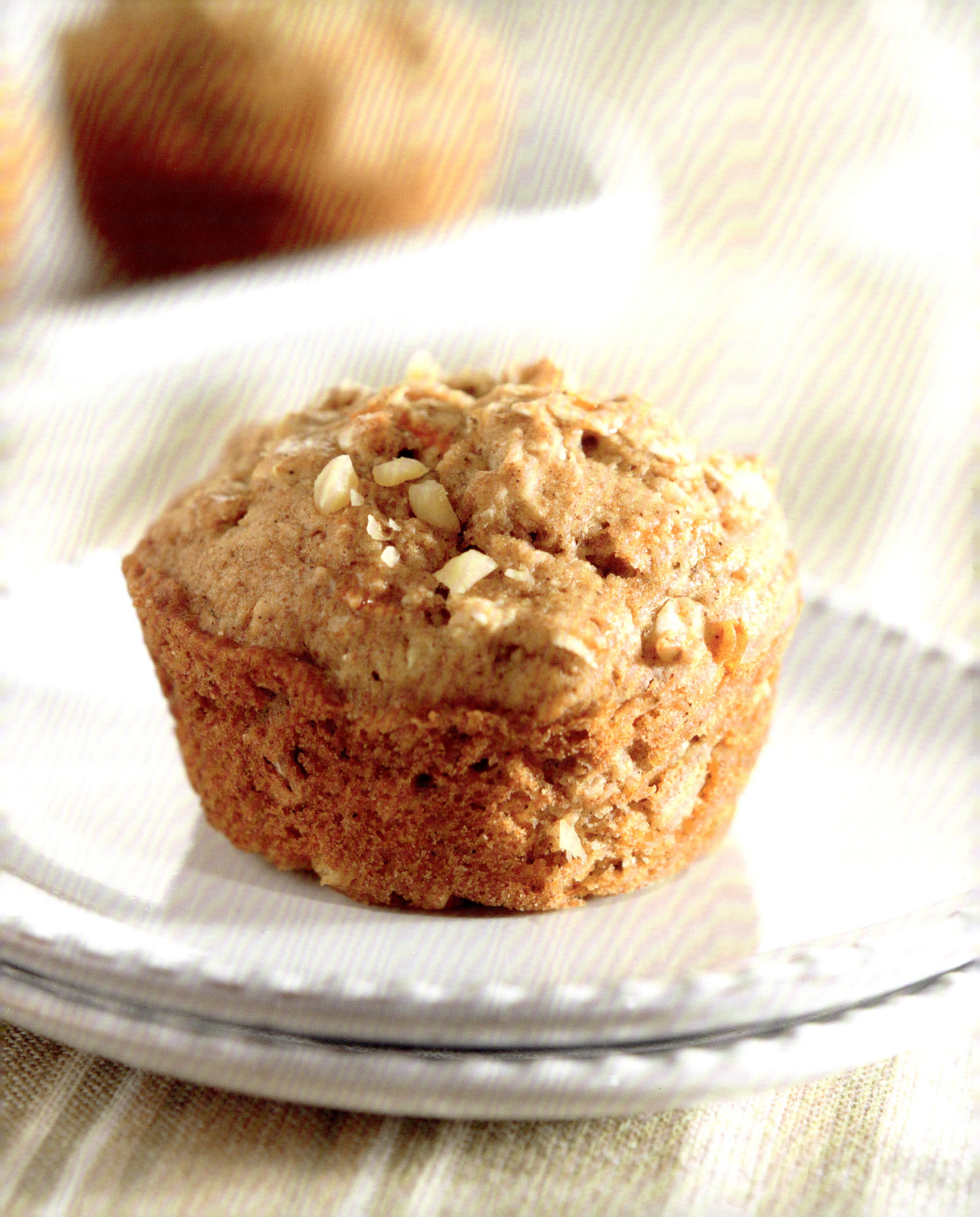

Sun-Dried Tomato Basil Muffins

MAKES 12 MUFFINS

- ½ cup sun-dried tomatoes (about 12 pieces, not oil-packed)
- 2 cups all-purpose flour
- 1 tablespoon baking powder
- 1½ teaspoons dried basil
- ½ teaspoon salt
- ¼ teaspoon black pepper
- ⅛ teaspoon garlic powder
- ¾ cup milk
- ½ cup (4 ounces) cottage cheese
- 1 egg
- ¼ cup vegetable or canola oil
- 2 teaspoons minced dried onion

1. Preheat oven to 400°F. Spray 12 standard (2½-inch) muffin cups with nonstick cooking spray or line with foil baking cups.

2. Place sun-dried tomatoes in small bowl; add hot water to cover. Let stand 10 minutes to soften. Drain and finely chop.

3. Combine flour, baking powder, basil, salt, pepper and garlic powder in large bowl; mix well.

4. Whisk milk, cottage cheese, egg, oil, onion and tomatoes in medium bowl until well blended. Add to flour mixture; stir just until dry ingredients are moistened. Spoon batter evenly into prepared muffin cups.

5. Bake 20 to 25 minutes or until toothpick inserted into center comes out clean. Cool in pan 5 minutes. Serve warm.

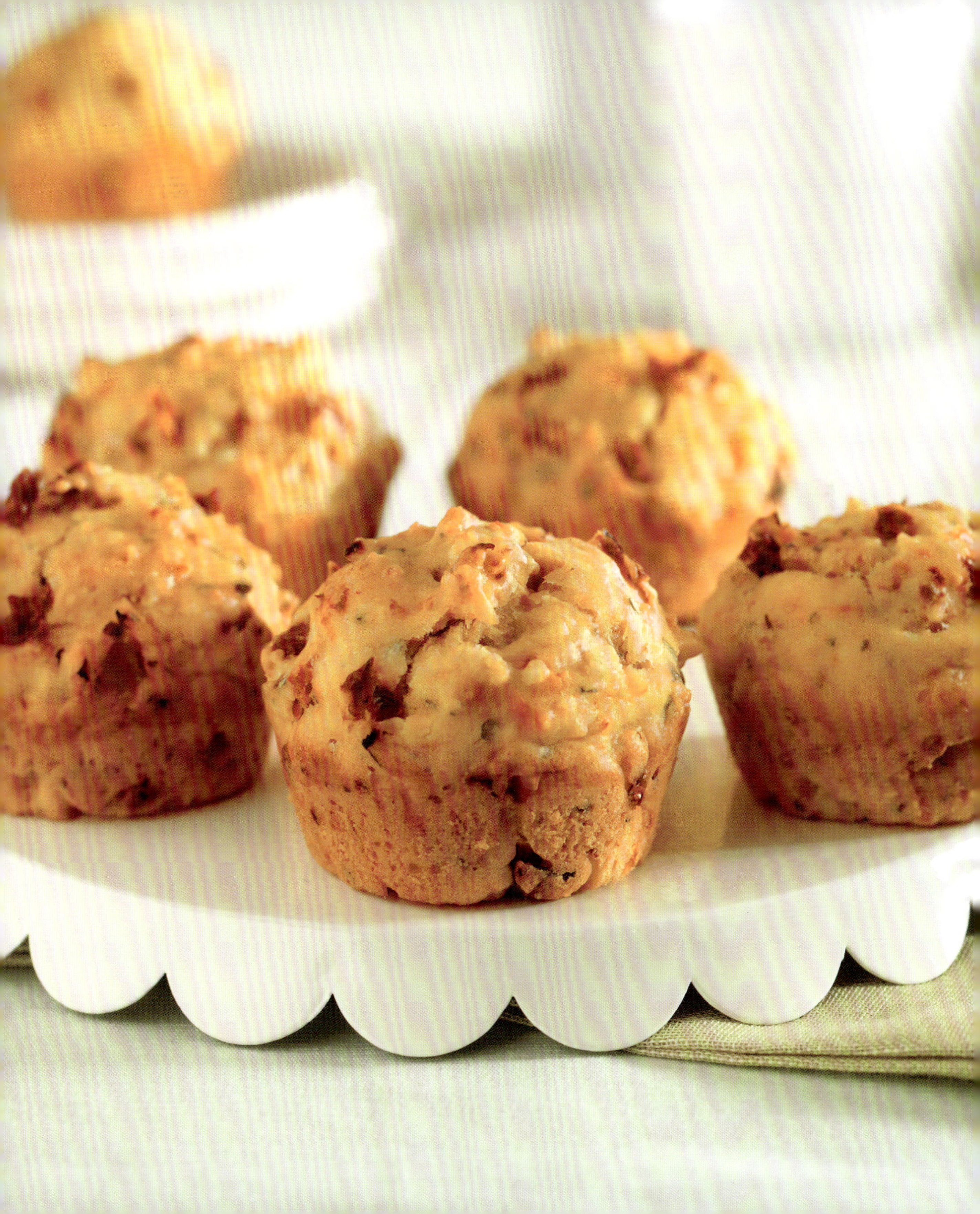

Blueberry Muffins

MAKES 12 MUFFINS

- 2 cups all-purpose flour
- 2¼ teaspoons baking powder
- ½ teaspoon salt
- ¼ teaspoon baking soda
- 1 cup granulated sugar
- ½ cup (1 stick) butter, melted
- ¾ cup buttermilk
- 2 eggs
- 1 teaspoon grated lemon peel
- 1½ cups blueberries
- 2 tablespoons sparkling sugar *or* 4 tablespoons turbinado sugar

1. Preheat oven to 375°F. Line 12 standard (2½-inch) muffin pan cups with paper baking cups or spray with nonstick cooking spray.

2. Combine flour, baking powder, salt and baking soda in medium bowl; mix well.

3. Whisk granulated sugar and butter in large bowl until well blended. Add buttermilk, eggs and lemon peel; whisk until well blended. Add flour; stir just until dry ingredients are moistened. Gently fold in blueberries.

4. Divide batter evenly between prepared muffin cups (cups will be almost full). Sprinkle ½ teaspoon sparkling sugar or 1 teaspoon turbinado sugar over each muffin.

5. Bake 20 to 22 minutes or until toothpick inserted into centers comes out clean. Cool in pan 10 minutes; remove to wire rack. Serve warm or cool completely.

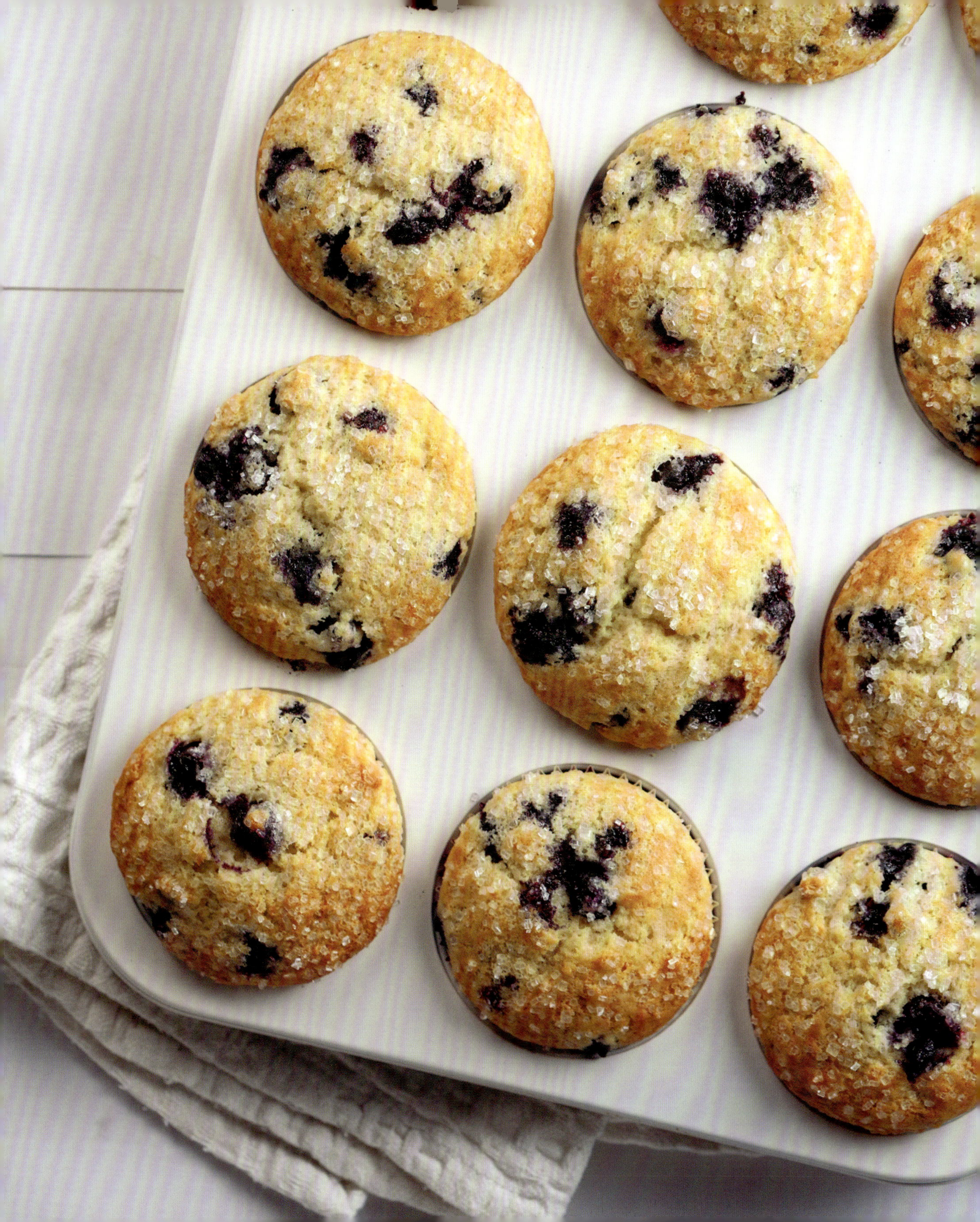

Cheddar Apple Muffins
MAKES 12 MUFFINS

- 2 cups all-purpose flour
- 3 tablespoons sugar
- 1 tablespoon baking powder
- 1 teaspoon salt
- ⅛ teaspoon ground red pepper
- 1½ cups chopped peeled Granny Smith apple (about 1 large)
- 1 cup (4 ounces) grated sharp Cheddar cheese
- 1 cup milk
- 2 eggs
- ¼ cup (½ stick) butter, melted

1. Preheat oven to 400°F. Spray 12 standard (2½-inch) muffin cups with nonstick cooking spray or line with paper baking cups.

2. Combine flour, sugar, baking powder, salt and red pepper in large bowl; mix well. Stir in apple and cheese until blended.

3. Whisk milk, eggs and butter in medium bowl until well blended. Add to flour mixture; stir just until dry ingredients are moistened. Spoon batter evenly into prepared muffin cups, filling almost full.

4. Bake 18 to 20 minutes or until toothpick inserted into centers comes out clean and muffins feel firm when lightly pressed. Cool in pan 5 minutes; remove to wire rack. Serve warm or cool completely.

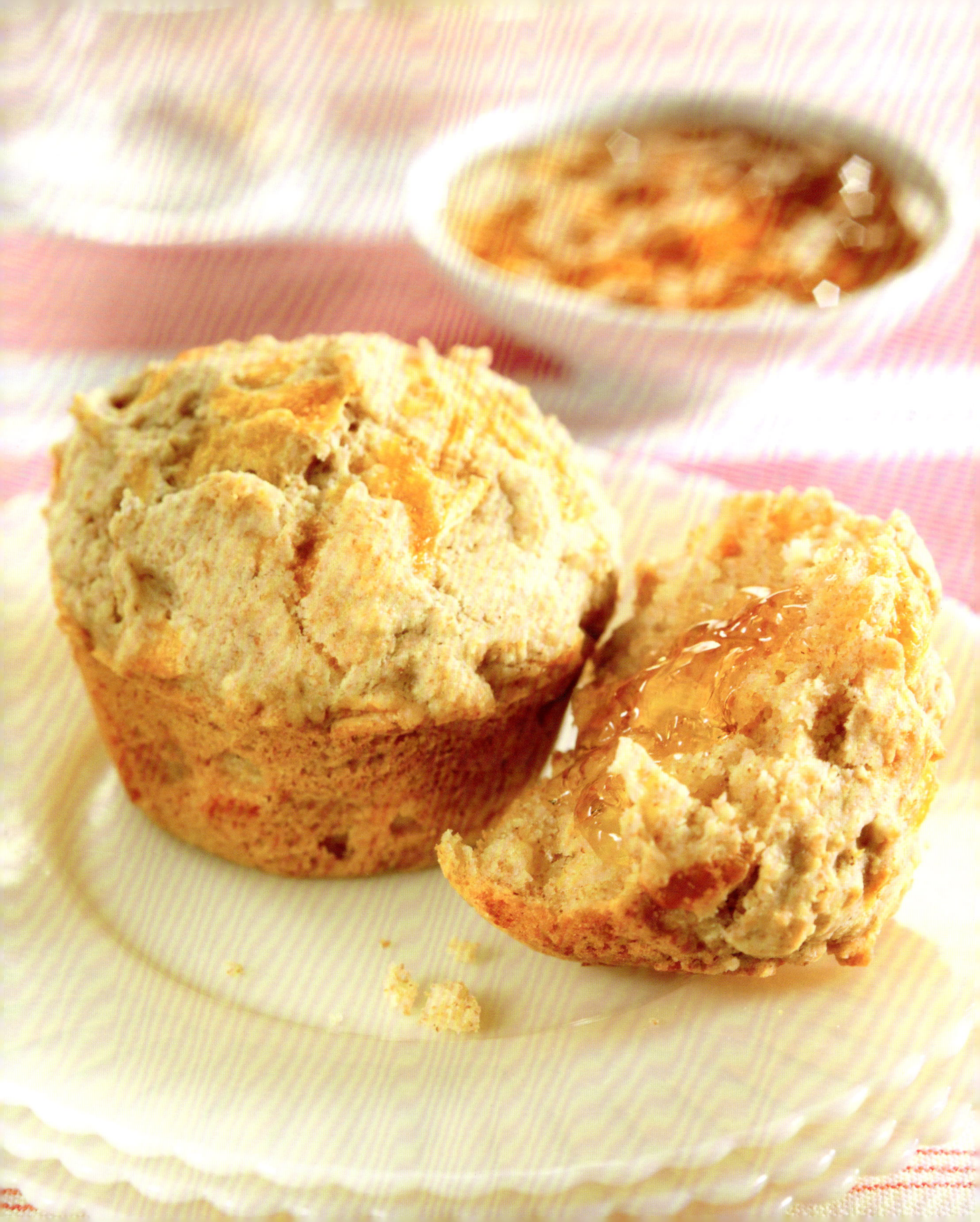

Chocolate Peanut Oatmeal Muffins

MAKES 12 MUFFINS

- 1 cup buttermilk
- 1 cup quick oats
- ¾ cup all-purpose flour
- ¼ cup Dutch process or regular unsweetened cocoa powder
- 1 teaspoon baking powder
- ¾ teaspoon salt
- ½ teaspoon baking soda
- ⅔ cup packed dark brown sugar
- ⅓ cup vegetable oil
- 1 egg
- 1 teaspoon vanilla
- ¾ cup roasted salted peanuts, chopped

1. Preheat oven to 400°F. Line 12 standard (2½-inch) muffin cups with paper baking cups or spray with nonstick cooking spray.

2. Combine buttermilk and oats in medium bowl; mix well. Let stand 15 minutes.

3. Meanwhile, combine flour, cocoa, baking powder, salt and baking soda in small bowl; mix well.

4. Whisk brown sugar, oil, egg and vanilla in large bowl until well blended. Add oat mixture; mix well. Add flour mixture; stir just until blended. Stir in peanuts. Spoon batter evenly into prepared muffin cups, filling almost full.

5. Bake 13 to 15 minutes or until toothpick inserted into centers comes out clean. Cool in pan 5 minutes; remove to wire rack. Serve warm or cool completely.

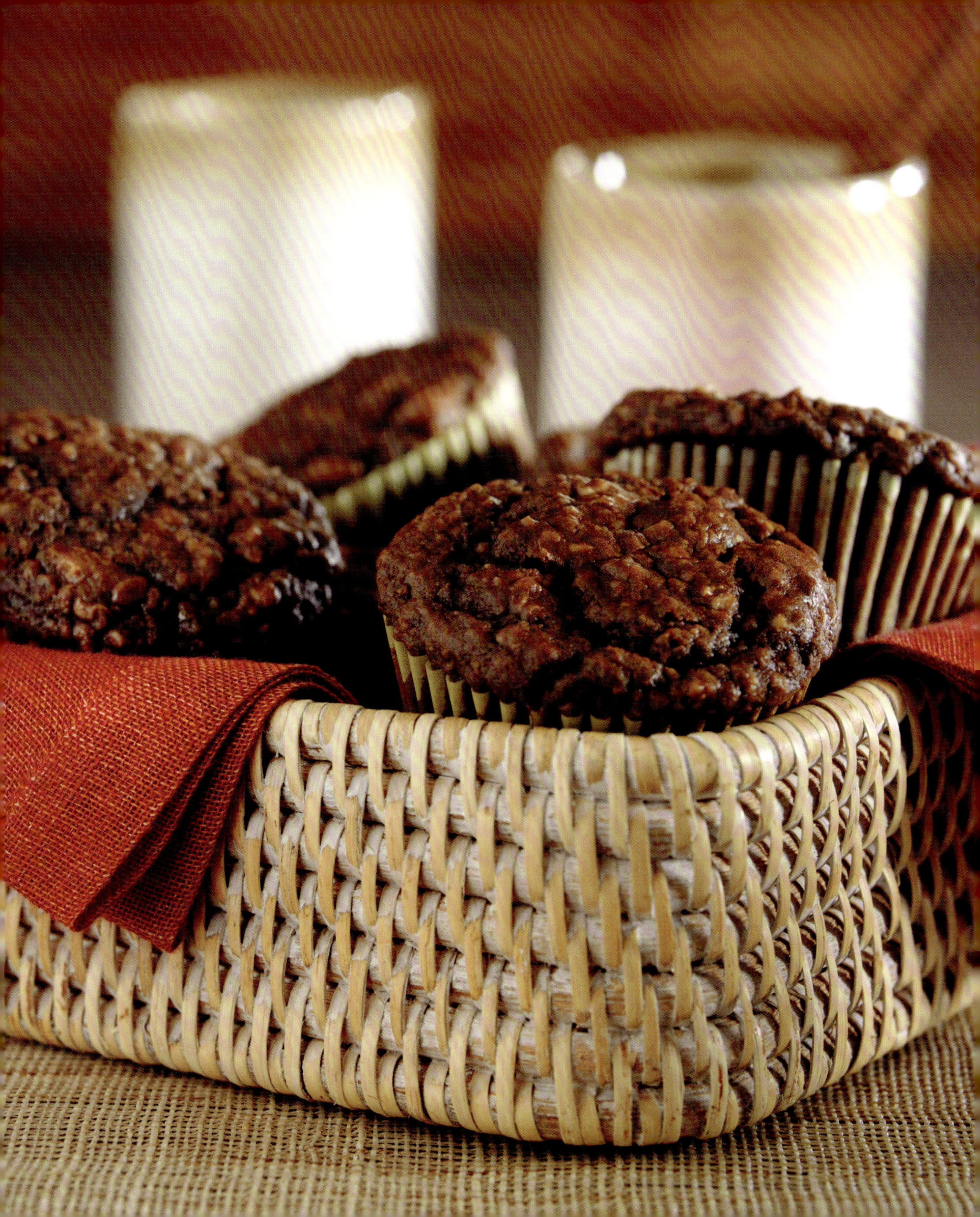

Corn Bread Muffins

MAKES 9 MUFFINS

- 1¼ cups yellow cornmeal
- 1 cup all-purpose flour
- ¼ cup granulated sugar
- 1 tablespoon baking powder
- 1 teaspoon salt
- ¾ cup milk
- 1 egg
- ¼ cup (½ stick) plus 1 tablespoon butter, melted, divided
- ¼ cup plus 1 tablespoon honey, divided

1. Preheat oven to 400°F. Spray 9 standard (2½-inch) muffin cups with nonstick cooking spray or line with paper baking cups.

2. Combine cornmeal, flour, sugar, baking powder and salt in large bowl; mix well.

3. Whisk milk, egg, ¼ cup melted butter and ¼ cup honey in medium bowl until well blended. Add to cornmeal mixture; stir just until combined. Divide batter evenly between prepared muffin cups. (Cups will be almost full.)

4. Bake 13 to 15 minutes or until toothpick inserted into centers comes out clean. Meanwhile, stir remaining 1 tablespoon melted butter and 1 tablespoon honey in small bowl until smooth.

5. Brush honey butter over muffins immediately after removing from oven. Cool muffins in pan 5 minutes; remove to wire rack. Serve warm.

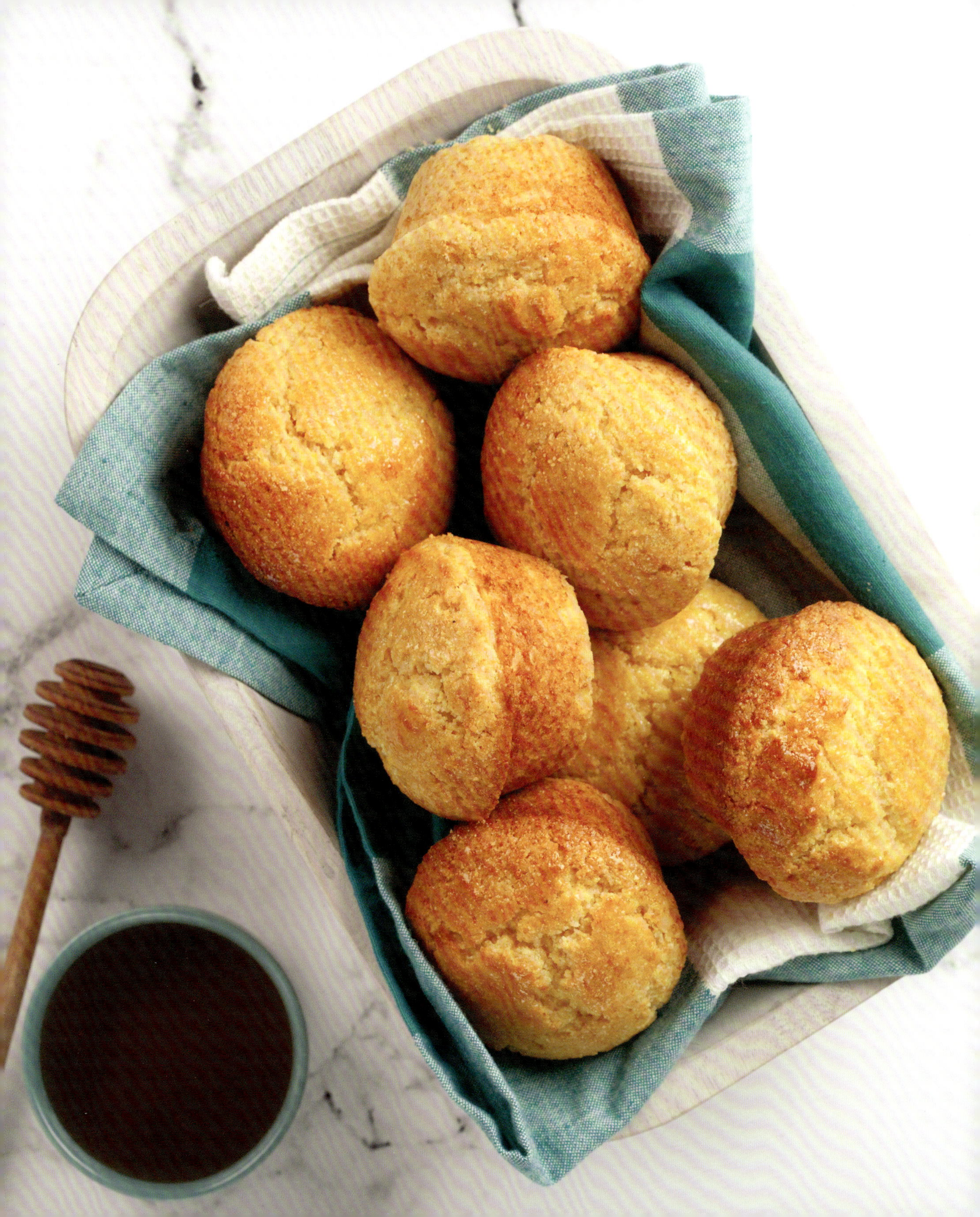

Maple Magic Muffins
MAKES 12 MUFFINS

- ½ cup plus 3 tablespoons maple syrup,* divided
- ¼ cup chopped walnuts
- 2 tablespoons butter, melted
- 2 cups all-purpose flour
- ¾ cup sugar
- 2 teaspoons baking powder
- ½ teaspoon baking soda
- ½ teaspoon salt
- ¼ teaspoon ground cinnamon
- ¾ cup plus 1 tablespoon milk
- ½ cup vegetable oil
- 1 egg
- ½ teaspoon vanilla

*For best flavor and texture, use pure maple syrup, not pancake syrup.

1. Preheat oven to 400°F. Spray 12 standard (2½-inch) muffin cups with nonstick cooking spray.

2. Pour 2 teaspoons maple syrup into each muffin cup; top with 1 teaspoon walnuts and ½ teaspoon butter.

3. Combine flour, sugar, baking powder, baking soda, salt and cinnamon in large bowl; mix well.

4. Whisk milk, oil, egg, remaining 3 tablespoons maple syrup and vanilla in medium bowl until well blended. Add to flour mixture; stir just until dry ingredients are moistened. Spoon batter into prepared muffin cups, filling two-thirds full. Place muffin pan on baking sheet to catch any drips (maple syrup may overflow slightly).

5. Bake 20 to 25 minutes or until toothpick inserted into centers comes out clean. Invert pan onto wire rack covered with waxed paper. Cool 5 to 10 minutes; serve warm.

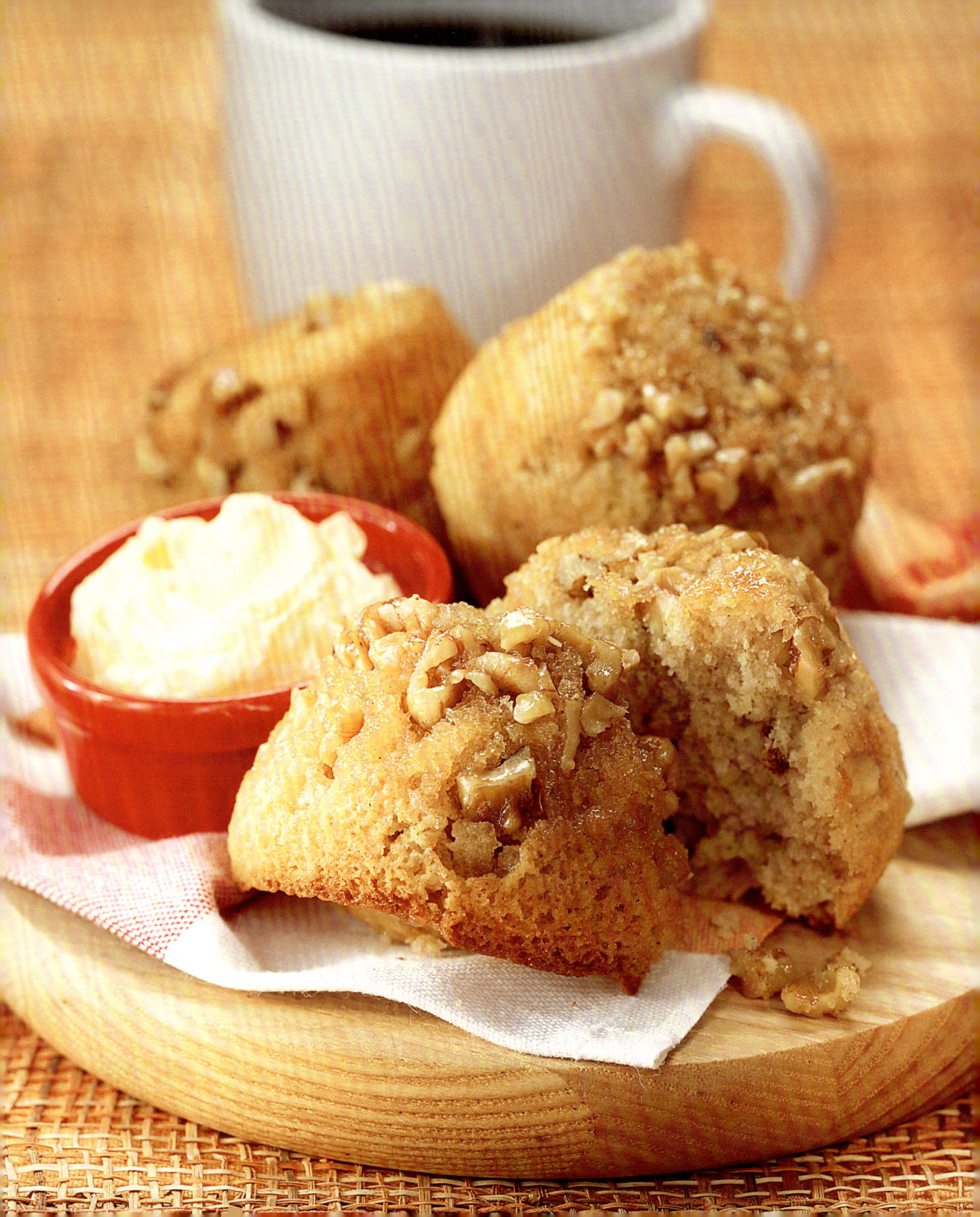

Peanut Butter Bran Muffins

MAKES 12 MUFFINS

- ½ cup peanut butter
- 2 tablespoons butter, softened
- ¼ cup packed brown sugar
- 1 egg
- 1 cup whole bran cereal
- 1 cup milk
- ¾ cup all-purpose flour
- 1 tablespoon baking powder
- ½ teaspoon salt
- ½ cup dark raisins

1. Heat oven to 400°F. Spray 12 standard (2½-inch) muffin cups with nonstick cooking spray or line with paper baking cups.

2. Combine peanut butter, butter, brown sugar and egg in food processor; process 5 to 10 seconds or until smooth. Add cereal and milk; pulse just until blended.

3. Add flour, baking powder and salt; pulse 2 to 3 times or just until flour is moistened. (Do not overprocess; batter should be lumpy.) Sprinkle raisins over batter; pulse just until raisins are incorporated into batter. Spoon batter into prepared muffin cups, filling about three-fourths full.

4. Bake 20 to 25 minutes or until golden brown. Cool in pan 5 minutes; remove to wire rack. Serve warm.

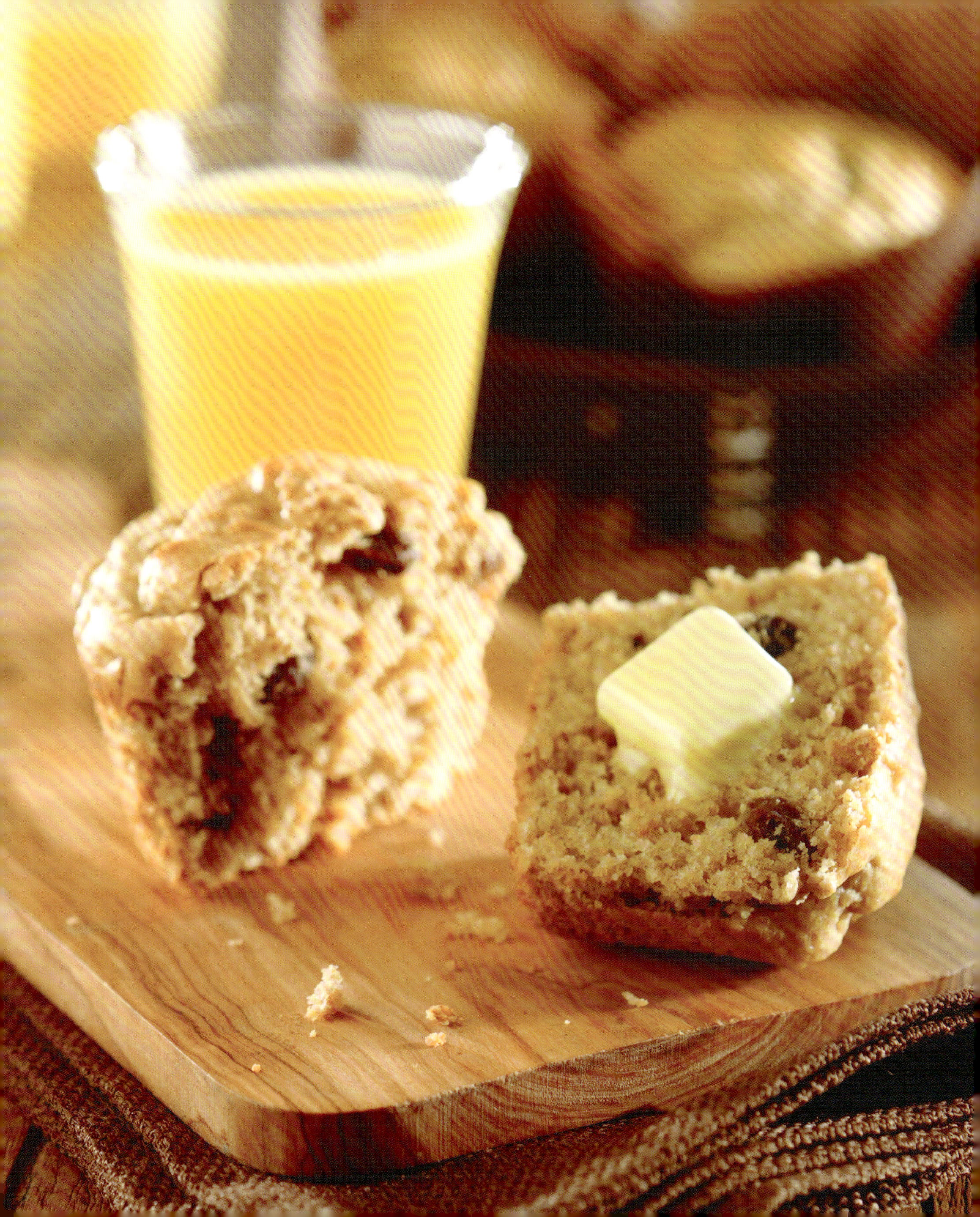

Banana Chocolate Chip Muffins

MAKES 15 MUFFINS

- 2 cups all-purpose flour
- ¼ cup granulated sugar
- ¼ cup packed brown sugar
- 1½ teaspoons baking powder
- ½ teaspoon salt
- ¼ teaspoon baking soda
- 1 cup mashed ripe bananas (about 2 large or 3 small)
- ½ cup (1 stick) butter, melted
- 2 eggs
- ⅓ cup buttermilk
- 1 teaspoon vanilla
- 1 package (about 11 ounces) semisweet chocolate chips

1. Preheat oven to 375°F. Spray 15 standard (2½-inch) muffin cups with nonstick cooking spray or line with paper baking cups.

2. Combine flour, granulated sugar, brown sugar, baking powder, salt and baking soda in large bowl; mix well. Whisk bananas, butter, eggs, buttermilk and vanilla in medium bowl until well blended. Add to flour mixture; stir just until blended. Stir in chocolate chips. Spoon batter evenly into prepared muffin cups, filling almost full. Smooth tops.

3. Bake about 20 minutes or until toothpick inserted into centers comes out clean. Cool in pans 5 minutes; remove to wire racks. Serve warm or cool completely.

Garden Vegetable Muffins
MAKES 12 MUFFINS

- 2 cups all-purpose flour
- 2 tablespoons sugar
- 1 tablespoon baking powder
- ¼ teaspoon salt
- 3 ounces cream cheese
- ¾ cup milk
- ½ cup finely shredded or grated carrots
- ¼ cup chopped green onions
- ¼ cup vegetable oil
- 1 egg

1. Preheat oven to 400°F. Line 12 standard (2½-inch) muffin cups with paper baking cups or spray with nonstick cooking spray.

2. Combine flour, sugar, baking powder and salt in large bowl; mix well. Cut in cream cheese with pastry blender or two knives until mixture resembles coarse crumbs.

3. Combine milk, carrots, green onions, oil and egg in small bowl; mix well. Add to flour mixture; stir just until moistened. Spoon batter evenly into prepared muffin cups.

4. Bake 25 to 30 minutes until toothpick inserted into centers comes out clean. Immediately remove muffins to wire rack; cool 10 minutes. Serve warm.

Lemon Poppy Seed Muffins
MAKES 18 MUFFINS

- 2 cups all-purpose flour
- 1¼ cups granulated sugar
- ¼ cup poppy seeds
- 2 tablespoons plus 2 teaspoons grated lemon peel, divided
- 2 teaspoons baking powder
- ½ teaspoon baking soda
- ½ teaspoon ground cardamom
- ¼ teaspoon salt
- 2 eggs
- ½ cup (1 stick) butter, melted
- ½ cup milk
- ½ cup plus 2 tablespoons lemon juice, divided
- 1 cup powdered sugar

1. Preheat oven to 400°F. Line 18 standard (2½-inch) muffin cups with paper baking cups or spray with nonstick cooking spray.

2. Combine flour, granulated sugar, poppy seeds, 2 tablespoons lemon peel, baking powder, baking soda, cardamom and salt in large bowl; mix well.

3. Beat eggs in medium bowl. Whisk in butter, milk and ½ cup lemon juice until well blended. Add to flour mixture; stir just until blended. Spoon batter evenly into prepared muffin cups, filling three-fourths full.

4. Bake 15 to 20 minutes or until toothpick inserted into centers comes out clean. Cool in pans on wire racks 10 minutes.

5. Meanwhile, prepare glaze. Combine powdered sugar and remaining 2 teaspoons lemon peel in small bowl; stir in enough remaining lemon juice to make pourable glaze. Place muffins on sheet of parchment or waxed paper; drizzle with glaze. Serve warm or at room temperature.

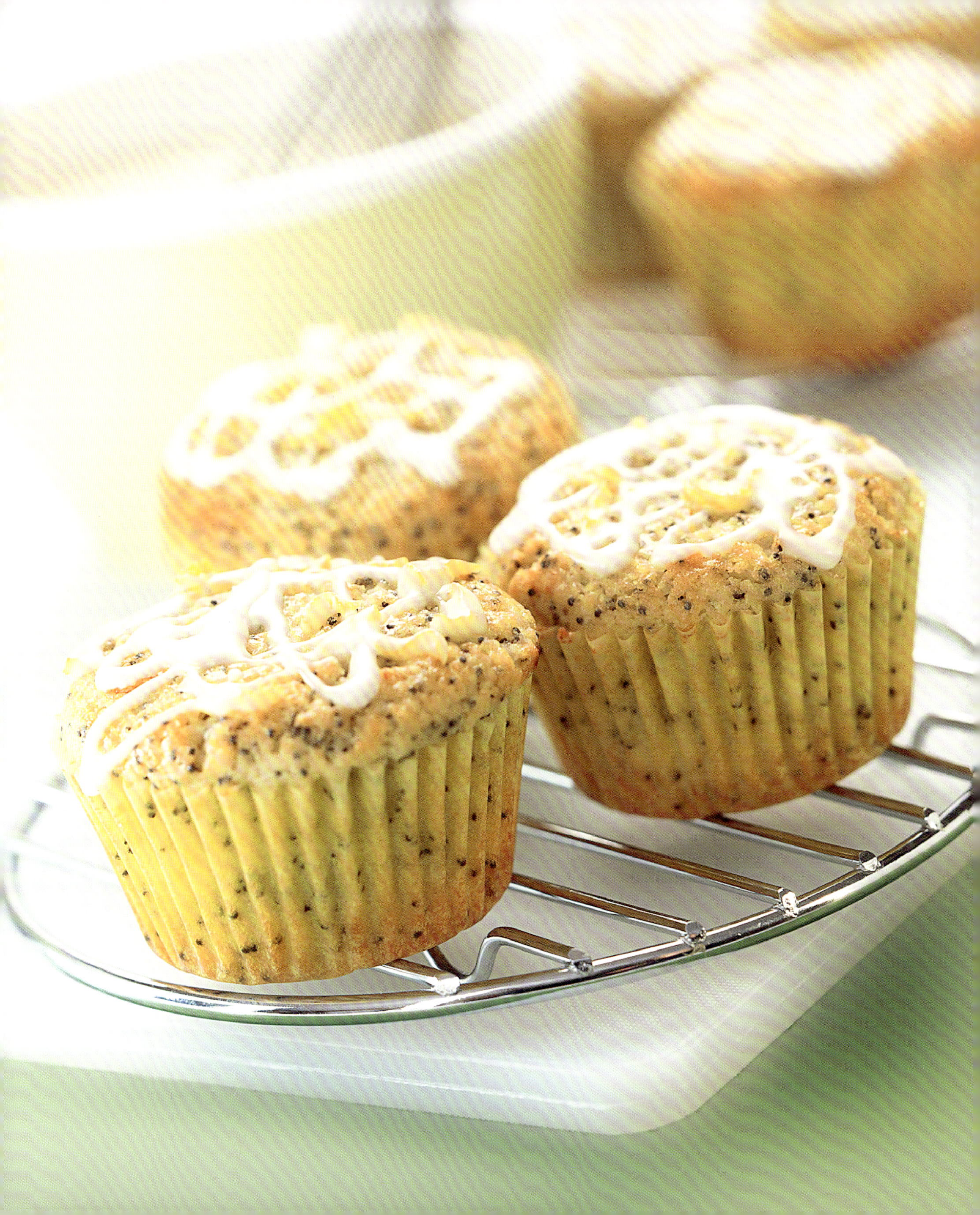

Cranberry Oatmeal Mini Muffins

MAKES 24 MUFFINS

1 cup quick oats
¾ cup milk
1 egg, beaten
2 tablespoons butter, melted
1 cup all-purpose flour
⅓ cup packed brown sugar
1 tablespoon baking powder
½ teaspoon baking soda
½ teaspoon cinnamon
¼ teaspoon salt
½ cup finely chopped dried cranberries *or* ¼ cup finely chopped dried cranberries and ¼ cup finely chopped walnuts

1. Preheat oven to 375°F. Spray 24 mini (1¾-inch) muffin cups with nonstick cooking spray.

2. Combine oats and milk in large bowl; mix well. Let stand 5 minutes. Stir in egg and butter until blended.

3. Combine flour, brown sugar, baking powder, baking soda, cinnamon and salt in small bowl; mix well. Add to oat mixture; stir just until dry ingredients are moistened. Stir in cranberries. Spoon batter into prepared pans, filling three-fourths full.

4. Bake 12 to 15 minutes or until toothpick inserted in centers comes out clean. Cool in pans 1 minute; remove to wire racks to cool completely.

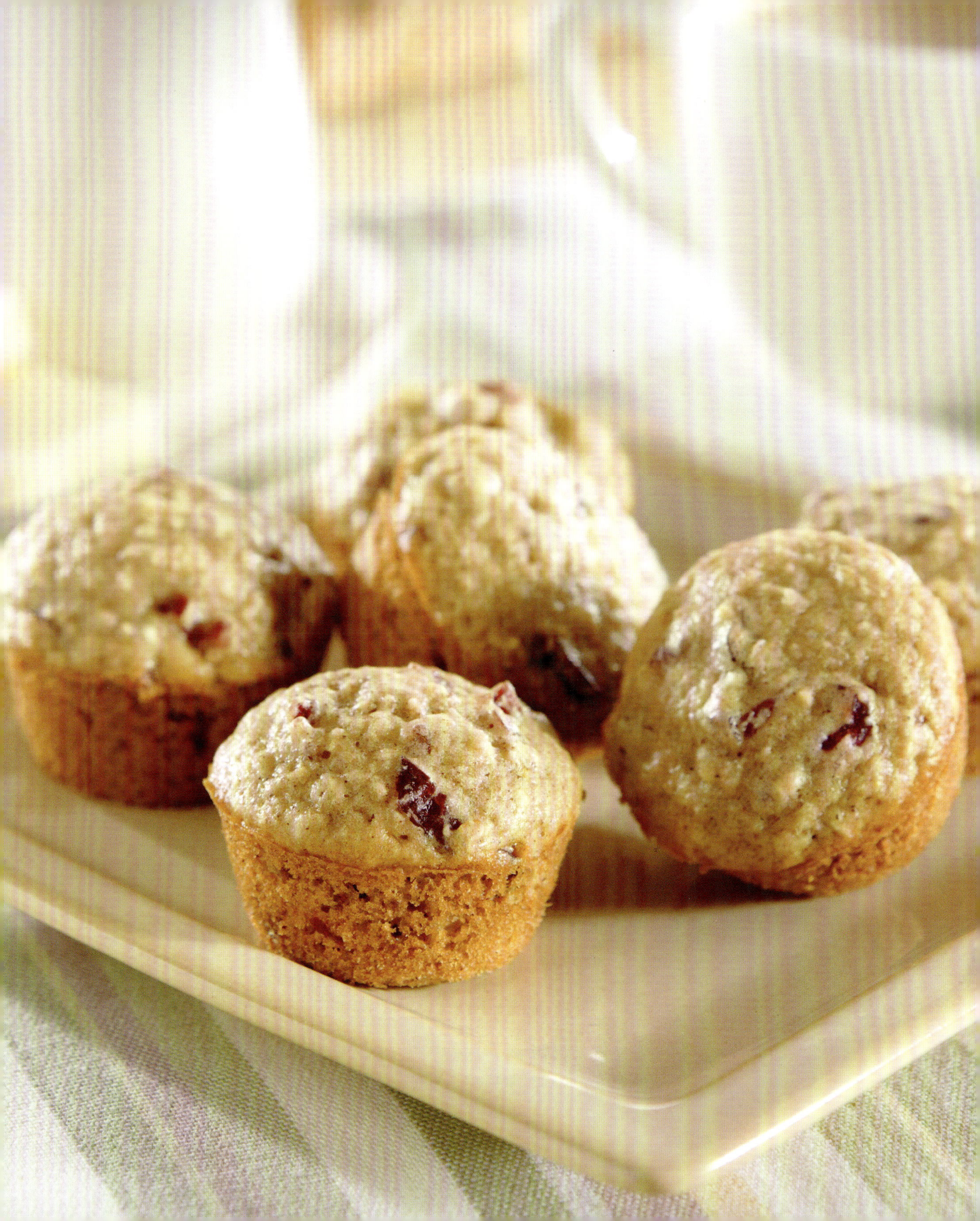

Apple Date Nut Muffins

MAKES 12 MUFFINS

1½ cups all-purpose flour
⅔ cup packed brown sugar
½ cup old-fashioned oats
1 tablespoon baking powder
1 teaspoon ground cinnamon
½ teaspoon salt
⅛ teaspoon ground nutmeg
⅛ teaspoon ground ginger
  Pinch ground cloves
1 cup coarsely chopped peeled apples
½ cup chopped walnuts
½ cup chopped pitted dates
½ cup (1 stick) butter, melted
2 eggs
¼ cup milk

1. Preheat oven to 400°F. Line 12 standard (2½-inch) muffin cups with paper baking cups or spray with nonstick cooking spray.

2. Combine flour, brown sugar, oats, baking powder, cinnamon, salt, nutmeg, ginger and cloves in large bowl; mix well. Stir in apples, walnuts and dates.

3. Whisk butter, eggs and milk in small bowl until blended. Add to flour mixture; stir just until dry ingredients are moistened. Spoon batter evenly into prepared muffin cups.

4. Bake 20 to 25 minutes or until toothpick inserted into centers comes out clean. Remove to wire rack to cool completely.

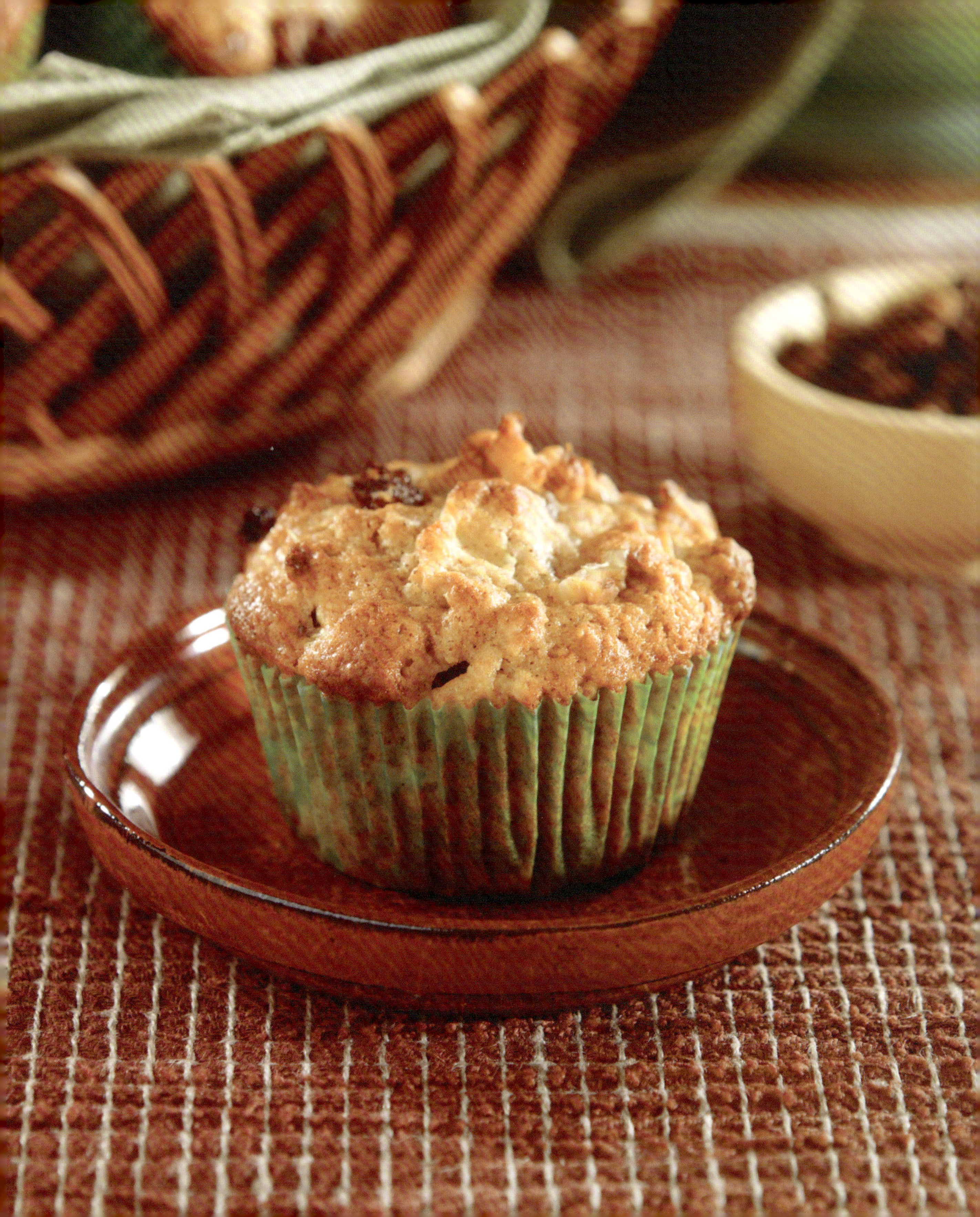

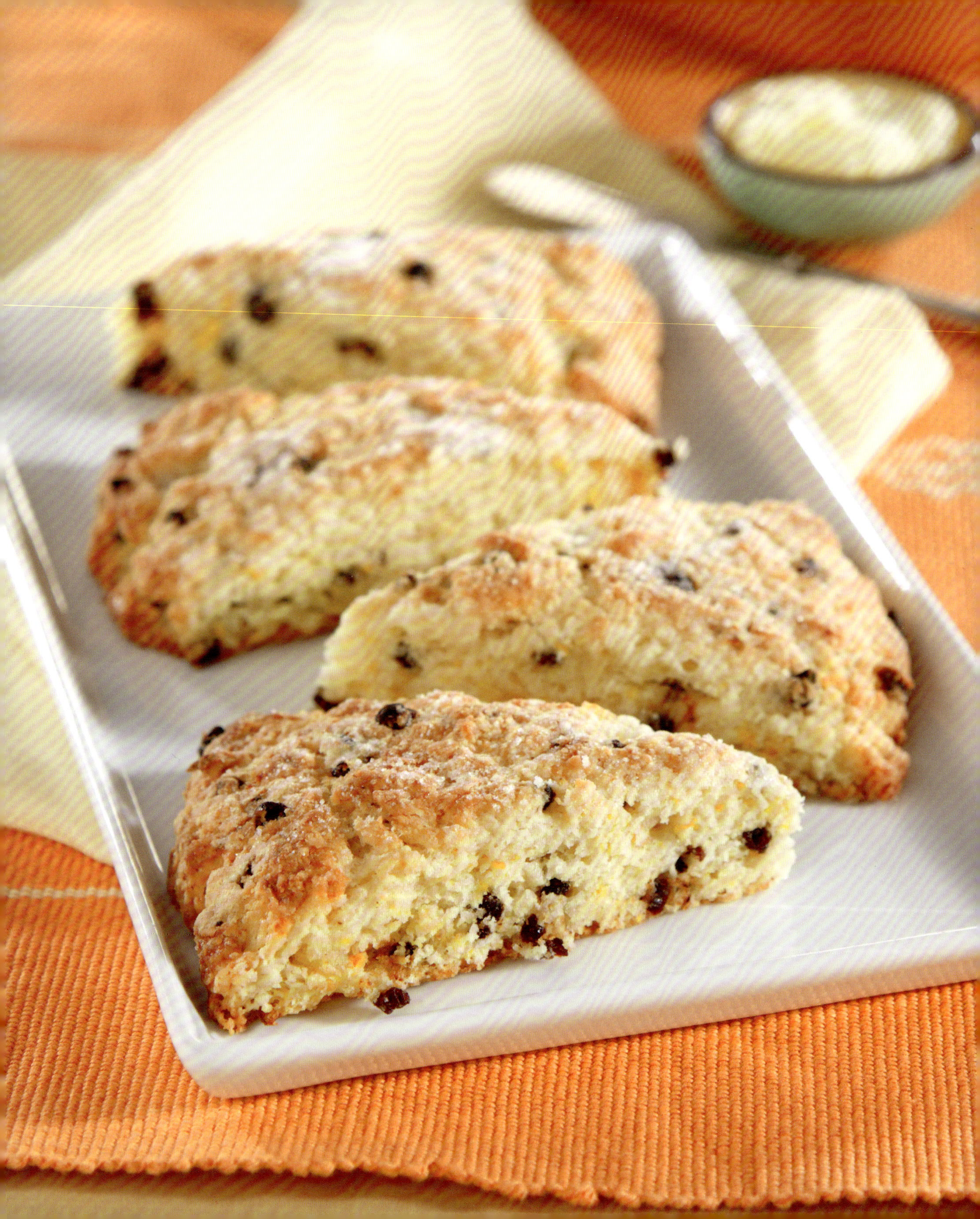

SCONES

Orange Currant Scones
MAKES 8 SCONES

- 1½ cups all-purpose flour
- ¼ cup plus 1 teaspoon sugar, divided
- 1 teaspoon baking powder
- ¼ teaspoon salt
- ¼ teaspoon baking soda
- ⅓ cup currants
- 1 tablespoon grated orange peel
- 6 tablespoons (¾ stick) cold butter, cut into small pieces
- ½ cup buttermilk, yogurt or sour cream

1. Preheat oven to 425°F. Line baking sheet with parchment paper or spray with nonstick cooking spray.

2. Combine flour, ¼ cup sugar, baking powder, salt and baking soda in large bowl; mix well. Stir in currants and orange peel. Cut in butter with pastry blender or two knives until mixture resembles coarse crumbs. Add buttermilk; stir to form soft, sticky dough that clings together.

3. Shape dough into a ball; pat into 8-inch round on prepared baking sheet. Cut dough into eight wedges with floured knife. Sprinkle with remaining 1 teaspoon sugar.

4. Bake 18 to 20 minutes or until lightly browned.

Walnut Ginger Scones

MAKES 8 SCONES

- 1 cup all-purpose flour
- 1 cup whole wheat flour
- 1 cup coarsely chopped walnuts, toasted*
- ¾ cup diced crystallized ginger
- ½ cup raisins
- ¼ cup plus 1 teaspoon sugar, divided
- 1 tablespoon baking powder
- ½ teaspoon salt
- ½ teaspoon ground cinnamon
- ½ cup (1 stick) cold butter, cut into small pieces
- ¾ to 1 cup half-and-half

*To toast walnuts, spread on ungreased baking sheet. Bake in preheated 350°F oven 8 to 10 minutes or until golden brown, stirring occasionally.

1. Preheat oven to 425°F. Line baking sheet with parchment paper or spray with nonstick cooking spray.

2. Combine all-purpose flour, whole wheat flour, walnuts, ginger, raisins, ¼ cup sugar, baking powder, salt and cinnamon in large bowl; mix well. Cut in butter with pastry blender or two knives until mixture is crumbly. Add half-and-half by ¼ cupfuls, stirring gently until dough comes together.

3. Pat dough into 10-inch circle on prepared baking sheet; sprinkle with remaining 1 teaspoon sugar. Cut dough into 10 wedges. Pull wedges apart, leaving 1 inch between wedges.

4. Bake 15 minutes or until golden brown. Cool on baking sheet 10 minutes; remove to wire rack to cool completely.

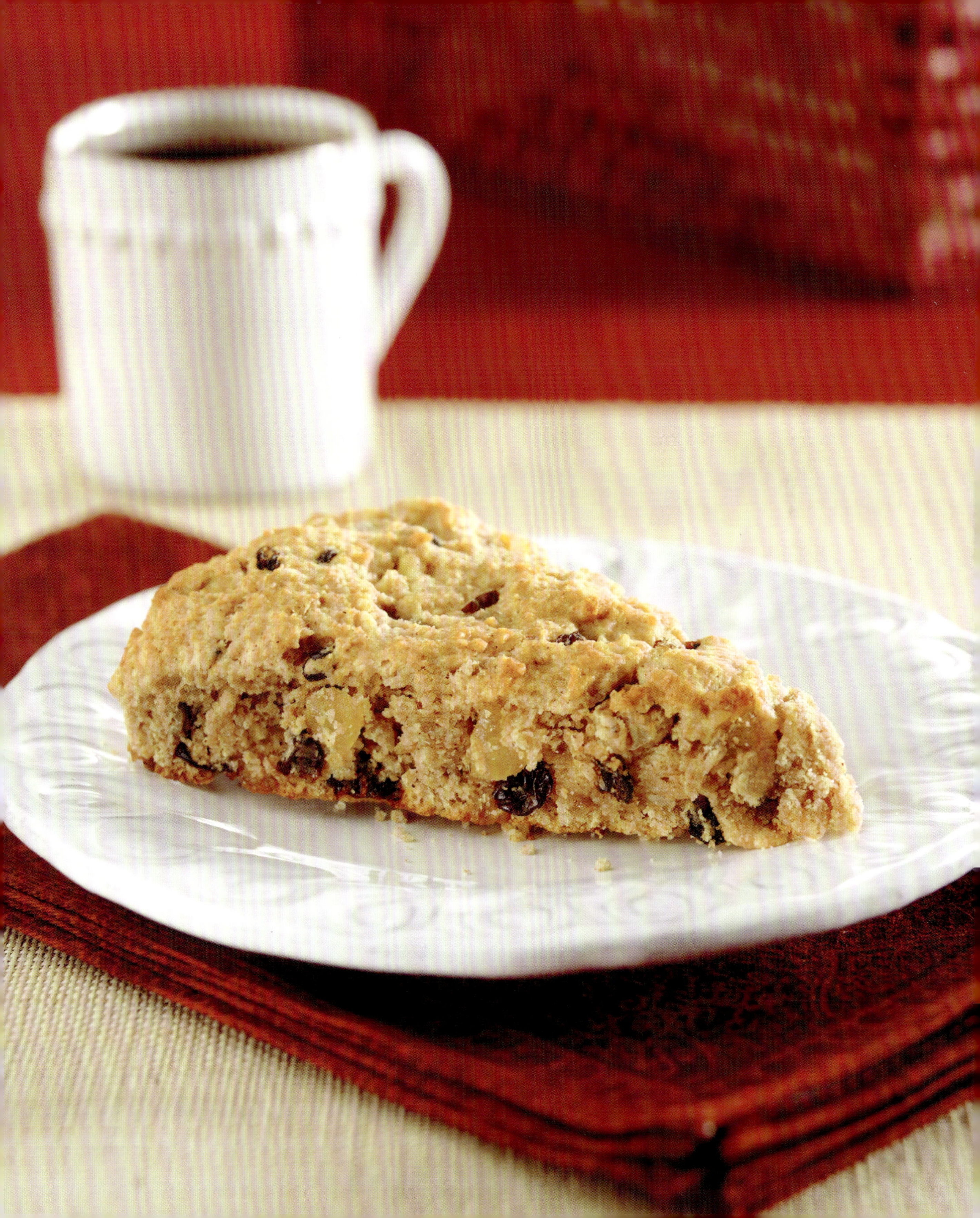

Cinnamon-Date Scones

MAKES 12 SCONES

4 tablespoons sugar, divided
¼ teaspoon ground cinnamon
2 cups all-purpose flour
2½ teaspoons baking powder
½ teaspoon salt
5 tablespoons cold butter, cut into small pieces
½ cup chopped pitted dates
2 eggs
⅓ cup half-and-half or milk

1. Preheat oven to 425°F. Combine 2 tablespoons sugar* and cinnamon in small bowl; mix well.

2. Combine flour, remaining 2 tablespoons sugar, baking powder and salt in large bowl; mix well. Cut in butter with pastry blender or two knives until mixture resembles coarse crumbs. Stir in dates.

3. Beat eggs in small bowl. Whisk in half-and-half until well blended. Reserve 1 tablespoon egg mixture; set aside for topping. Add remaining egg mixture to flour mixture; stir to form soft dough that clings together and forms a ball.

4. Turn out dough onto well-floured surface; knead gently 10 to 12 times. Roll out dough into 9×6-inch rectangle. Cut into six 3-inch squares; cut each square diagonally in half to make 12 triangles. Place 2 inches apart on ungreased baking sheets. Brush with reserved egg mixture; sprinkle with cinnamon-sugar.

5. Bake 10 to 12 minutes or until golden brown. Remove to wire racks to cool 10 minutes. Serve warm.

For extra sparkle and crunch, substitute 2 tablespoons sparkling or coarse sugar for the granulated sugar in the cinnamon-sugar mixture.

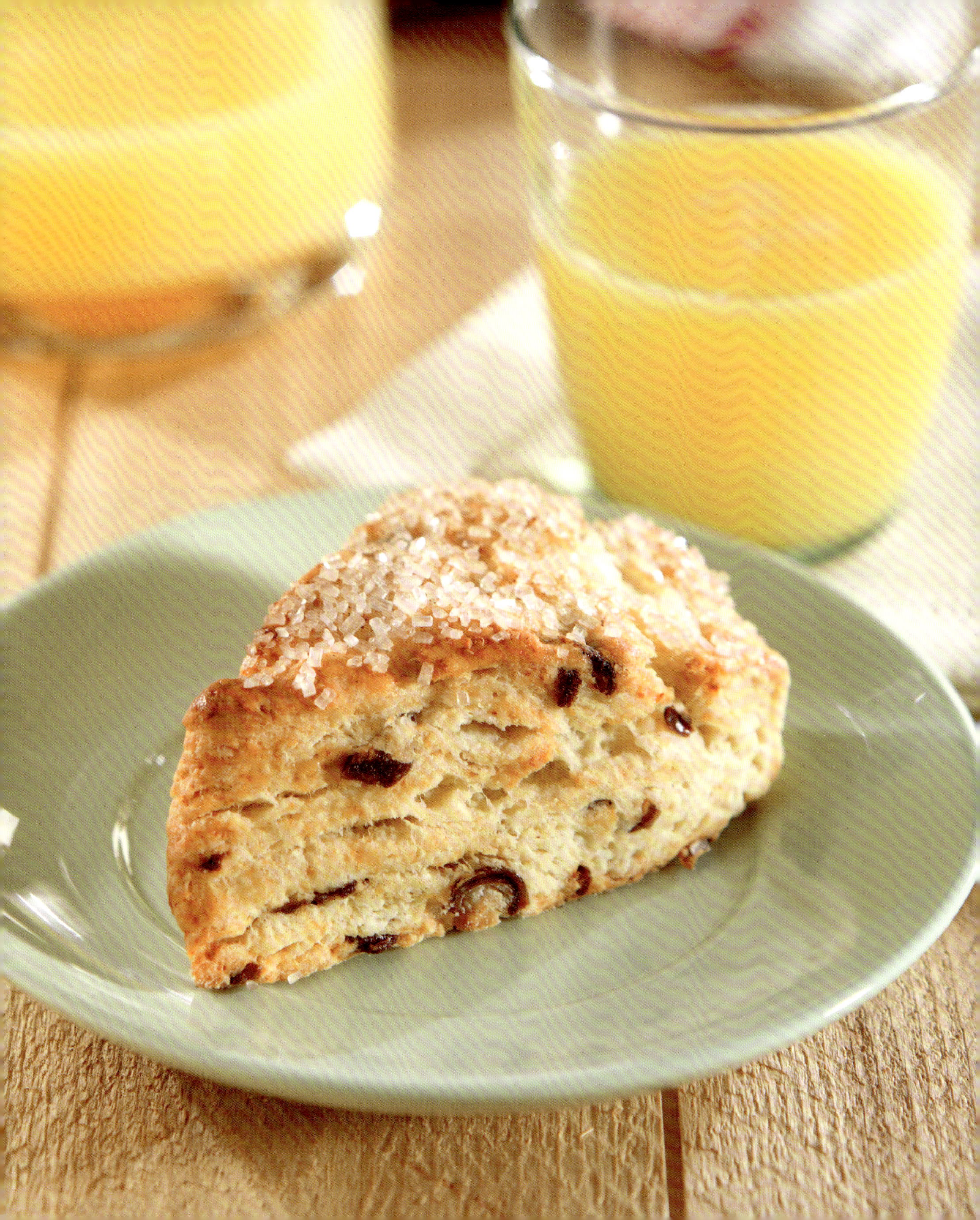

Pumpkin Ginger Scones

MAKES 12 SCONES

- ½ cup sugar, divided
- 2 cups all-purpose flour
- 2 teaspoons baking powder
- 1 teaspoon ground cinnamon
- ½ teaspoon baking soda
- ½ teaspoon salt
- ¼ cup (½ stick) cold butter, cut into small pieces
- 1 egg
- ½ cup canned pumpkin
- ¼ cup sour cream
- ½ teaspoon grated fresh ginger *or* 2 tablespoons finely chopped crystallized ginger
- 1 tablespoon butter, melted

1. Preheat oven to 425°F.
2. Reserve 1 tablespoon sugar; set aside for topping. Combine remaining sugar, flour, baking powder, cinnamon, baking soda and salt in large bowl; mix well. Cut in ¼ cup cold butter with pastry blender or two knives until mixture resembles coarse crumbs.
3. Beat egg in medium bowl. Whisk in pumpkin, sour cream and ginger until well blended. Add to flour mixture; stir to form soft dough that leaves side of bowl.
4. Turn out dough onto well-floured surface; knead 10 times. Roll out dough into 9×6-inch rectangle with floured rolling pin. Cut into six 3-inch squares; cut each square diagonally in half to make 12 triangles. Place 2 inches apart on ungreased baking sheets. Brush tops with 1 tablespoon melted butter; sprinkle with reserved sugar.
5. Bake 10 to 12 minutes or until golden brown. Cool on wire racks 10 minutes. Serve warm.

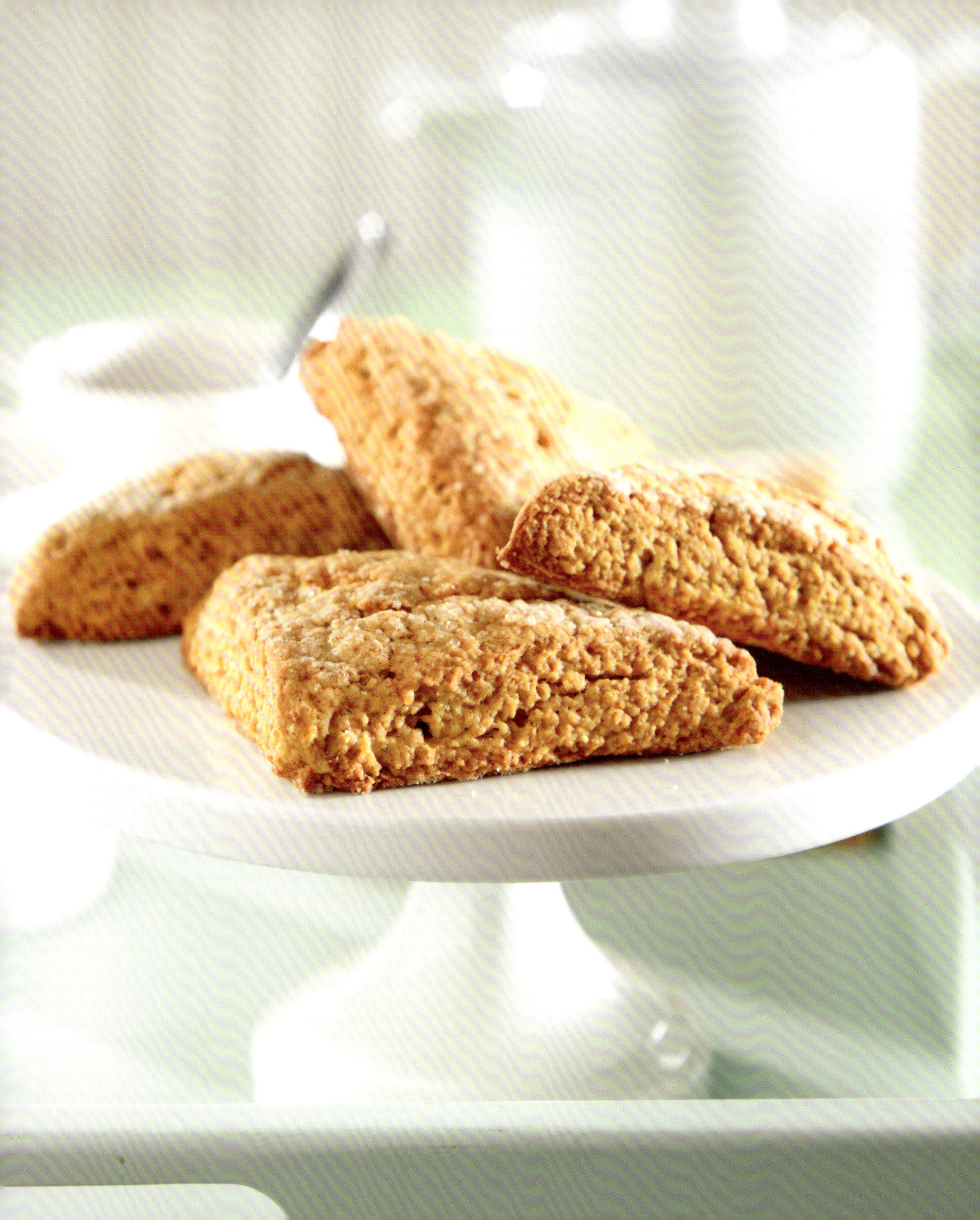

English-Style Scones

MAKES 6 SCONES

- 3 eggs, divided
- ½ cup whipping cream
- 1½ teaspoons vanilla
- 2 cups all-purpose flour
- 2 teaspoons baking powder
- ¼ teaspoon salt
- ¼ cup (½ stick) cold butter, cut into small pieces
- ¼ cup finely chopped pitted dates
- ¼ cup golden raisins or currants
- 1 teaspoon water

1. Preheat oven to 375°F. Line baking sheet with parchment paper.

2. Whisk 2 eggs, cream and vanilla in medium bowl until blended. Combine flour, baking powder and salt in medium bowl; mix well. Cut in butter with pastry blender or two knives until mixture resembles coarse crumbs. Stir in dates and raisins. Add cream mixture; stir just until dry ingredients are moistened.

3. Turn out dough onto lightly floured surface; knead four times with floured hands. Place dough on prepared baking sheet; pat into 8-inch circle.

4. Gently score dough into six wedges with sharp wet knife, cutting three fourths of the way through dough. Beat remaining egg and water in small bowl; brush lightly over dough.

5. Bake 18 to 20 minutes or until golden brown. Remove to wire rack to cool 5 minutes. Cut into wedges; serve warm.

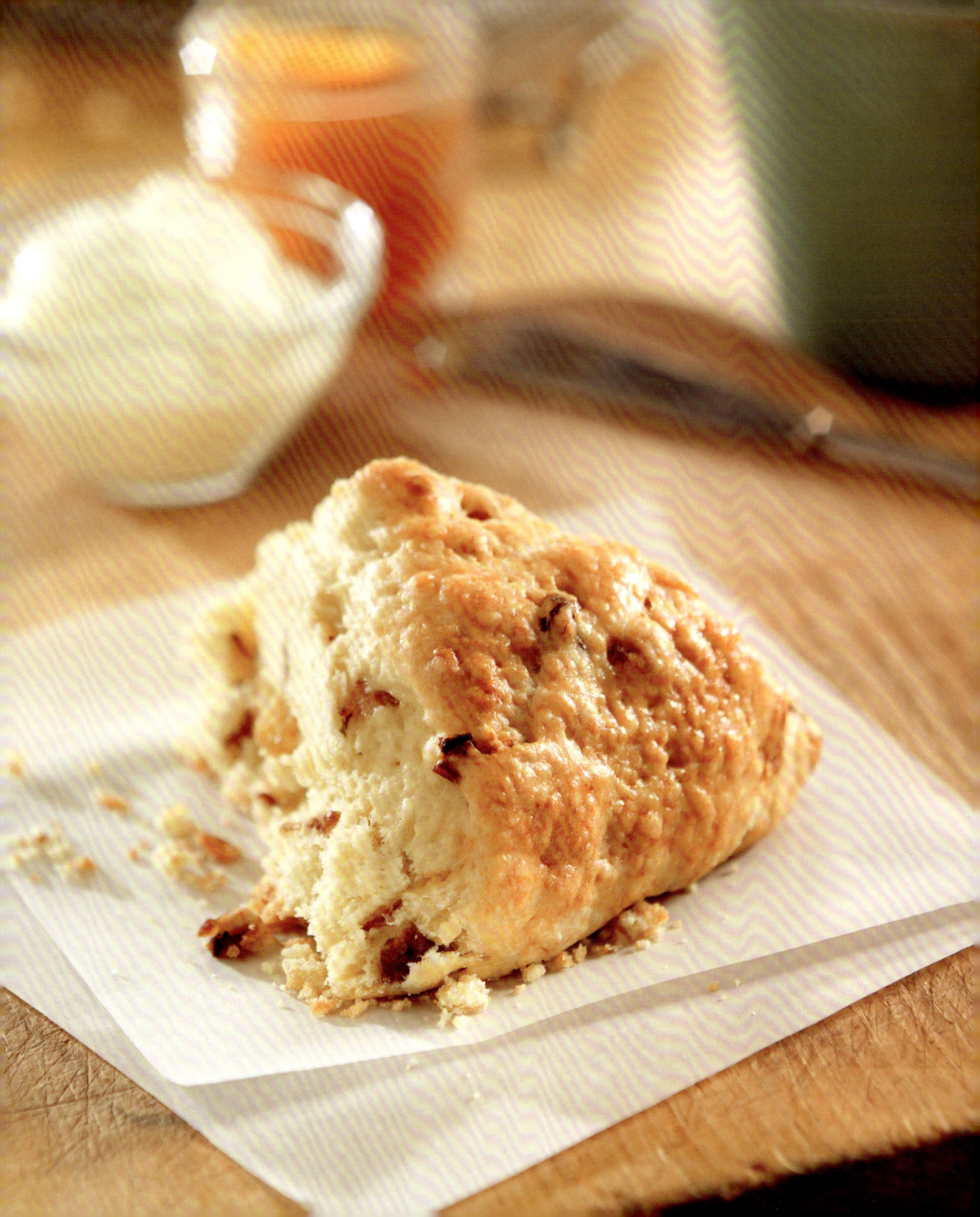

Cranberry Scones

MAKES 8 SCONES

- 2 cups all-purpose flour
- ¼ cup sugar
- 2 teaspoons baking powder
- ½ teaspoon salt
- ¼ teaspoon baking soda
- ½ cup (1 stick) cold butter, cut into small pieces
- ⅔ cup buttermilk
- 1 egg
- ½ teaspoon vanilla
- ½ cup chopped pecans, toasted*
- ½ cup dried cranberries or cherries

*To toast pecans, spread on baking sheet. Bake in preheated 350°F oven 8 to 10 minutes or until golden brown, stirring frequently.

1. Preheat oven to 350°F.
2. Combine flour, sugar, baking powder, salt and baking soda in large bowl; mix well. Cut in butter with pastry blender or two knives until mixture resembles coarse crumbs.
3. Whisk buttermilk, egg and vanilla in small bowl until well blended. Add to flour mixture; stir just until dry ingredients are moistened. Stir in pecans and cranberries.
4. Turn out dough onto floured surface. Shape into 6-inch circle; cut into eight wedges. Place 2 inches apart on ungreased baking sheet.
5. Bake 30 to 35 minutes or until golden brown. Serve warm.

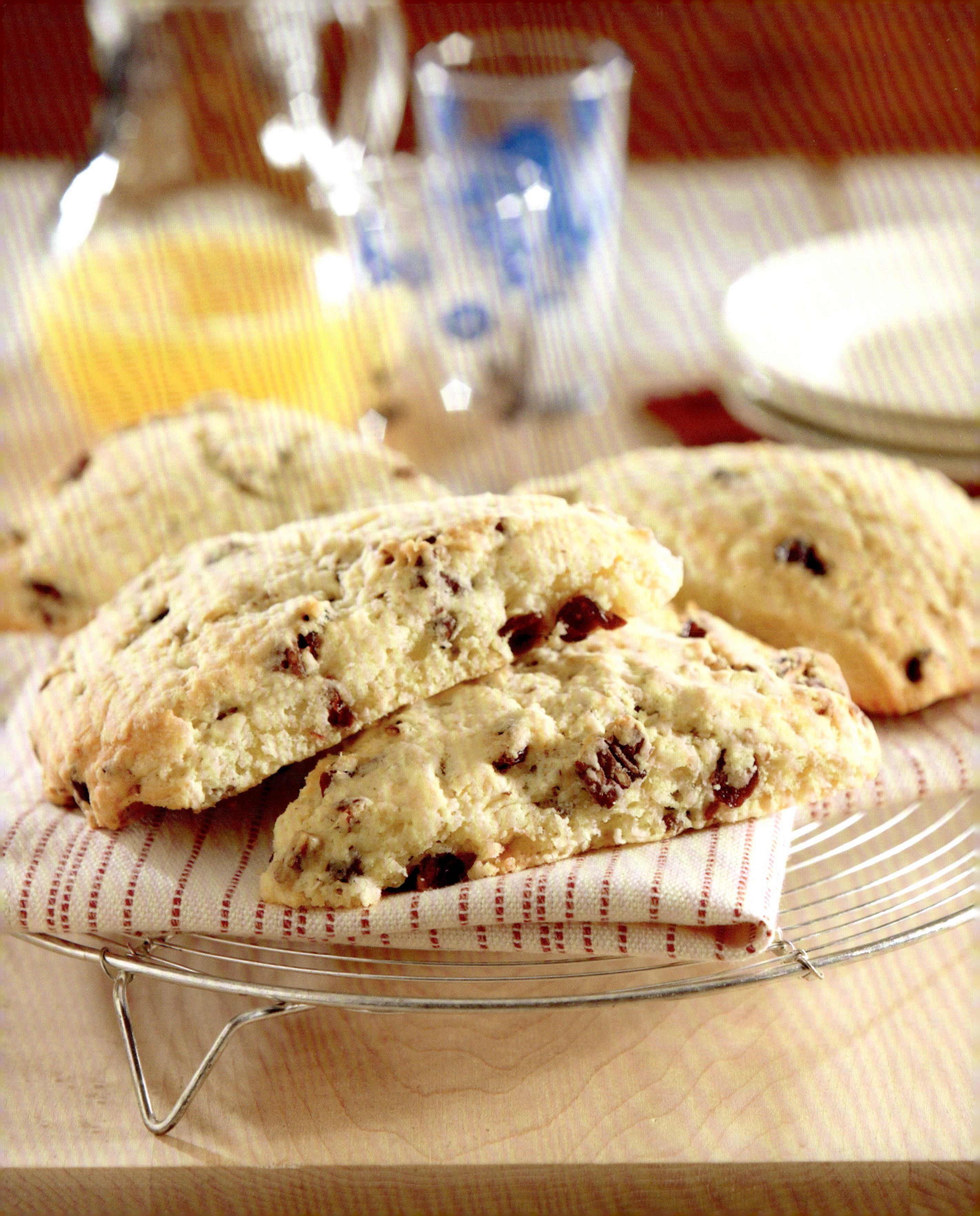

Berry Buckwheat Scones

MAKES 8 SCONES

- 1¼ cups all-purpose flour
- ¾ cup buckwheat flour
- ¼ cup packed brown sugar
- 1 tablespoon baking powder
- ½ teaspoon salt
- ½ cup (1 stick) cold butter, cubed
- ¾ cup fresh raspberries
- ¾ cup fresh blackberries
- 1 egg
- ½ cup whipping cream
- 1 tablespoon granulated sugar

1. Preheat oven to 375°F. Line baking sheet with parchment paper.

2. Combine all-purpose flour, buckwheat flour, brown sugar, baking powder and salt in food processor; pulse until combined. Add butter; pulse until pea-sized pieces of butter remain. Transfer to large bowl; gently stir in berries.

3. Whisk egg and cream in small bowl until blended. Add to flour mixture; stir to form soft dough.

4. Turn out dough onto surface lightly dusted with buckwheat flour. Gently pat dough into 8-inch round about ¾ inch thick. Cut into eight wedges. Place 1½ inches apart on prepared baking sheet; sprinkle with granulated sugar.

5. Bake 20 to 25 minutes or until golden brown. Remove to wire rack to cool 10 minutes. Serve warm.

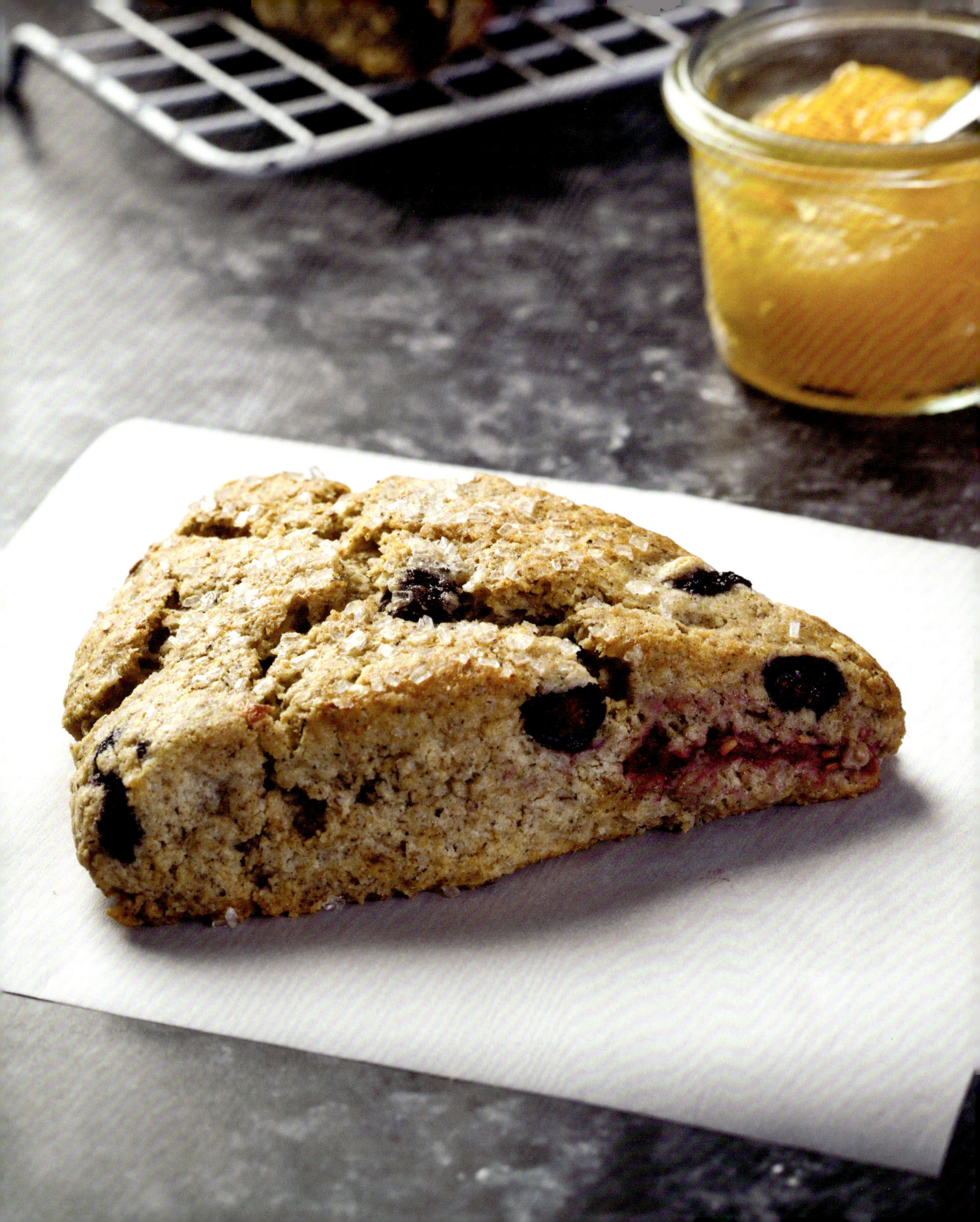

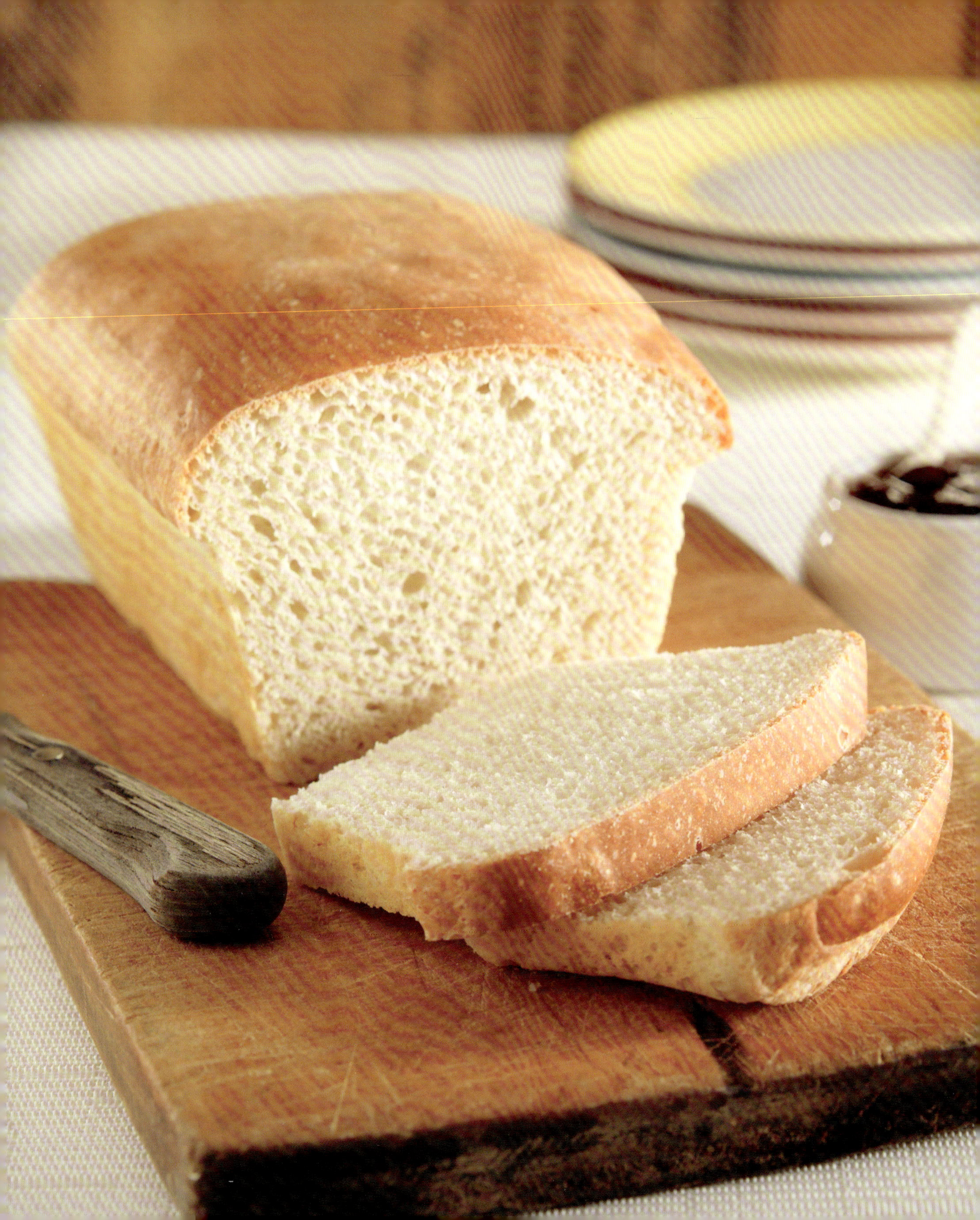

YEAST BREADS

Sandwich Bread
MAKES 2 LOAVES

½ cup milk
3 tablespoons sugar
2 teaspoons salt
3 tablespoons butter
2 packages (¼ ounce each) active dry yeast
1½ cups warm water (105° to 115°F)
5 to 6 cups all-purpose flour, divided

1. Combine milk, sugar, salt and butter in small saucepan; heat over low heat until butter melts and sugar dissolves. Cool to lukewarm (about 105°F).

2. Dissolve yeast in warm water in large bowl of stand mixer. Add lukewarm milk mixture and 3 cups flour; mix with dough hook at low speed 2 minutes. Add remaining flour, ½ cup at a time; mix until soft dough forms. Mix about 5 minutes or until dough is slightly sticky and elastic.

3. Shape dough into a ball. Place dough in large greased bowl; turn to grease top. Cover and let rise in warm place about 1 hour or until doubled in size.

4. Spray two 8×4-inch loaf pans with nonstick cooking spray. Punch down dough. Divide dough in half; shape each half into a loaf. Place in prepared pans; cover and let rise in warm place about 1 hour or until doubled in size. Preheat oven to 400°F.

5. Bake 30 minutes or until bread is golden brown. Remove to wire racks to cool completely.

Red Pepper Bread

MAKES 1 LARGE LOAF OR 2 SMALL LOAVES

- 2 to 2½ cups all-purpose flour, divided
- 1 cup whole wheat flour
- 2 tablespoons grated Parmesan cheese
- 1 teaspoon dried rosemary, plus additional for topping
- 1 package (¼ ounce) instant yeast
- ½ teaspoon salt
- ¼ teaspoon dried thyme
- 1¼ cups hot water (130°F)
- 1 tablespoon olive or vegetable oil
- ½ cup chopped roasted red pepper
- 1 egg white, beaten
- 2 teaspoons water

1. Combine 1 cup all-purpose flour, whole wheat flour, cheese, 1 teaspoon rosemary, yeast, salt and thyme in large bowl; mix well. Stir in hot water and oil until mixture is smooth. Stir in roasted pepper. Stir in enough remaining all-purpose flour to form soft dough.

2. Turn out dough onto lightly floured surface; flatten slightly. Knead gently 2 to 3 minutes or until smooth and elastic, adding additional all-purpose flour to prevent sticking, if necessary. Place dough in large greased bowl; turn to grease top. Cover and let rise in warm place 30 minutes or until doubled in size.

3. Line baking sheet with parchment paper. Punch down dough. Shape dough into one large or two small round loaves on prepared baking sheet. Cover and let rise 30 minutes or until doubled in size.

4. Preheat oven to 375°F. Slash top of dough with sharp knife. Whisk egg white and 2 teaspoons water in small bowl; brush over dough. Sprinkle with additional rosemary, if desired.

5. Bake 35 to 40 minutes for one large loaf, 25 to 30 minutes for two small loaves or until bread is golden brown and sounds hollow when gently tapped. Remove to wire rack to cool completely.

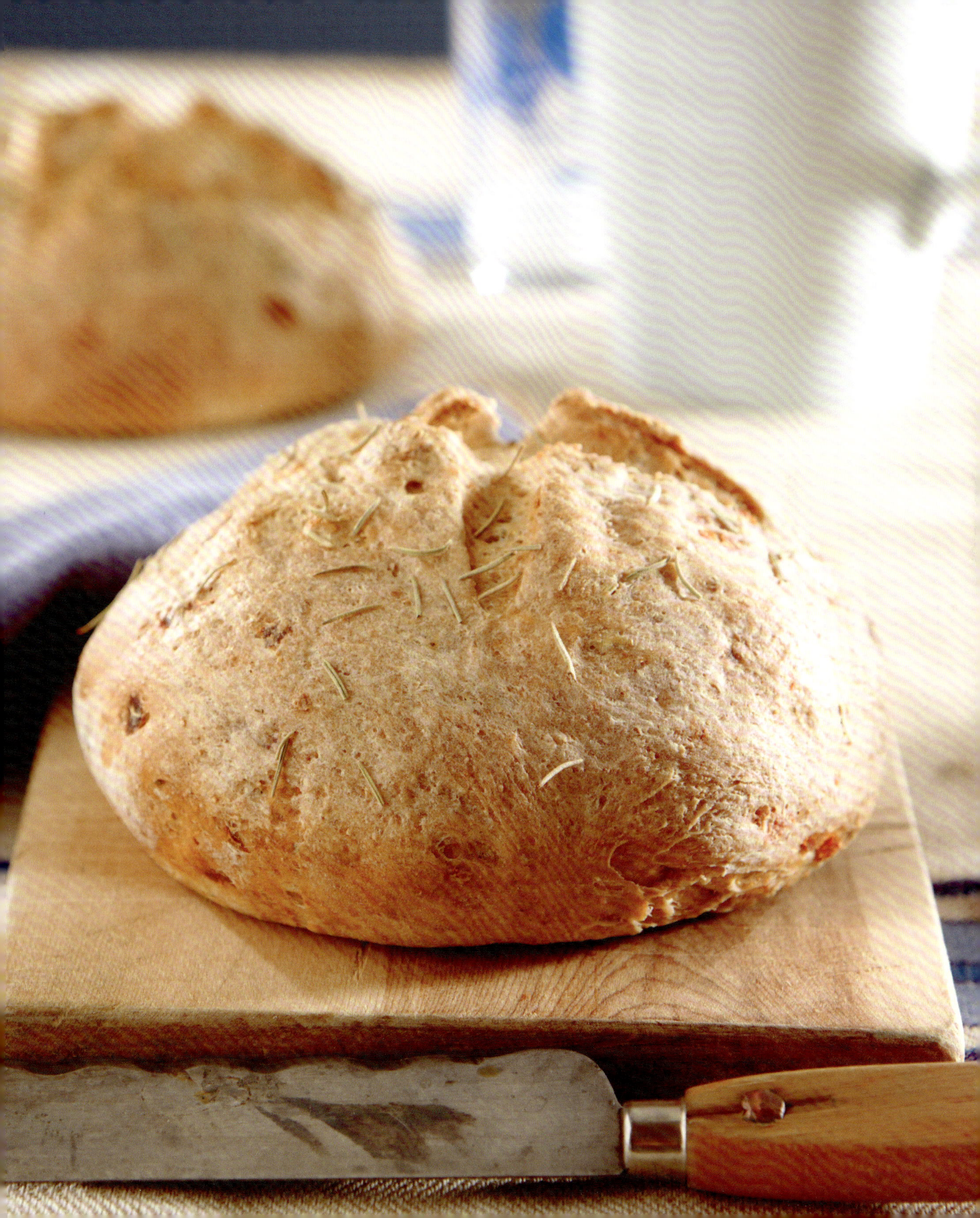

Oatmeal Honey Bread

MAKES 1 LOAF

1½ to 2 cups all-purpose flour
1 cup plus 1 tablespoon old-fashioned oats, divided
½ cup whole wheat flour
1 package (¼ ounce) instant yeast
1 teaspoon salt
1⅓ cups plus 1 tablespoon water, divided
¼ cup honey
2 tablespoons butter
1 egg

1. Combine 1½ cups all-purpose flour, 1 cup oats, whole wheat flour, yeast and salt in large bowl of stand mixer.

2. Combine 1⅓ cups water, honey and butter in small saucepan; heat over low heat until honey dissolves and butter melts. Cool to 130°F (temperature of very hot tap water). Add to flour mixture; beat with paddle attachment at medium speed 2 minutes. Add additional all-purpose flour by tablespoonfuls until dough begins to cling together. Dough should be shaggy and very sticky, not dry. (Dough should not form a ball and/or clean side of bowl.)

3. Replace paddle attachment with dough hook; mix at low speed 4 minutes. Place dough in large greased bowl; turn to grease top. Cover and let rise in warm place 45 minutes or until doubled in size.

4. Spray 8×4-inch loaf pan with nonstick cooking spray. Punch down dough; turn out onto floured surface. Flatten and stretch dough into 8-inch-long oval. Bring long sides together and pinch to seal; fold over short ends and pinch to seal. Place dough seam side down in prepared pan. Cover and let rise in warm place 20 to 30 minutes or until dough reaches top of pan.

5. Preheat oven to 375°F. Beat egg and remaining 1 tablespoon water in small bowl. Brush top of loaf with egg mixture; sprinkle with remaining 1 tablespoon oats.

6. Bake 30 to 35 minutes or until bread sounds hollow when tapped (internal temperature of 190°F). Cool in pan 10 minutes; remove to wire rack to cool completely.

French Cheese Bread

MAKES 1 LOAF

- 1 package (¼ ounce) active dry yeast
- 1 teaspoon sugar
- 4 to 6 tablespoons warm water (105° to 115°F)
- 2½ cups all-purpose flour
- ¼ cup (½ stick) butter, at room temperature
- 1 teaspoon salt
- 2 eggs
- 4 ounces Emmentaler Swiss, Gruyère, sharp Cheddar or Swiss cheese, shredded
- 1 teaspoon vegetable oil

1. Dissolve yeast and sugar in 4 tablespoons warm water in small bowl; let stand 5 minutes or until bubbly.

2. Combine flour, butter and salt in food processor; process 15 seconds or until blended. Add yeast mixture and eggs; process 15 seconds or just until blended.

3. With motor running, slowly drizzle just enough water through feed tube so dough forms a ball that cleans side of bowl. Process until ball turns around bowl about 25 times. Let dough rest 1 to 2 minutes. With motor running, drizzle in enough remaining water to make dough soft, smooth and satiny. Process until dough turns around bowl about 15 times.

4. Turn out dough onto lightly floured surface. Shape dough into a ball. Place dough in large greased bowl; turn to grease top. Cover and let rise in warm place about 1 hour or until doubled in size.

5. Spray 9-inch round cake pan or pie plate with nonstick cooking spray. Punch down dough. Place dough on lightly greased surface; knead cheese into dough. Roll or pat into 8-inch round; brush with oil. Let rise in warm place about 45 minutes or until doubled in size. Preheat oven to 375°F.

6. Bake 30 to 35 minutes or until bread is golden brown and sounds hollow when tapped. Remove to wire rack to cool completely.

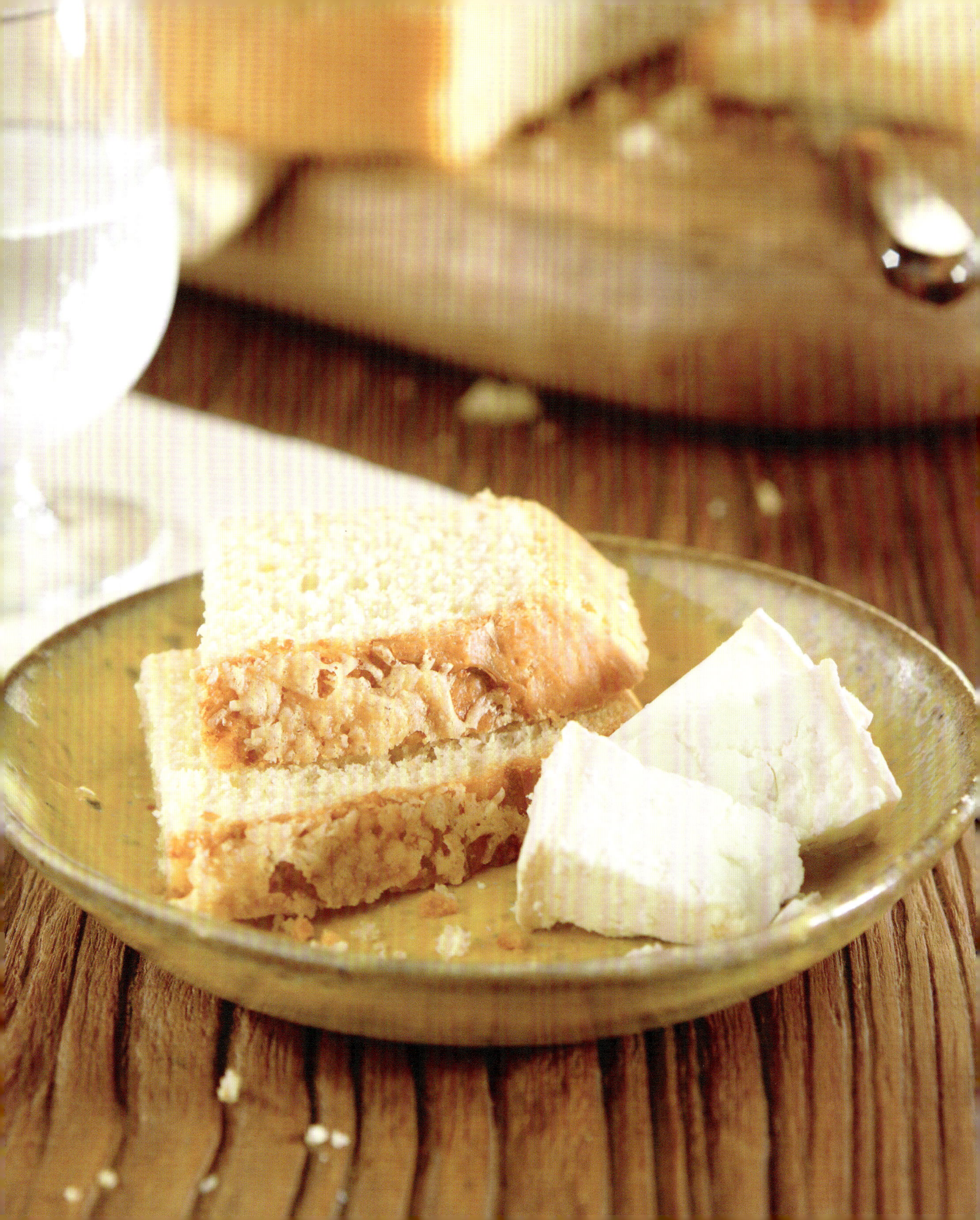

Walnut Fig Bread

MAKES 1 LOAF

- 1 cup honey beer or water
- 2 tablespoons butter or olive oil
- 1 tablespoon honey
- 2¼ cups all-purpose flour, divided
- 1 cup whole wheat flour
- 1 package (¼ ounce) active dry yeast
- 1 tablespoon whole fennel seeds
- 1½ teaspoons salt
- 1 egg, beaten
- 1 cup chopped dried figs or dates
- ½ cup chopped walnuts, toasted*

To toast walnuts, cook in medium skillet over medium heat 2 minutes or until lightly browned, stirring frequently.

1. Combine beer, butter and honey in small saucepan; heat over low heat to 120°F.

2. Combine 1 cup all-purpose flour, whole wheat flour, yeast, fennel seeds and salt in large bowl of stand mixer. Add beer mixture; beat with paddle attachment at medium-low speed 3 minutes. Add egg; beat until blended.

3. Replace paddle attachment with dough hook. Add remaining all-purpose flour, ¼ cup at a time; mix at low speed to form soft dough. Add figs and walnuts; mix about 5 minutes or until dough is smooth and elastic.

4. Shape dough into a ball. Place dough in large greased bowl; turn to grease top. Cover and let rise in warm place about 1 hour or until doubled in size.

5. Line baking sheet with parchment paper. Punch down dough. Shape dough into round loaf; place on prepared baking sheet. Cover and let rise in warm place 40 minutes or until doubled in size. Preheat oven to 350°F.

6. Bake 30 to 35 minutes or until bread is golden brown and sounds hollow when tapped. Remove to wire rack to cool completely.

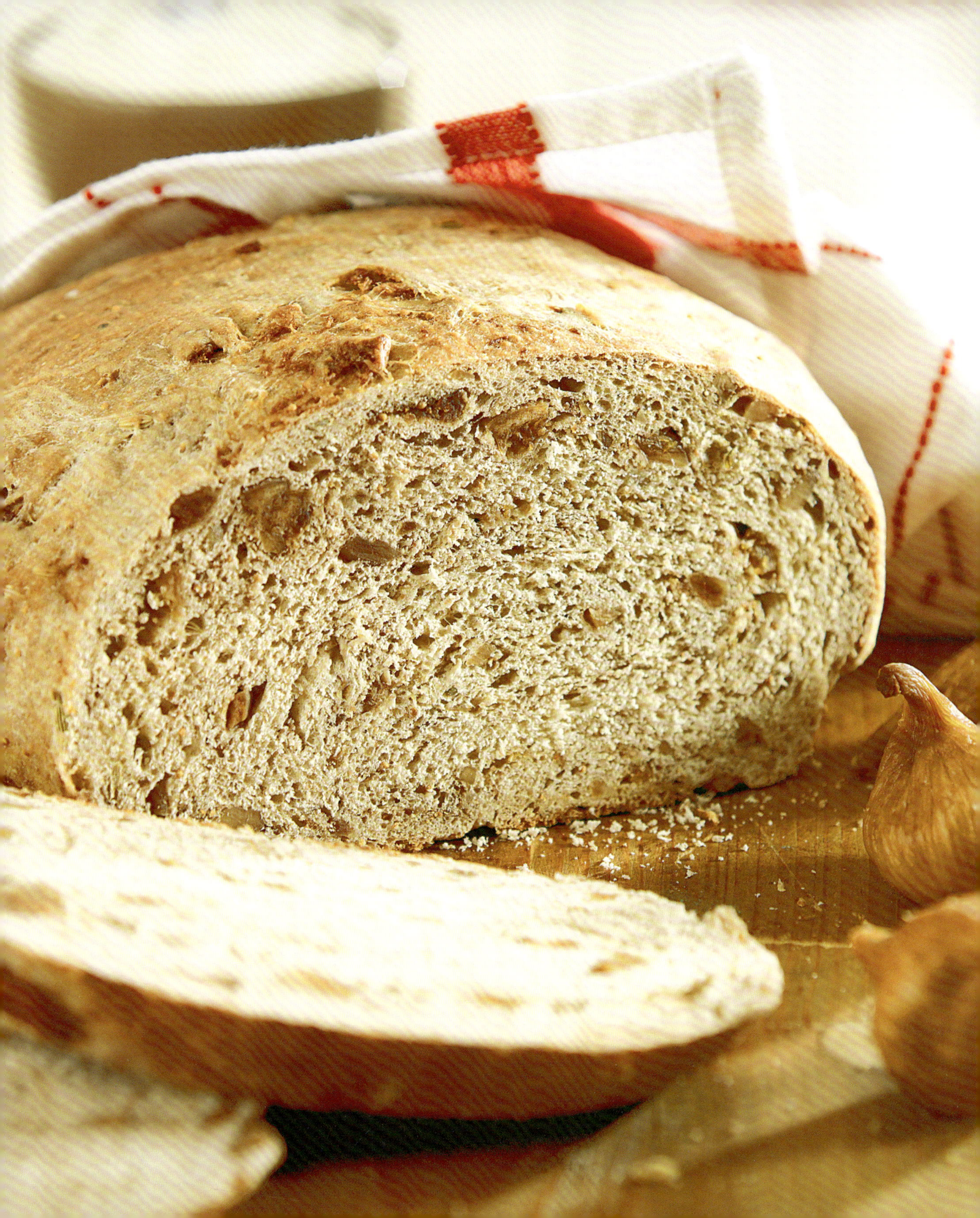

Quick Casserole Bread

MAKES 1 LOAF

2¾ cups all-purpose flour
3 tablespoons nonfat dry milk powder
1 package (¼ ounce) instant yeast
2 tablespoons sugar
1 teaspoon salt
1 cup warm water (120°F)
2 tablespoons vegetable oil
1 tablespoon sesame or poppy seeds (optional)

1. Combine flour, milk powder, yeast, sugar and salt in large bowl of stand mixer. Mix with dough hook at low speed 1 minute. With mixer running, add water and oil; mix at low speed 5 minutes.

2. Spray 1½-quart round baking dish with nonstick cooking spray. Scrape batter into prepared baking dish; smooth top. Sprinkle with sesame seeds, if desired. Cover and let stand in warm place 45 minutes or until almost doubled in size. Preheat oven to 375°F.

3. Bake 25 to 30 minutes or until wooden skewer inserted into center comes out clean (internal temperature of 190° to 200°F). Cool in baking dish 10 minutes; remove to wire rack to cool completely.

CASSEROLE CHEESE BREAD Prepare batter as directed for Quick Casserole Bread. Pour half of batter into greased 1½-quart baking dish. Sprinkle with 1 cup cubed Cheddar or Swiss cheese; pour remaining batter over cheese. Stir gently to mix in cheese. Let rise and bake as directed above.

HONEY WHOLE WHEAT CASSEROLE BREAD Prepare batter as directed for Quick Casserole Bread using 1½ cups all-purpose flour and 1 cup whole wheat flour, and substituting honey for sugar. Let rise and bake as directed above.

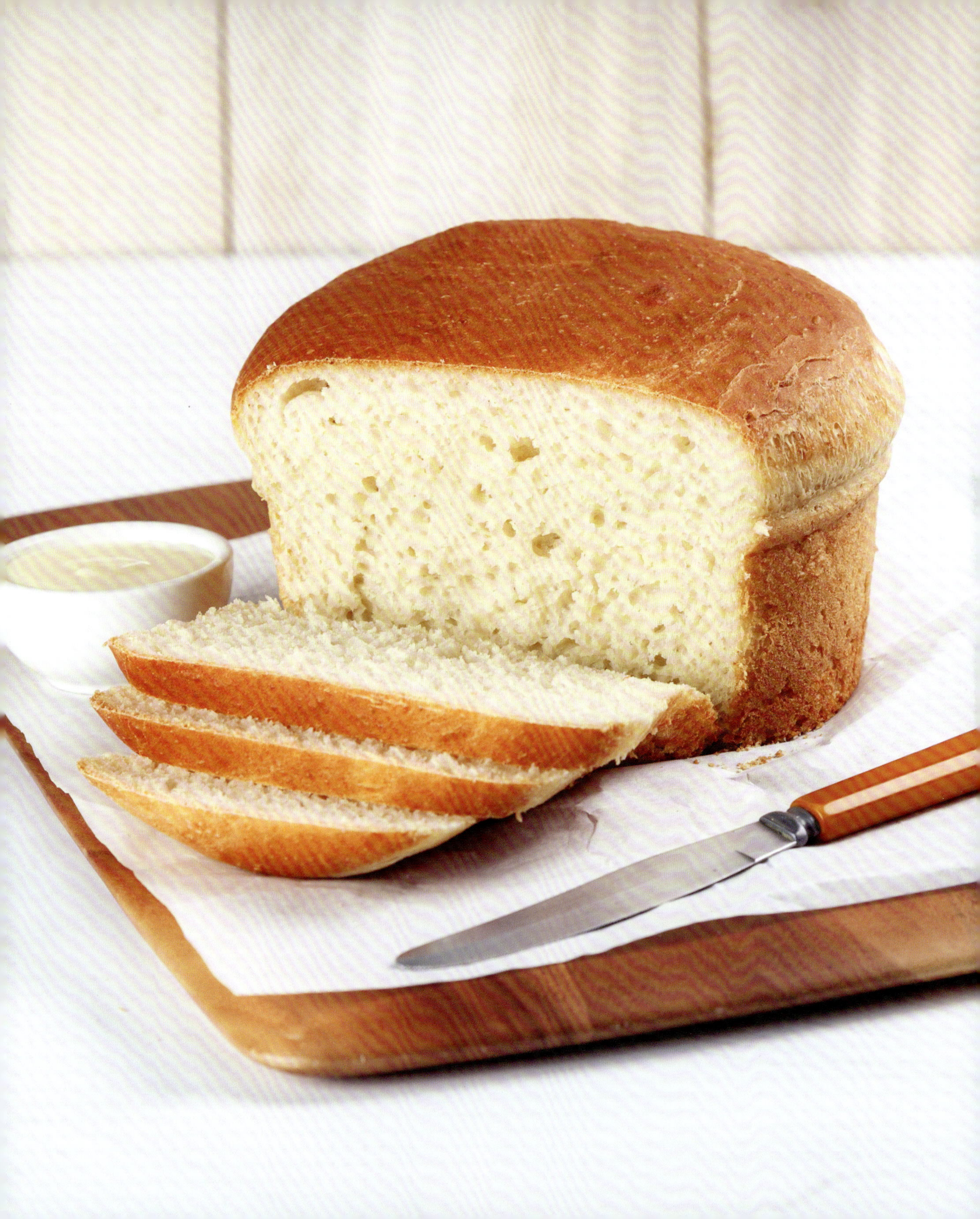

Sugar and Spice Bread

MAKES 1 LOAF

- 1 cup milk
- ¼ cup (½ stick) butter
- 3 cups bread flour, divided
- ¼ cup packed brown sugar
- 1 package (¼ ounce) instant yeast
- 2 teaspoons ground cinnamon
- 1 teaspoon salt
- ¼ teaspoon ground nutmeg
- ⅛ teaspoon ground cloves

1. Combine milk and butter in small saucepan; heat to 120°F. Combine 1 cup flour, brown sugar, yeast, cinnamon, salt, nutmeg and cloves in large bowl of stand mixer. Add milk mixture; beat with paddle attachment at medium speed 2 minutes.

2. Replace paddle attachment with dough hook; mix in enough remaining flour to form soft dough. Mix at medium-low speed 5 to 8 minutes or until dough is smooth and elastic. Place dough in large greased bowl; turn to grease top. Cover and let rise in warm place about 20 minutes or until doubled in size.

3. Spray 9×5-inch loaf pan with nonstick cooking spray. Punch down dough. Shape dough into loaf; place in prepared pan. Cover and let rise in warm place about 30 minutes or until doubled in size. Preheat oven to 375°F.

4. Bake 35 to 40 minutes or until bread is golden brown and sounds hollow when tapped (internal temperature of 195° to 200°F). Remove to wire rack to cool completely.

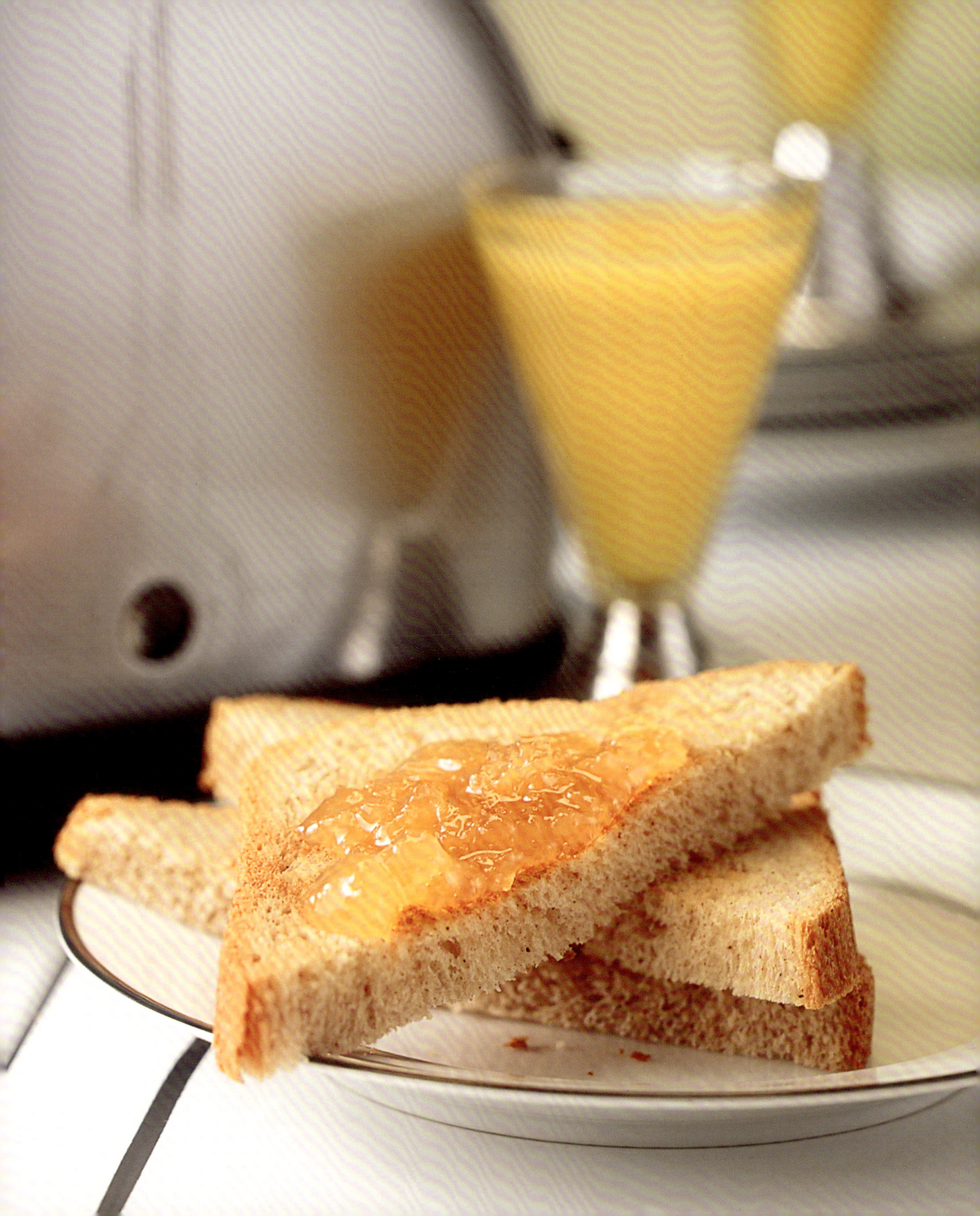

Crunchy Whole Grain Bread

MAKES 2 LOAVES

- 2 cups warm water (105° to 115°F), divided
- 1/3 cup honey
- 2 tablespoons vegetable oil
- 1 tablespoon salt
- 2 packages (1/4 ounce each) active dry yeast
- 2 to 2 1/2 cups whole wheat flour, divided
- 1 cup bread flour
- 1 1/4 cup quick oats, divided
- 1/2 cup hulled pumpkin seeds or sunflower kernels
- 1/2 cup assorted grains and seeds
- 1 egg white
- 1 tablespoon water

1. Combine 1 1/2 cups warm water, honey, oil and salt in small saucepan; heat over low heat until warm (115° to 120°F), stirring occasionally.

2. Dissolve yeast in remaining 1/2 cup warm water in large bowl of stand mixer; let stand 5 minutes. Stir in honey mixture. Add 1 cup whole wheat flour and bread flour; mix with dough hook at low speed 2 minutes. Slowly add 1 cup oats, pumpkin seeds and assorted grains; mix until incorporated. Add remaining whole wheat flour, 1/2 cup at a time; mix until dough begins to form a ball. Mix 6 to 8 minutes or until dough is smooth and elastic.

3. Place dough in large greased bowl; turn to grease top. Cover and let rise in warm place 1 1/2 to 2 hours or until doubled in size.

4. Spray two 9×5-inch loaf pans with nonstick cooking spray. Punch down dough. Divide dough in half; shape each half into a loaf. Place in prepared pans. Cover and let rise in warm place 1 hour or until almost doubled in size.

5. Preheat oven to 375°F. Beat egg white and 1 tablespoon water in small bowl. Brush over tops of loaves; sprinkle with remaining 1/4 cup oats.

6. Bake 35 to 45 minutes or until bread sounds hollow when tapped. Cool in pans 10 minutes; remove to wire racks to cool completely.

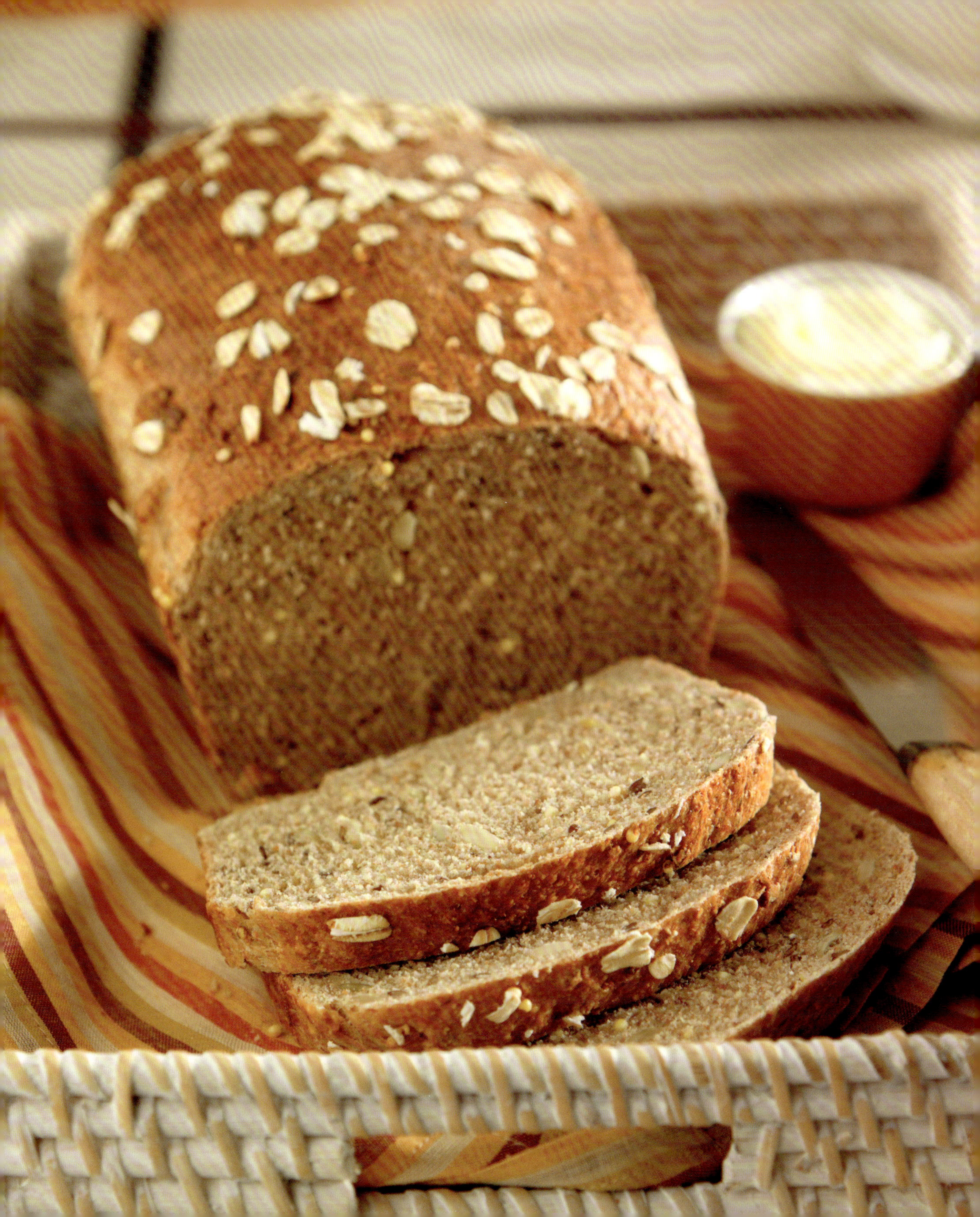

Pepperoni Cheese Bread

MAKES 2 LOAVES

- 1 package (¼ ounce) active dry yeast
- 1 cup warm beer
- ½ cup warm milk
- 2¼ cups all-purpose flour, divided
- 1 cup rye flour
- 1 tablespoon dried basil
- 1 teaspoon sugar
- 1 teaspoon salt
- 1 teaspoon red pepper flakes
- 1 cup (4 ounces) shredded sharp Cheddar cheese
- 1 cup finely chopped pepperoni
- 1 tablespoon olive oil

1. Dissolve yeast in warm beer and milk in large bowl.

2. Stir in 2 cups all-purpose flour, rye flour, basil, sugar, salt and red pepper flakes until smooth. Stir in enough remaining all-purpose flour to form stiff dough.

3. Turn out dough onto well-floured surface; sprinkle with cheese and pepperoni. Knead 5 to 6 minutes or until smooth and elastic. Transfer dough to large greased bowl; turn to grease top. Cover and let rise in warm place about 1 hour or until doubled in size.

4. Line two baking sheets with parchment paper. Punch down dough. Divide dough in half; shape each half into 12-inch loaf. Place on prepared baking sheets; cover and let rise in warm place about 45 minutes or until doubled in size. Preheat oven to 350°F.

5. Bake 30 to 35 minutes or until bread is golden brown.

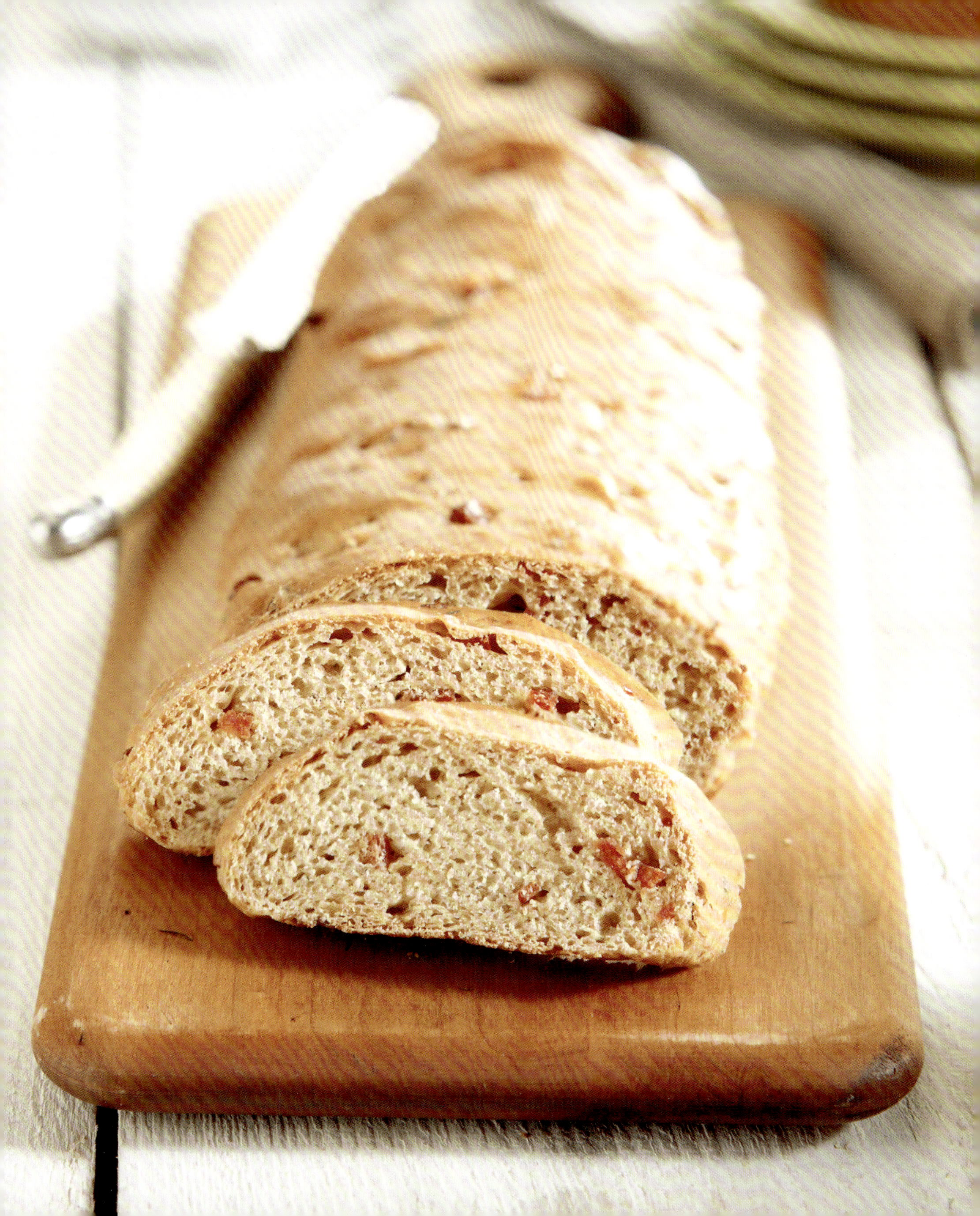

Rustic Sour Cream Bread
MAKES 1 LOAF

- 1 cup sour cream
- 3 tablespoons water
- 2½ to 3 cups all-purpose flour, divided
- 1 package (¼ ounce) active dry yeast
- 2 tablespoons sugar
- 1½ teaspoons salt
- ¼ teaspoon baking soda
- 1 teaspoon vegetable oil
- 1 tablespoon sesame or poppy seeds

1. Combine sour cream and water in small saucepan; heat over low heat to 110° to 120°F.

2. Combine 2 cups flour, yeast, sugar, salt and baking soda in large bowl of stand mixer. Add sour cream mixture; mix with dough hook at low speed 3 minutes. Add remaining flour, ¼ cup at a time; mix 5 minutes or until dough is smooth and elastic.

3. Line baking sheet with parchment paper. Shape dough into a ball; place on prepared baking sheet. Flatten into 8-inch round. Brush top with oil; sprinkle with sesame seeds. Cover and let rise in warm place 1 hour or until doubled in size. Preheat oven to 350°F.

4. Bake 22 to 27 minutes or until bread is golden brown. Remove to wire rack to cool completely.

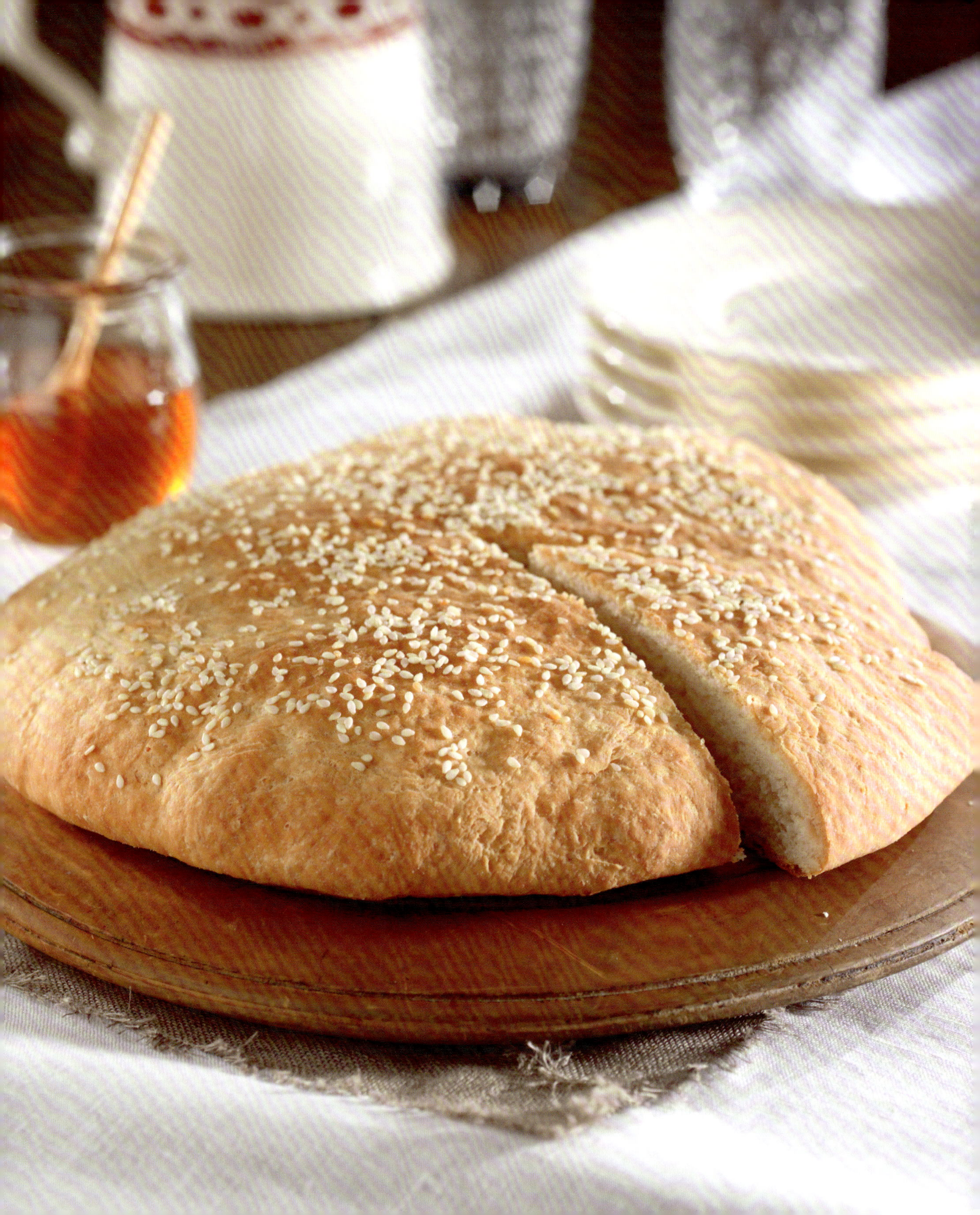

Whole Wheat Herb Bread

MAKES 4 SMALL LOAVES

- ⅔ cup water
- ⅔ cup milk
- 2 teaspoons sugar
- 2 packages (¼ ounce each) active dry yeast
- 3 egg whites, lightly beaten
- 3 tablespoons olive oil
- 1 teaspoon salt
- ½ teaspoon dried basil
- ½ teaspoon dried oregano
- 4 to 4½ cups whole wheat flour, divided

1. Bring water to a boil in small saucepan. Remove from heat; stir in milk and sugar. When mixture cools to 110° to 115°F, stir in yeast; let stand 10 minutes or until bubbly.

2. Combine egg whites, oil, salt, basil and oregano in large bowl of stand mixer; beat with paddle attachment at medium speed until blended. Beat in yeast mixture; mix well. Add 1½ cups flour; beat 2 minutes.

3. Replace paddle attachment with dough hook. Add 2½ cups flour, ½ cup at a time; mix at low speed until dough forms a rough ball. Add enough remaining flour, 1 tablespoon at a time, if necessary to clean side of bowl. Mix at low speed 5 to 7 minutes or until dough is smooth and elastic.

4. Shape dough into a ball. Place dough in large greased bowl; turn to grease top. Cover and let rise in warm place about 1 hour or until doubled in size.

5. Preheat oven to 350°F. Line baking sheet with parchment paper. Punch down dough; turn out onto lightly floured surface. Divide dough into four pieces; roll each piece into a ball. Place on prepared baking sheet.

6. Bake 30 to 35 minutes or until golden brown and breads sound hollow when tapped. Remove to wire racks to cool completely.

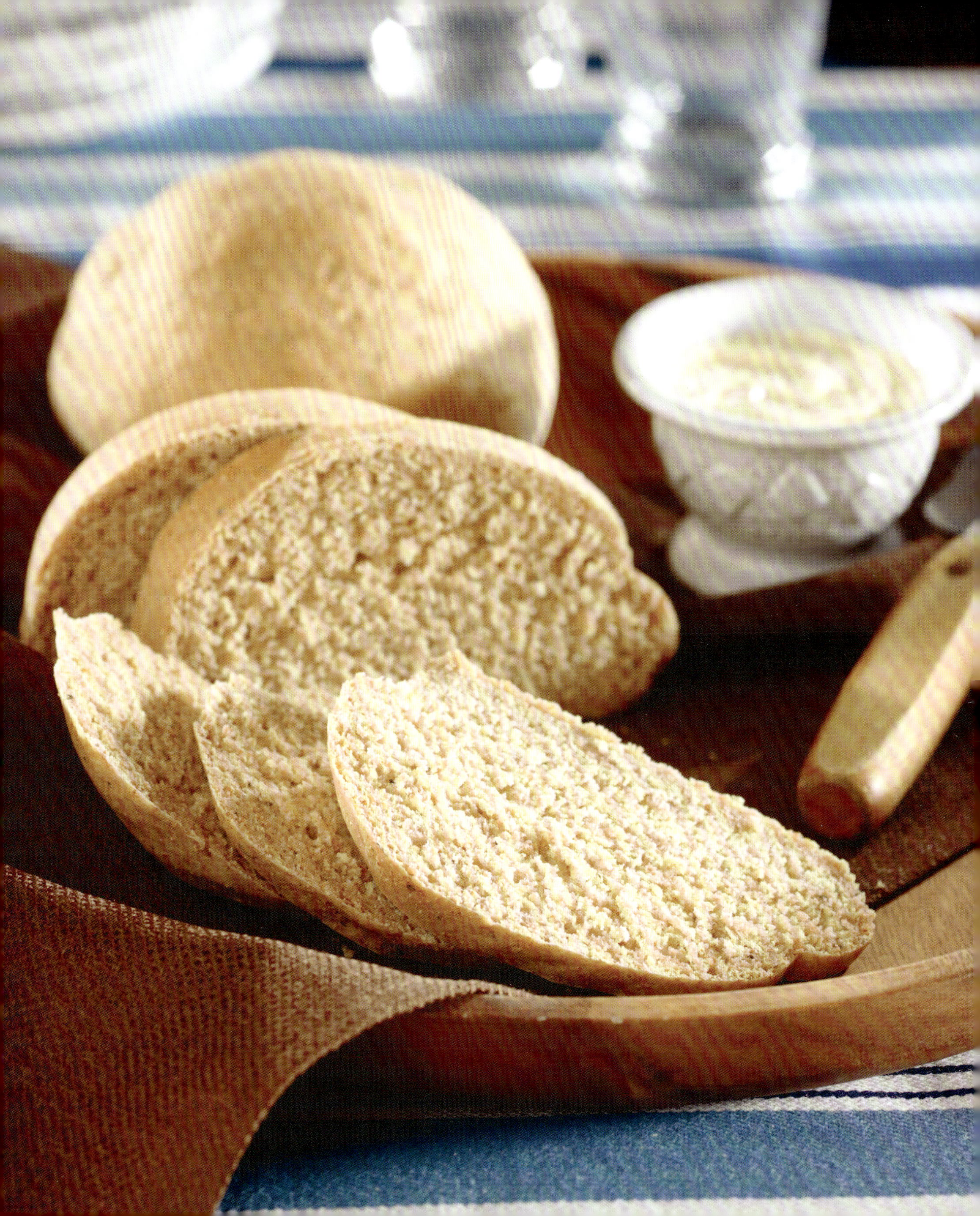

Chili Cheese Bread

MAKES 1 LOAF

- 2 tablespoons butter
- ½ cup finely chopped onion
- 1 clove garlic, minced
- ¾ cup milk
- 2¾ cups bread flour, divided
- 1 tablespoon sugar
- 1 package (¼ ounce) instant yeast
- 2 to 3 teaspoons chili powder
- 1 teaspoon salt
- 1 teaspoon dried basil
- 1 egg
- 1¼ cups (5 ounces) shredded sharp Cheddar cheese

1. Melt butter in medium saucepan over medium heat. Add onion and garlic; cook and stir 5 minutes or until onion is tender. Add milk; heat to 120°F.

2. Combine 1 cup flour, sugar, yeast, chili powder, salt and basil in large bowl of stand mixer. Add milk mixture; beat with paddle attachment at medium speed 2 minutes. Add egg; beat 1 minute.

3. Replace paddle attachment with dough hook. Add 1 cup flour and cheese; mix at low speed 2 minutes. Add enough remaining flour, ¼ cup at a time, to form firm dough. Mix 5 minutes or until dough is smooth and elastic.

4. Shape dough into a ball. Place dough in large greased bowl; turn to grease top. Cover and let rise in warm place about 30 minutes or until doubled in size.

5. Spray 9×5-inch loaf pan with nonstick cooking spray. Punch down dough. Shape dough into a loaf; place in prepared pan. Cover and let rise in warm place about 20 minutes or until doubled in size. Preheat oven to 375°F.

6. Bake 30 to 35 minutes or until bread is golden brown and sounds hollow when tapped.

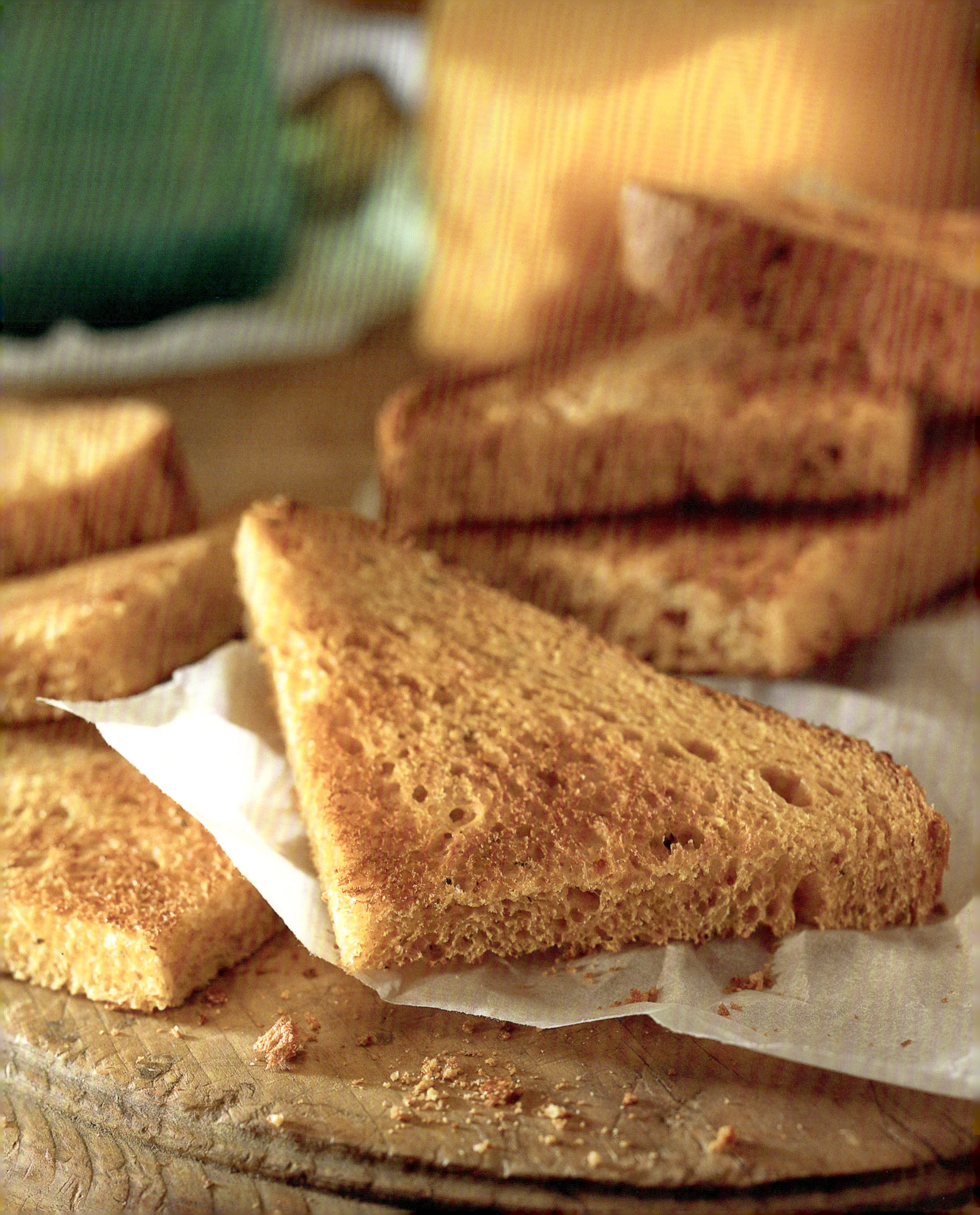

Three-Grain Bread

MAKES 1 LOAF

- 1 cup whole wheat flour
- ¾ cup all-purpose flour
- 1 package (¼ ounce) instant yeast
- 1 cup milk
- 2 tablespoons honey
- 1 tablespoon olive oil
- 1 teaspoon salt
- ½ cup plus 1 tablespoon old-fashioned oats, divided
- ¼ cup whole grain cornmeal
- 1 egg beaten with 1 tablespoon water

1. Combine whole wheat flour, all-purpose flour and yeast in large bowl of stand mixer. Combine milk, honey, oil and salt in small saucepan; heat over low heat until warm (110°F to 120°F). Add to flour mixture; beat with paddle attachment at medium-high speed 3 minutes. Add ½ cup oats and cornmeal; beat at low speed until blended. If dough is too wet, add additional flour by teaspoonfuls until it begins to come together.

2. Replace paddle attachment with dough hook; mix at low speed 5 minutes or until dough forms a ball. Place dough in large greased bowl; turn to grease top. Cover and let rise in warm place about 1 hour or until dough is puffy and does not spring back when touched.

3. Punch down dough. Shape dough into 8-inch loaf; place on baking sheet lightly sprinkled with cornmeal. Cover and let rise in warm place about 45 minutes or until almost doubled in size. Preheat oven to 375°F.

4. Make shallow slash down center of loaf with sharp knife. Brush lightly with egg mixture; sprinkle with remaining 1 tablespoon oats.

5. Bake 30 minutes or until bread sounds hollow when tapped (internal temperature of 200°F). Remove to wire rack to cool completely.

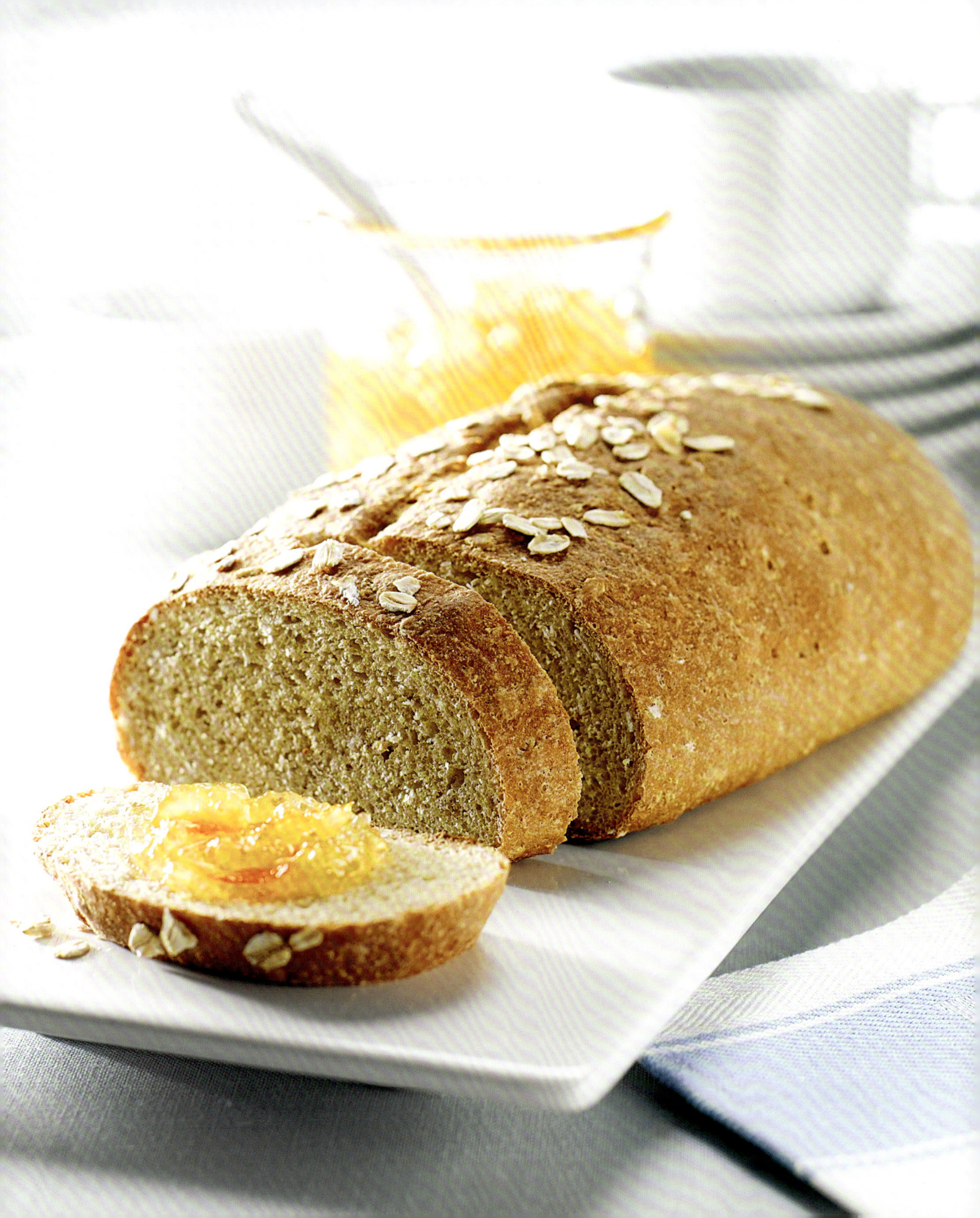

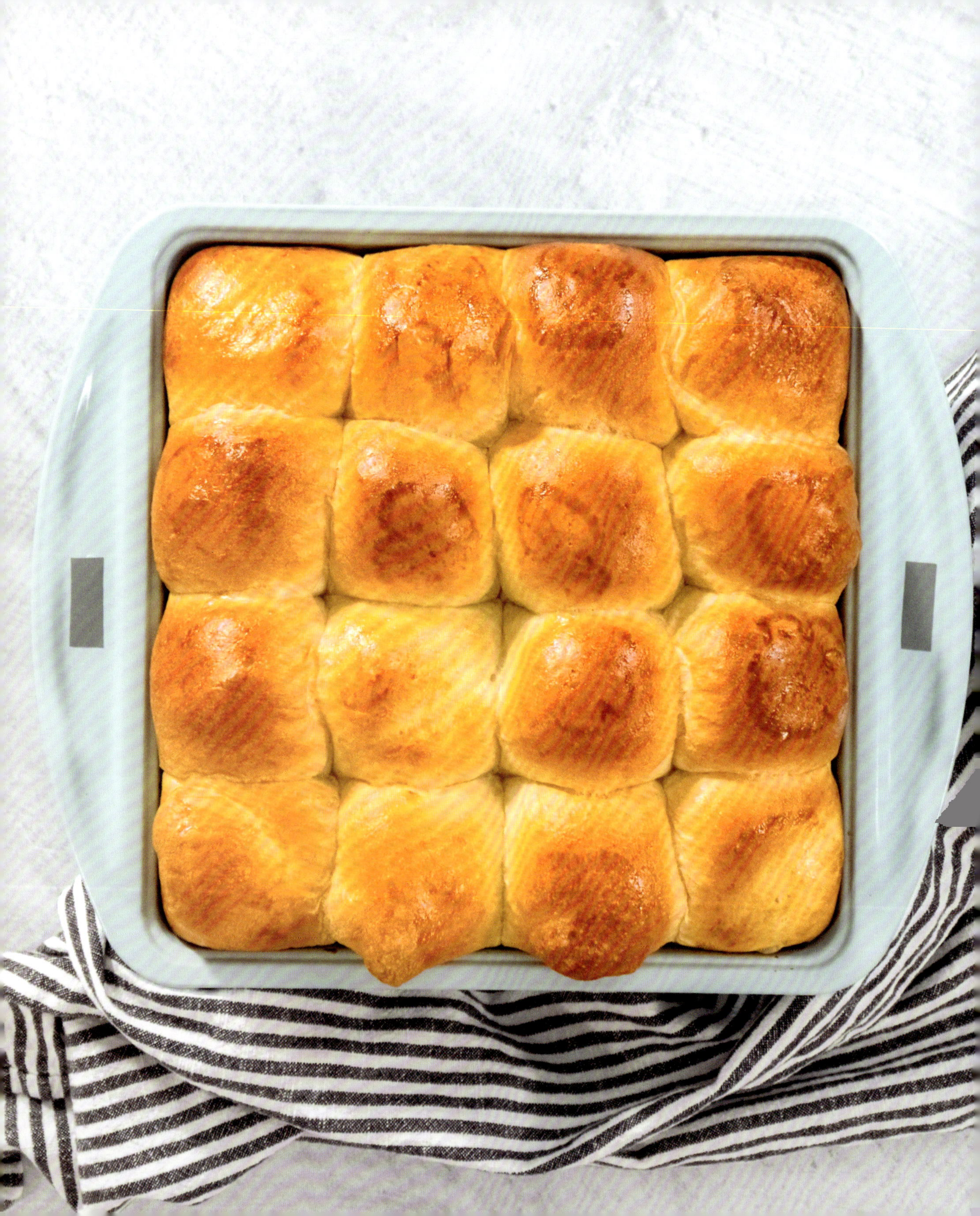

ROLLS & BUNS

Quick Honey Butter Rolls
MAKES 16 ROLLS

- 16 frozen bread dough rolls
- 3 tablespoons butter
- 3 tablespoons honey
- Pinch salt
- Pinch ground red pepper

1. Spray 9-inch square baking dish with nonstick cooking spray. Arrange rolls evenly in pan. Cover with greased plastic wrap; let stand at room temperature 2 to 3 hours or until doubled in size (or refrigerate 8 to 16 hours or until doubled).

2. Preheat oven to 350°F. Combine butter, honey, salt and red pepper in small microwavable bowl; microwave on HIGH 30 to 40 seconds or until butter is melted. Stir until smooth. Brush 2 tablespoons mixture evenly over rolls.

3. Bake rolls 18 minutes. Brush rolls with remaining butter mixture; bake 2 minutes or until golden brown. Serve warm.

Cinnamon Pecan Rolls

MAKES ABOUT 18 ROLLS

- 4 tablespoons (½ stick) butter, melted, divided
- 1 loaf (16 ounces) frozen bread dough, thawed according to package directions
- ½ cup packed dark brown sugar
- 2 teaspoons ground cinnamon
- ½ cup chopped pecans

1. Brush large (10-inch) ovenproof skillet with ½ tablespoon melted butter. Roll out dough into 18×8-inch rectangle on lightly floured surface.

2. Combine brown sugar, 3 tablespoons butter and cinnamon in medium bowl; mix well. Brush mixture evenly over dough; sprinkle with pecans. Starting with long side, roll up dough jelly-roll style; pinch seam to seal.

3. Cut dough crosswise into 1-inch slices; arrange slices cut sides up in prepared skillet. Cover loosely; let rise in warm place 30 minutes or until doubled in size.

4. Preheat oven to 350°F. Brush tops of rolls with remaining ½ tablespoon butter.

5. Bake 20 to 25 minutes or until golden brown. Serve warm.

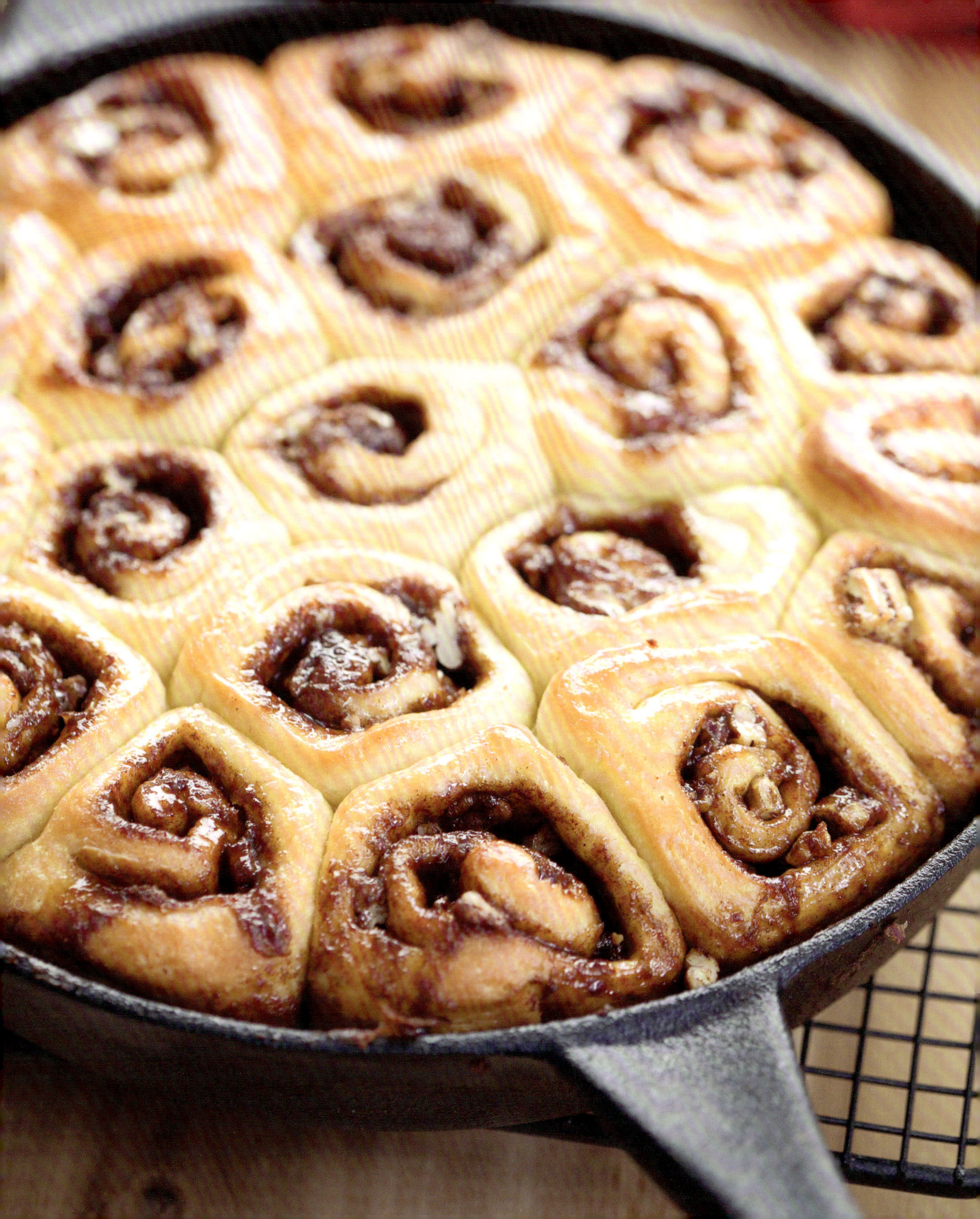

Reuben Rolls

MAKES 8 ROLLS

1 cup sauerkraut
1 can (about 14 ounces) refrigerated pizza dough
6 thin slices Swiss cheese (about 4 ounces)
1 teaspoon caraway seeds
½ teaspoon black pepper
⅓ pound thinly sliced corned beef
½ cup Thousand Island dressing

1. Preheat oven to 400°F. Line baking sheet with parchment paper. Squeeze sauerkraut as dry as possible to yield about ⅔ cup.

2. Unroll dough on work surface or cutting board; press into 13×9-inch rectangle. Arrange cheese slices over dough, leaving 1 inch border on all sides. Sprinkle with sauerkraut, caraway seeds and pepper. Top with corned beef.

3. Starting with long side, gently roll up dough jelly-roll style. Trim off ends. Cut crosswise into eight 1½-inch slices with serrated knife; place slices cut sides up on prepared baking sheet.

4. Bake 20 to 25 minutes or until dough is golden brown and cheese is melted. Immediately remove from baking sheet; serve warm with dressing for dipping.

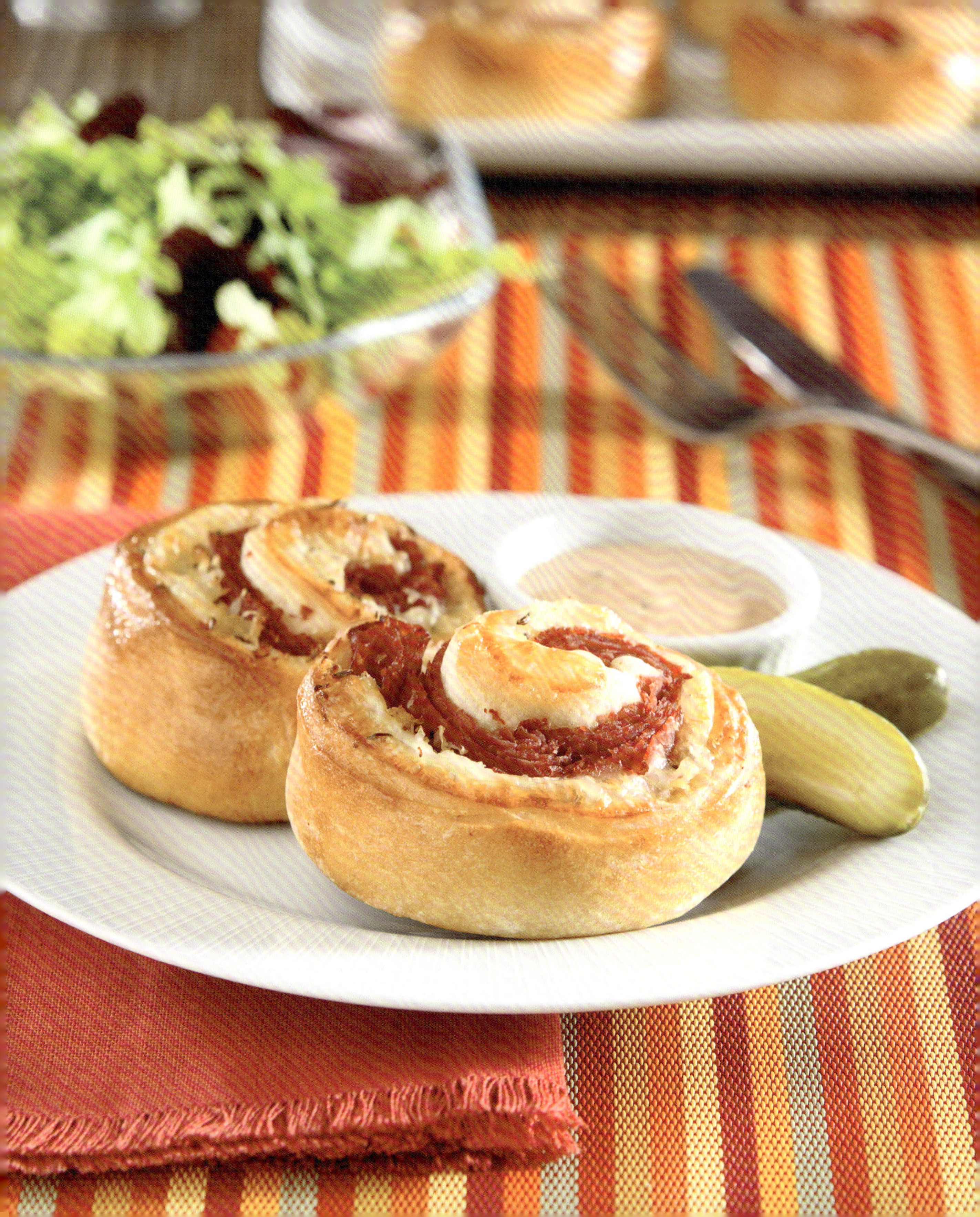

Pepperoni Pizza Rolls

MAKES 12 ROLLS

- 1 package (16 ounces) frozen pizza dough or 1 loaf (16 ounces) white bread dough, thawed according to package directions
- ½ cup pizza sauce, plus additional sauce for serving
- ⅓ cup chopped pepperoni or mini pepperoni slices (half of 2½-ounce package)
- 9 to 10 slices (about 1 ounce each) fontina, provolone or provolone-mozzarella blend cheese*

*For best results, use thinner cheese slices which are less than 1 ounce each.

1. Spray 12 standard (2½-inch) muffin pan cups with nonstick cooking spray.

2. Roll out dough into 12×10-inch rectangle on lightly floured surface. Spread ½ cup pizza sauce over dough, leaving ½-inch border on long sides. Sprinkle with pepperoni; top with cheese, cutting slices to fit as necessary. Starting with long side, tightly roll up dough jelly-roll style; pinch seam to seal.

3. Cut dough crosswise into 1-inch slices; place slices cut sides up in prepared muffin cups. Cover and let rise in warm place 30 to 40 minutes or until nearly doubled in size. Preheat oven to 350°F.

4. Bake 25 minutes or until golden brown. Loosen bottom and sides with small spatula or knife; remove to wire rack. Serve warm with additional sauce for dipping, if desired.

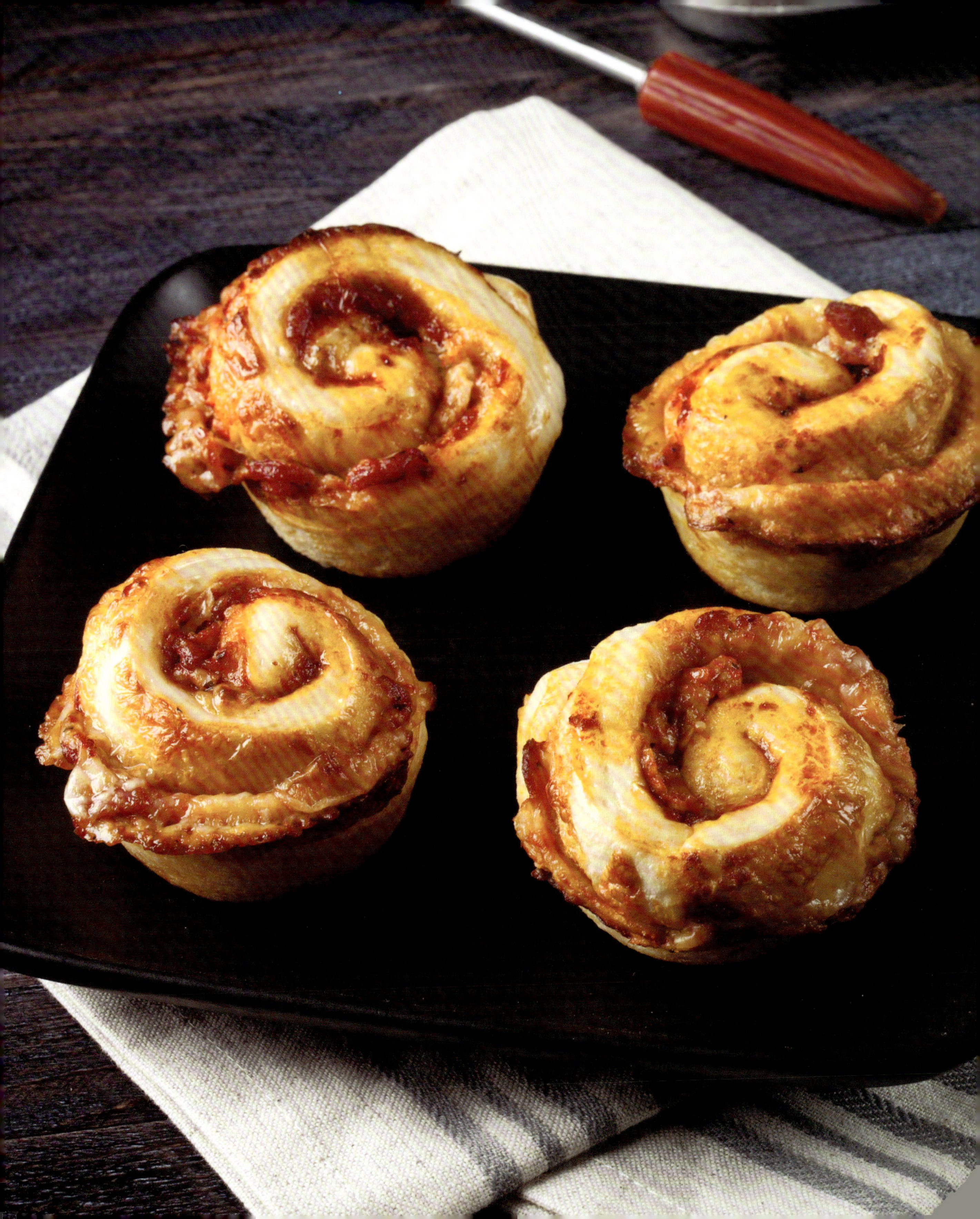

Pull-Apart Rye Rolls
MAKES 24 ROLLS

- ¾ cup water
- 2 tablespoons butter
- 2 tablespoons molasses
- 2¼ cups all-purpose flour, divided
- ½ cup rye flour
- ⅓ cup nonfat dry milk powder
- 1 package (¼ ounce) active dry yeast
- 1½ teaspoons salt
- 1½ teaspoons caraway seeds
- 2 teaspoons vegetable oil

1. Combine water, butter and molasses in small saucepan; heat over low heat to 120°F. Combine 1¼ cups all-purpose flour, rye flour, milk powder, yeast, salt and caraway seeds in large bowl of stand mixer. Slowly add water mixture; beat with paddle attachment at low speed to form soft, sticky dough.

2. Replace paddle attachment with dough hook. Gradually add enough additional all-purpose flour, about ¾ cup, to form rough dough. Add remaining flour, 1 tablespoon at a time, if necessary to prevent sticking. Mix at low speed 5 minutes or until dough is smooth and elastic.

3. Shape dough into a ball. Place dough in large greased bowl; turn to grease top. Cover and let rise in warm place 35 to 40 minutes or until dough has increased in size by one third.

4. Spray 8- or 9-inch round cake pan with nonstick cooking spray. Punch down dough. Divide dough in half; roll each half into 12-inch log. Cut each log into 12 pieces with sharp knife; shape each piece into a tight ball. Place balls in single layer in prepared pan; brush with oil. Cover loosely with lightly greased sheet of plastic wrap; let rise in warm place 45 minutes or until doubled in size. Preheat oven to 375°F.

5. Bake 15 to 20 minutes or until rolls are golden brown. Cool in pan 5 minutes; remove to wire rack to cool completely.

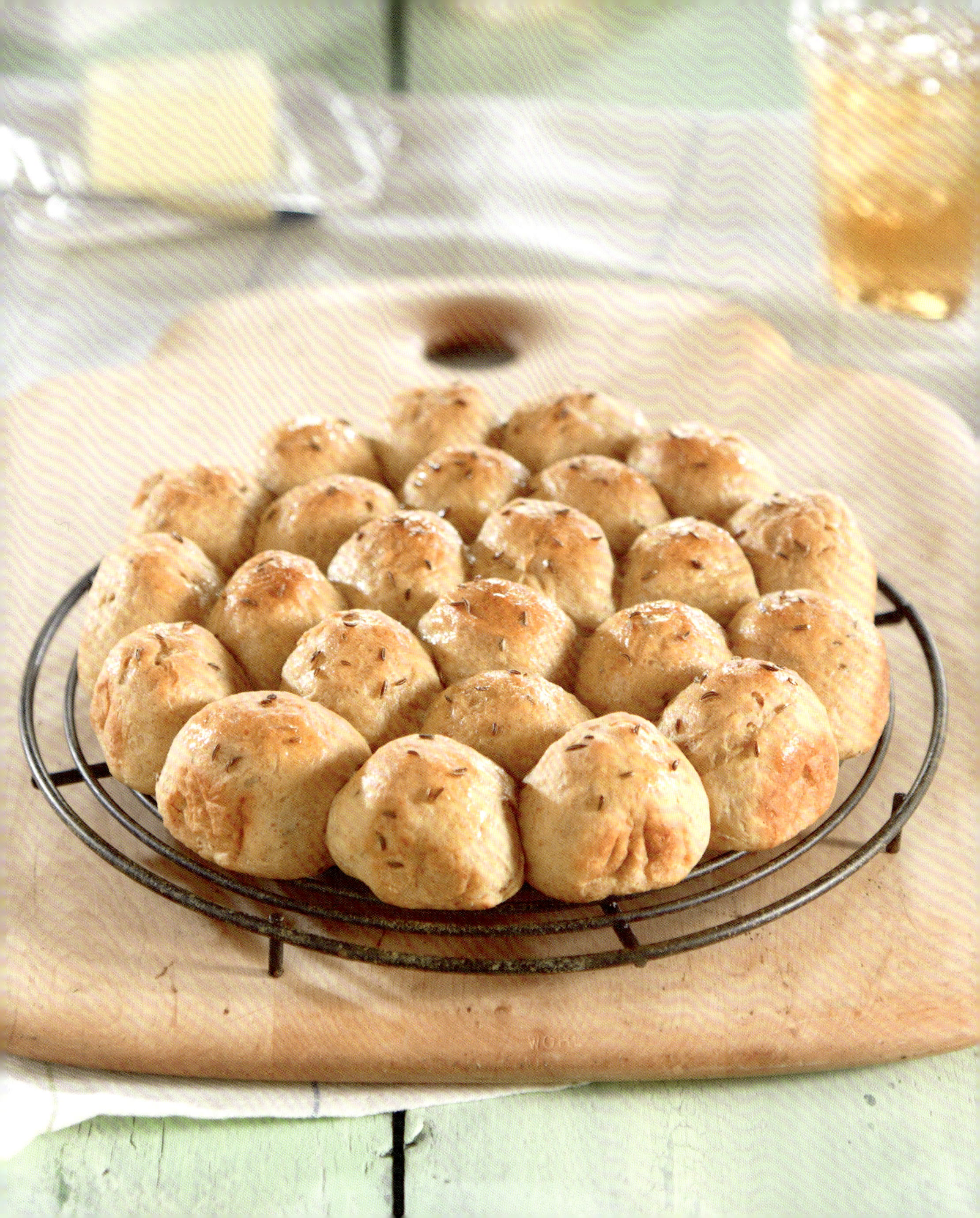

Greek Spinach Cheese Rolls

MAKES 15 ROLLS

- 1 loaf (16 ounces) frozen bread dough, thawed according to package directions
- 1 package (10 ounces) frozen chopped spinach, thawed and squeezed dry
- ¾ cup (3 ounces) crumbled feta cheese
- ½ cup (2 ounces) shredded Monterey Jack cheese
- 4 green onions, thinly sliced
- 1 teaspoon dried dill weed
- ½ teaspoon garlic powder
- ½ teaspoon black pepper

1. Spray 15 standard (2½-inch) muffin cups with nonstick cooking spray. Roll out dough into 15×9-inch rectangle on lightly floured surface. (If dough is springy and difficult to roll, cover with plastic wrap and let rest 5 minutes.)

2. Combine spinach, feta, Monterey Jack, green onions, dill weed, garlic powder and pepper in medium bowl; mix well. Spread spinach mixture evenly over dough, leaving 1-inch border on long sides.

3. Starting with long side, roll up dough jelly-roll style; pinch seam to seal. Cut dough crosswise into 1-inch slices with serrated knife; place slices cut sides up in prepared muffin cups. Cover and let rise in warm place 30 minutes or until dough is slightly puffy. Preheat oven to 375°F.

4. Bake 20 to 25 minutes or until golden brown. Serve warm or at room temperature.

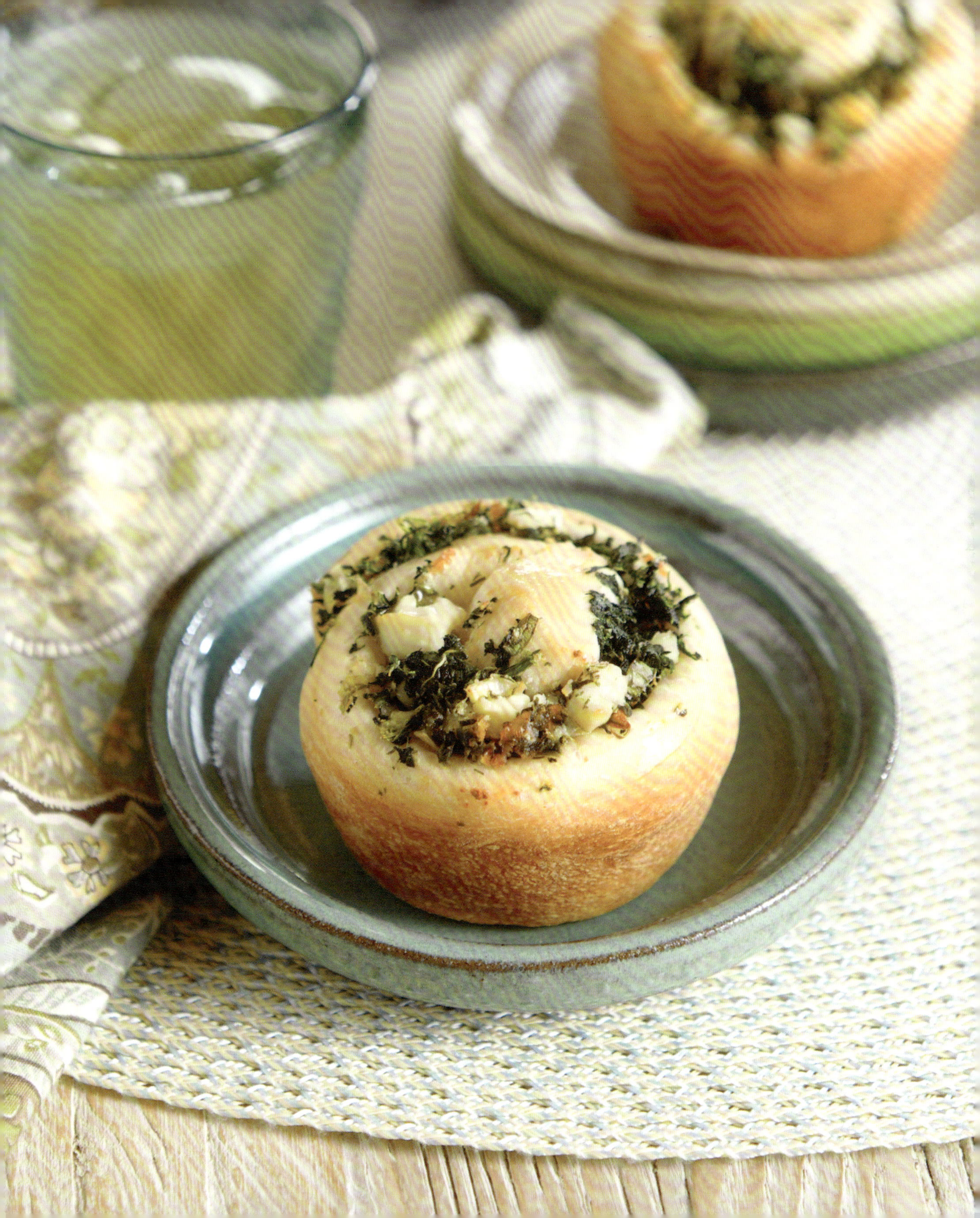

Quick Chocolate Chip Sticky Buns

MAKES 8 STICKY BUNS

- 2 tablespoons butter
- 1 can (11 ounces) refrigerated French bread dough
- ¼ cup sugar
- 1 teaspoon ground cinnamon
- ½ cup mini semisweet chocolate chips
- ⅓ cup pecan pieces, toasted*
- 1 tablespoon maple syrup

*To toast pecans, spread on ungreased baking sheet. Bake in preheated 350°F oven 6 to 8 minutes or until golden brown, stirring frequently.

1. Preheat oven to 350°F. Place butter in 9-inch round cake pan; place pan in oven while preheating to melt butter.

2. Meanwhile, unroll dough on cutting board or work surface. Combine sugar and cinnamon in small bowl; sprinkle evenly over dough. Top with chocolate chips. Starting with short side, roll up dough jelly-roll style. Cut dough crosswise into eight slices with serrated knife.

3. Remove pan from oven. Stir pecans and maple syrup into melted butter; mix well. Place dough slices cut sides up in pan, pressing gently into pecan mixture.

4. Bake 20 to 22 minutes or until golden brown. Immediately invert pan onto serving plate; scrape any pecans or butter mixture remaining in pan over buns. Serve warm.

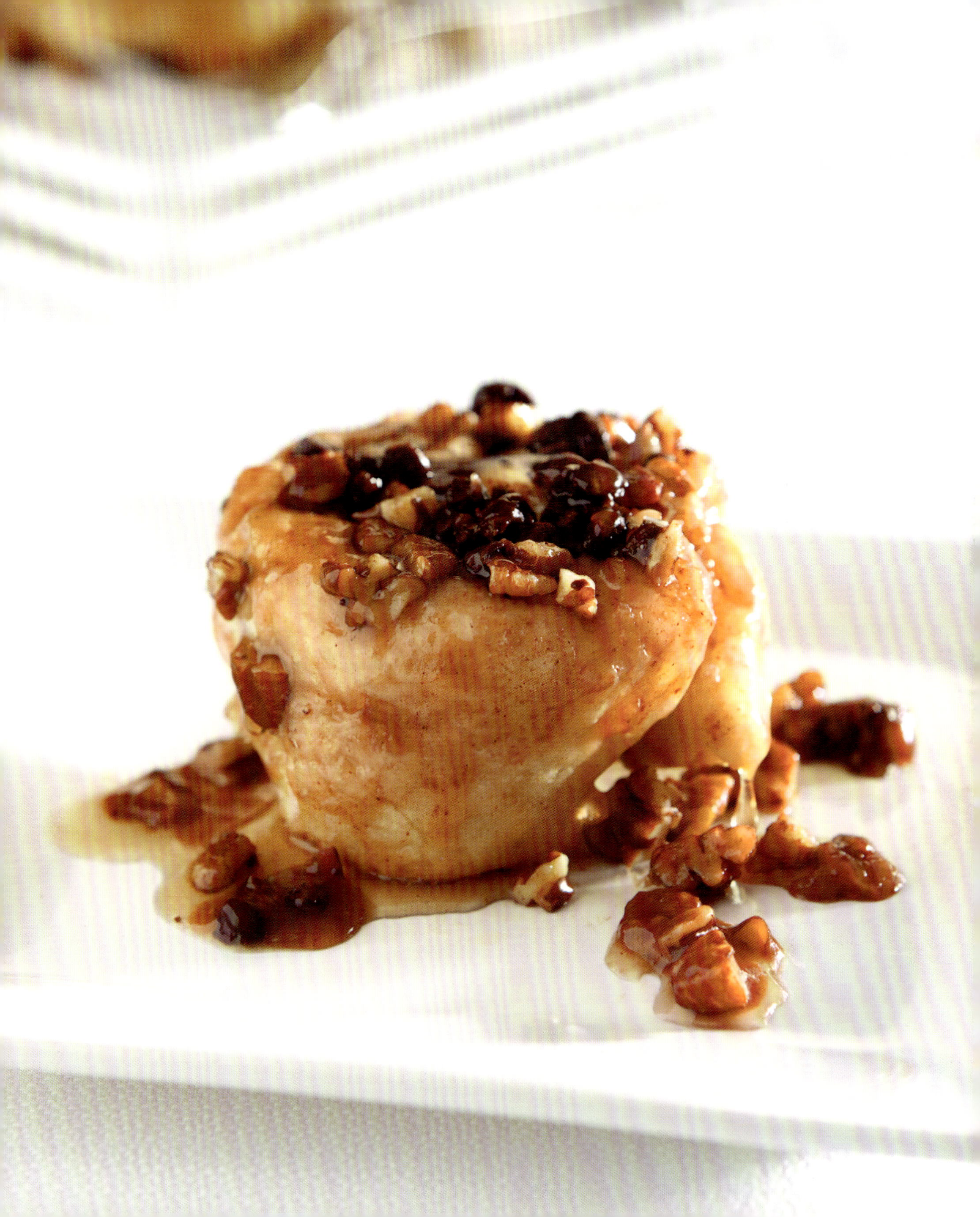

Easy Rosemary Rolls

MAKES 24 ROLLS

- 24 frozen bread dough rolls
- ½ cup (1 stick) butter, melted
- 2 cloves garlic, crushed
- 1 teaspoon minced fresh rosemary
- ¼ teaspoon salt
- Coarse salt (optional)

1. Spray 13×9-inch baking pan with nonstick cooking spray. Arrange rolls evenly in pan.

2. Melt butter in small saucepan over low heat. Add garlic, rosemary and ¼ teaspoon salt; cook and stir 2 minutes. Brush some of butter over rolls. Cover with plastic wrap; let stand at room temperature 2 to 3 hours or until doubled (or refrigerate 8 to 16 hours or until doubled). Cover remaining butter mixture and refrigerate until ready to bake.

3. Preheat oven to 350°F. Heat remaining butter mixture until melted.

4. Bake rolls 15 to 18 minutes or until golden brown. Remove crushed garlic cloves from butter mixture; brush over rolls immediately after removing from oven. Sprinkle with coarse salt, if desired. Serve warm.

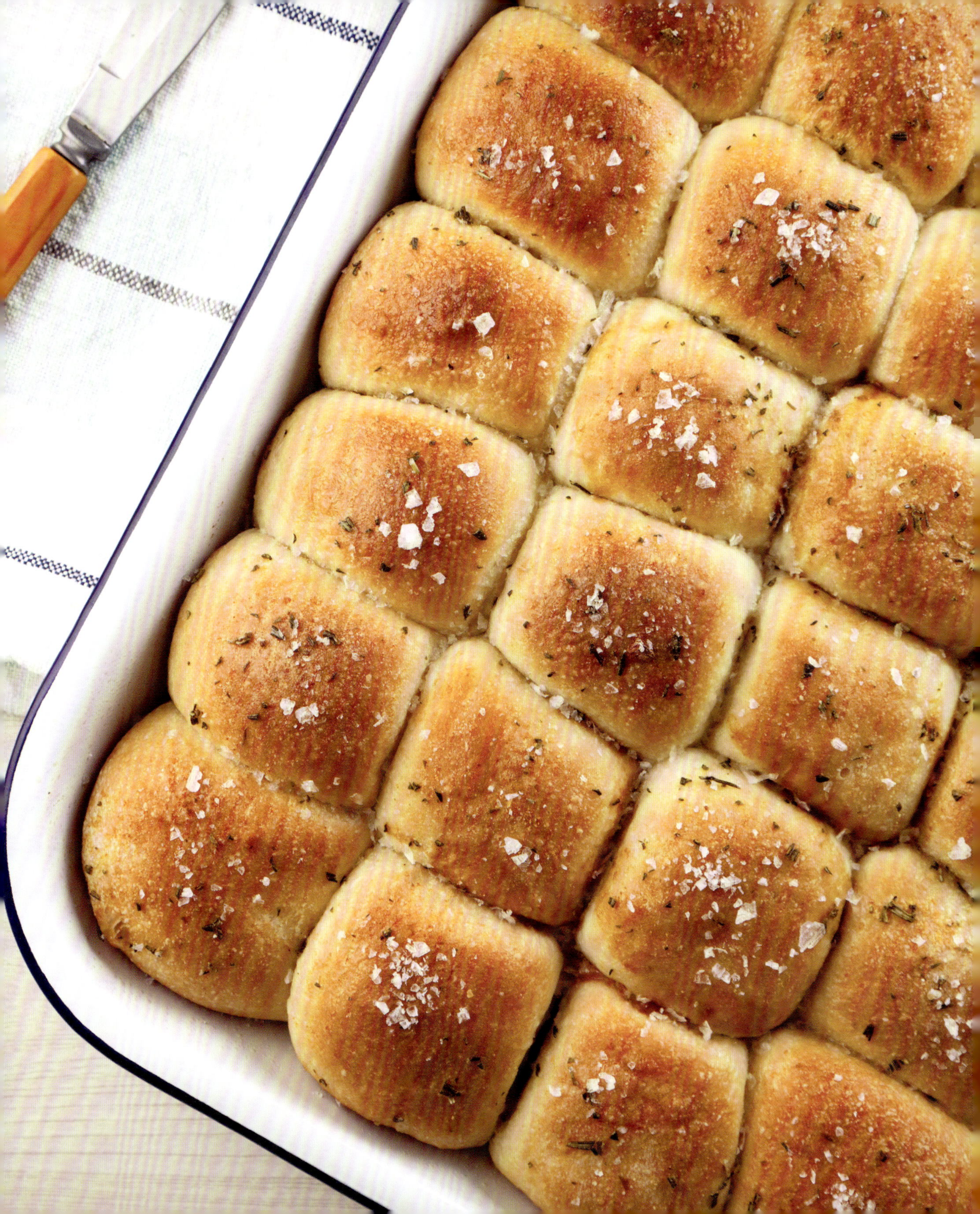

Hawaiian Pizza Rolls

MAKES 6 ROLLS

- 2 tablespoons cornmeal, divided
- 1 can (about 14 ounces) refrigerated pizza dough
- 6 ounces thinly sliced Canadian bacon
- ⅓ cup crushed pineapple, drained
- ⅓ cup pizza sauce, plus additional sauce for serving
- 3 pieces (1 ounce each) string cheese

1. Preheat oven to 400°F. Spray baking sheet with nonstick cooking spray. Sprinkle with 1 tablespoon cornmeal.

2. Roll out dough into 16½×11-inch rectangle on lightly floured surface. Sprinkle with remaining 1 tablespoon cornmeal. Cut into six squares. Top each square with bacon, pineapple and pizza sauce.

3. Cut each piece of string cheese in half; place one piece of cheese in center of each square. Bring up two opposite sides of each square and crimp ends of each roll to seal. Place rolls, seam side down, on prepared baking sheet.

4. Bake 15 to 17 minutes or until golden brown. Serve with additional sauce for dipping.

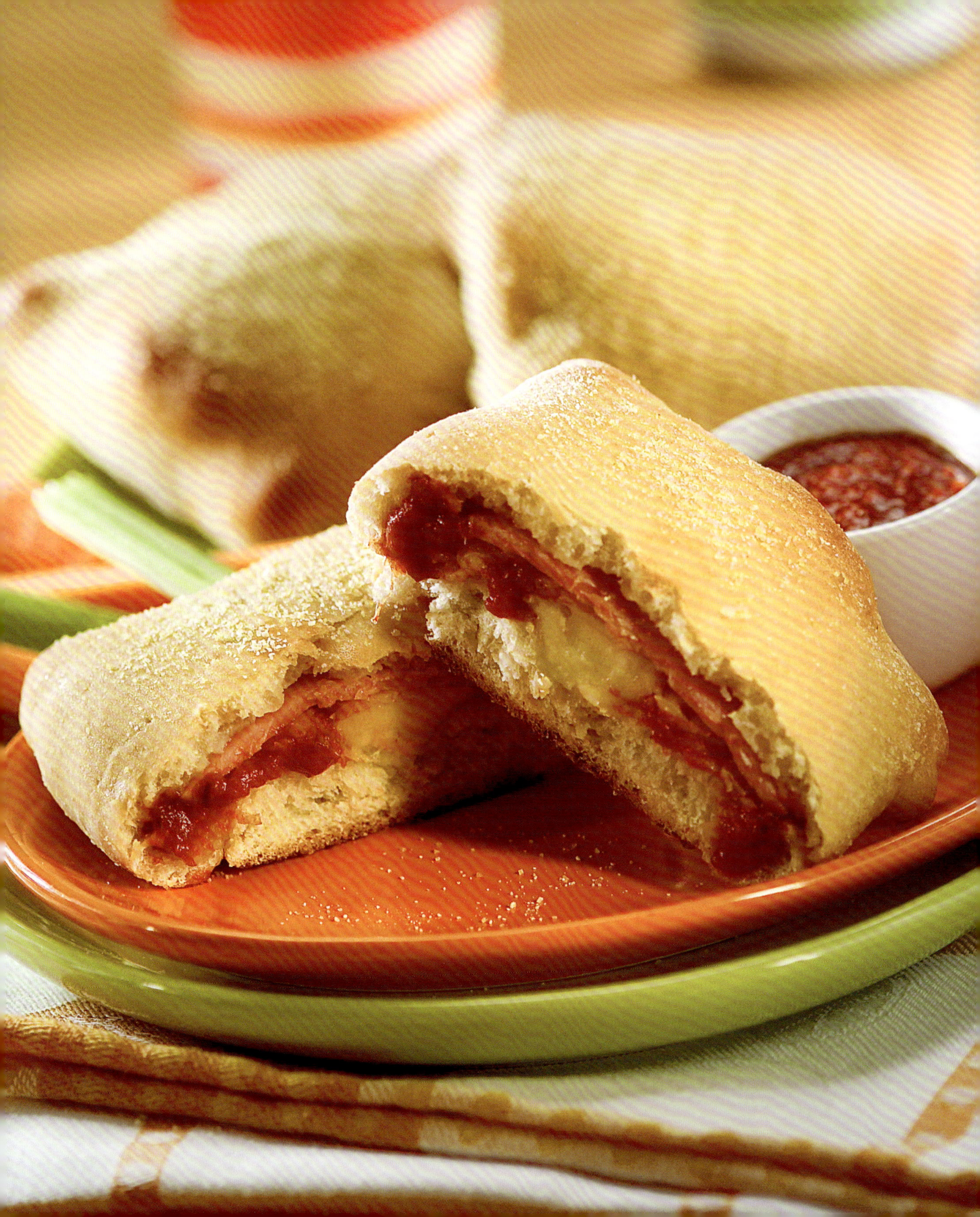

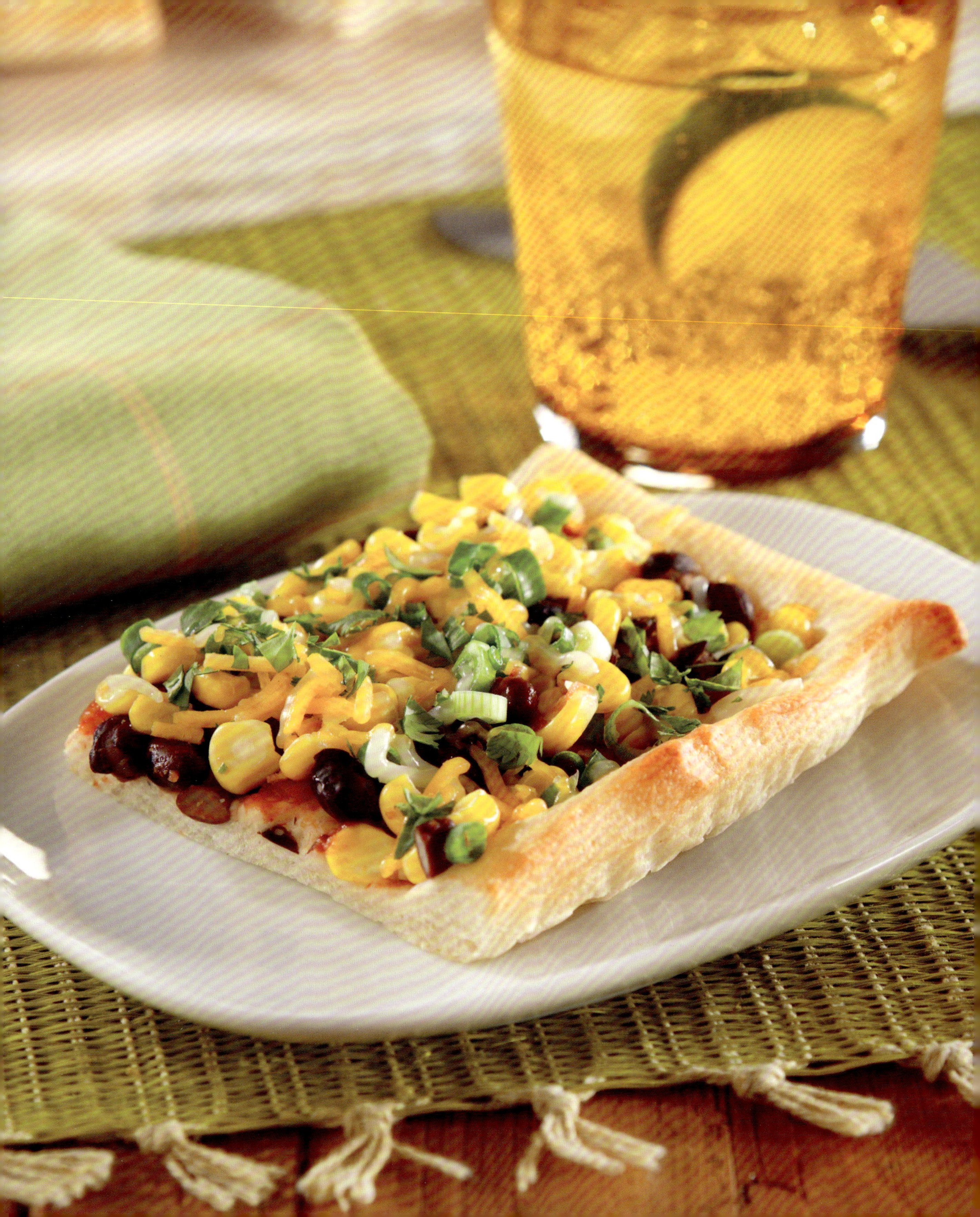

PIZZAS & FLATBREADS

Mexican Pizza
MAKES 8 SERVINGS

- 1 can (about 14 ounces) refrigerated pizza dough
- 1 cup chunky salsa
- 1 teaspoon ground cumin
- 1 cup canned black beans, rinsed and drained*
- 1 cup frozen corn, thawed
- ½ cup sliced green onions
- 1½ cups (6 ounces) shredded Mexican cheese blend
- ½ cup chopped fresh cilantro (optional)

*Save the remaining ¾ cup beans (from a 15-ounce can) in the refrigerator for up to 4 days to add to salads or soups.

1. Preheat oven to 425°F. Spray 15×10-inch baking pan with nonstick cooking spray.
2. Unroll dough on prepared baking sheet; press dough evenly to edges of pan. Bake 8 minutes.
3. Combine salsa and cumin in small bowl; spread over partially baked crust. Top with beans, corn and green onions.
4. Bake 8 minutes or until crust is golden brown. Sprinkle with cheese; bake 2 minutes or until cheese is melted. Cut into squares; garnish with cilantro, if desired.

Quattro Formaggio Focaccia

MAKES 12 SERVINGS

- 1 tablespoon sugar
- 1 package (¼ ounce) instant yeast
- 1¼ cups warm water (100° to 105°F)
- 3 to 3¼ cups all-purpose flour
- ¼ cup plus 2 tablespoons olive oil, divided
- 1 teaspoon salt
- ¼ cup marinara sauce with basil
- 1 cup (4 ounces) shredded Italian cheese blend

1. Dissolve sugar and yeast in warm water in large bowl of stand mixer; let stand 5 minutes or until bubbly. Stir in 3 cups flour, ¼ cup oil and salt with spoon or spatula to form rough dough. Mix with dough hook at low speed 5 minutes, adding additional flour, 1 tablespoon at a time, if necessary for dough to come together. (Dough will be sticky and will not clean side of bowl.)

2. Shape dough into a ball. Place dough in large greased bowl; turn to grease top. Cover and let rise 1 to 1½ hours or until doubled in size.

3. Punch down dough. Pour remaining 2 tablespoons oil into 13×9-inch baking pan; pat and stretch dough to fill pan. Make indentations in top of dough with fingertips.

4. Spread marinara sauce evenly over dough; sprinkle with cheese. Cover and let rise 30 minutes or until puffy. Preheat oven to 425°F.

5. Bake 17 to 20 minutes or until golden brown. Cut into squares or strips.

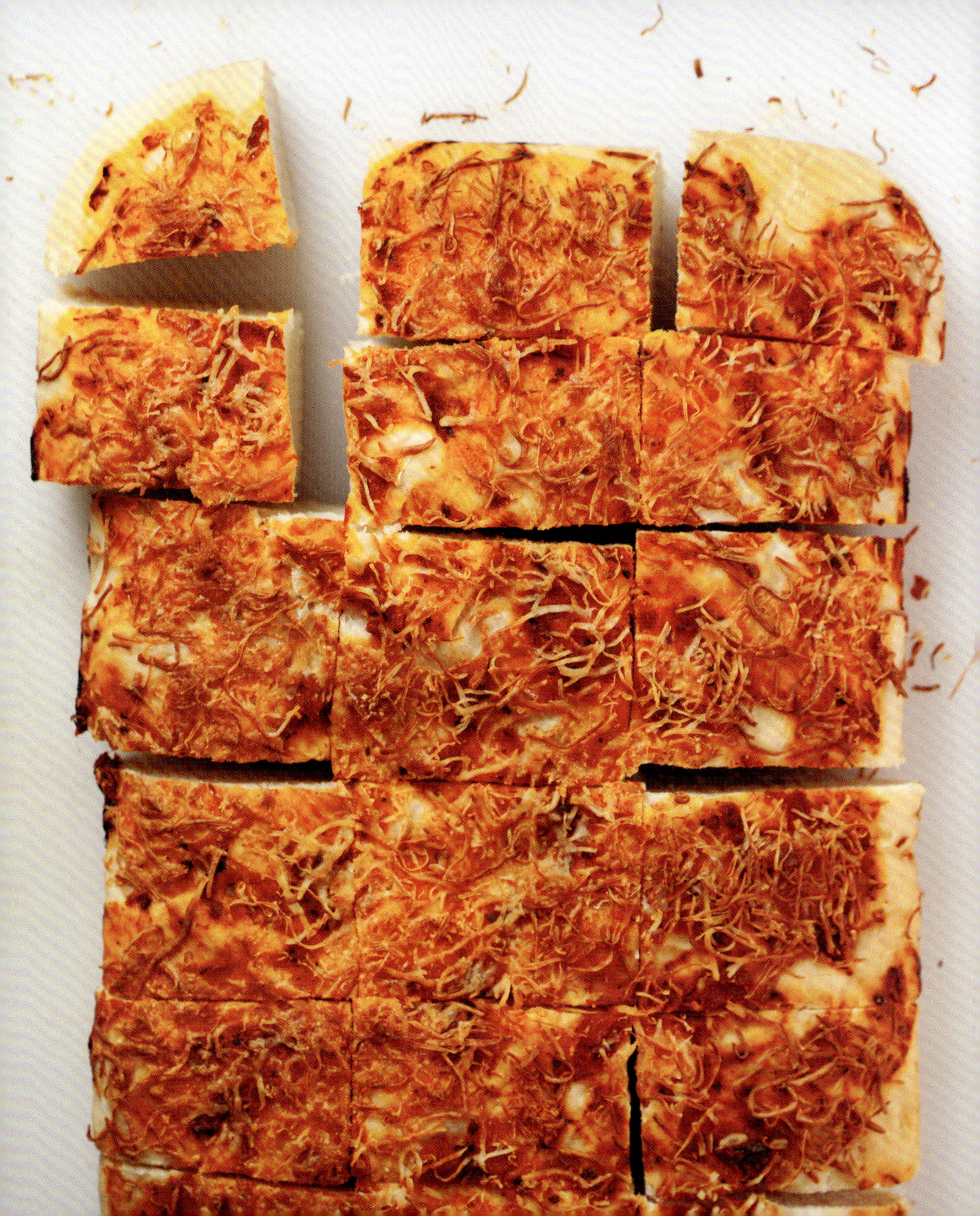

Barbecue Chicken Flatbread

MAKES 4 SERVINGS

- 3 tablespoons red wine vinegar
- 2 teaspoons sugar
- ¼ red onion, thinly sliced (about ⅓ cup)
- 3 cups shredded rotisserie chicken
- ½ cup barbecue sauce
- 1 can (about 14 ounces) refrigerated pizza dough
- All-purpose flour, for dusting
- 1½ cups (6 ounces) shredded mozzarella cheese
- 1 green onion, thinly sliced
- 2 tablespoons chopped fresh cilantro

1. Preheat oven to 400°F. Line baking sheet with parchment paper.

2. For pickled onion, combine vinegar and sugar in small bowl; stir until sugar is dissolved. Stir in red onion; cover and let stand at room temperature while preparing flatbread.

3. Combine chicken and barbecue sauce in medium bowl; toss to coat.

4. Roll out dough into 11×9-inch rectangle on lightly floured surface. Transfer dough to prepared baking sheet; top with cheese and chicken mixture.

5. Bake about 12 minutes or until crust is golden brown and cheese is melted. Drain red onion. Sprinkle red onion, green onion and cilantro over flatbread. Serve immediately.

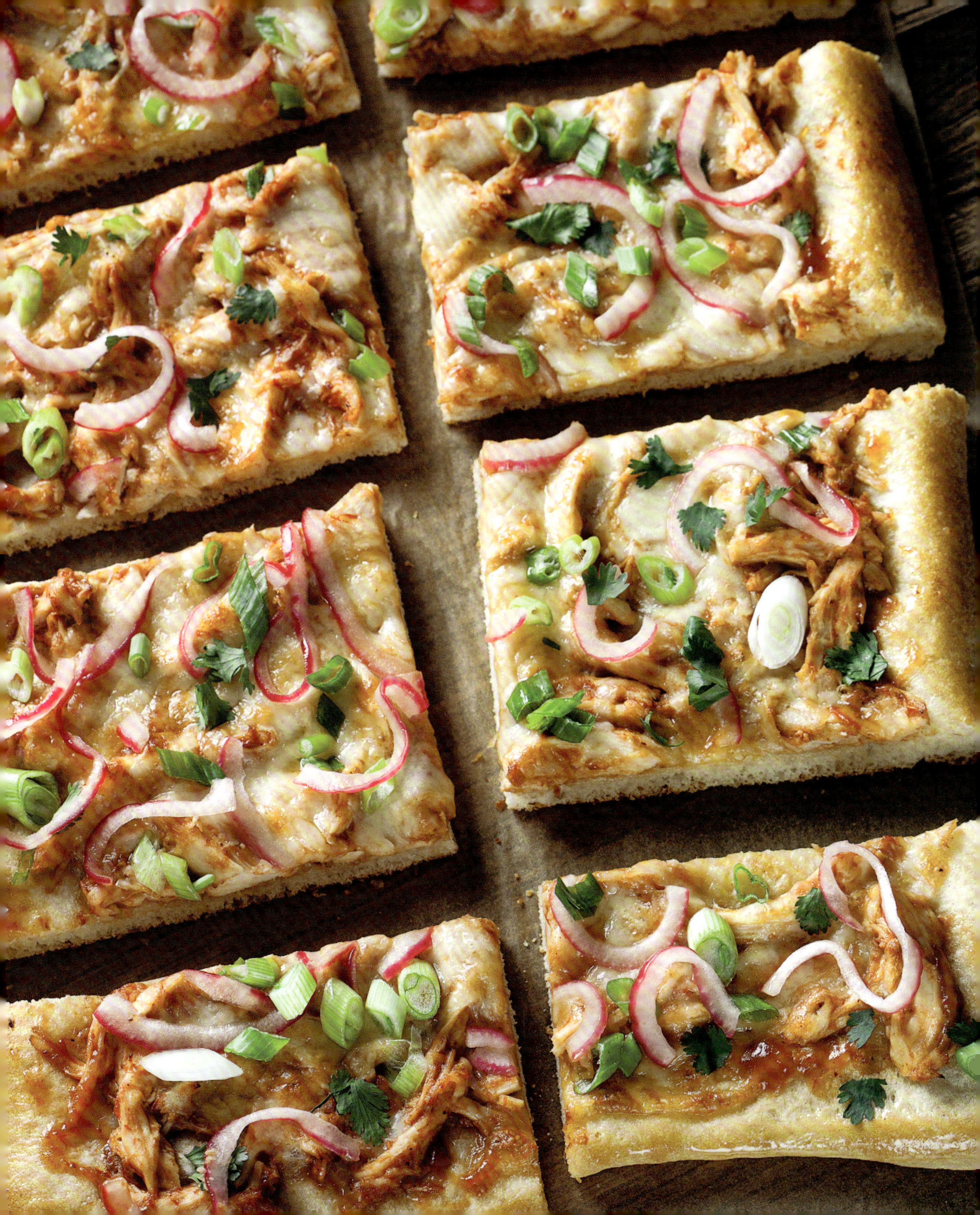

Olive and Herb Focaccia

MAKES ABOUT 12 SERVINGS

3½ to 3¾ cups bread flour
1¼ cups warm water (120°F)
½ cup extra virgin olive oil, divided
1 package (¼ ounce) instant yeast
2 teaspoons honey
1 teaspoon salt
1 cup chopped pitted Kalamata olives
3 tablespoons chopped fresh rosemary
2 tablespoons chopped fresh thyme
3 cloves garlic, minced
Black pepper
¼ cup grated Romano cheese

1. Combine 3½ cups flour, water, 3 tablespoons oil, yeast, honey and 1 teaspoon salt in large bowl of stand mixer. Mix with dough hook at low speed 2 minutes or until soft dough forms, adding additional flour, 1 tablespoon at a time, if necessary to clean side of bowl. Mix 5 minutes or until dough is smooth and elastic.

2. Shape dough into a ball. Place dough in large greased bowl; turn to grease top. Cover and let rise in warm place about 1 hour or until doubled in size.

3. Preheat oven to 450°F. Brush each of two 9-inch cake pans or deep-dish pizza pans with 1 tablespoon oil. Divide dough in half. Roll out each half into 9-inch circle on lightly floured surface. Place dough in prepared pans; cover and let rest 10 minutes.

4. Make indentations in top of dough with fingertips or handle of wooden spoon. Sprinkle with olives, rosemary, thyme and garlic; drizzle with remaining 3 tablespoons oil. Sprinkle with additional salt and pepper.

5. Bake about 15 minutes or until lightly browned. Immediately sprinkle with cheese. Remove to wire racks to cool slightly. Serve warm.

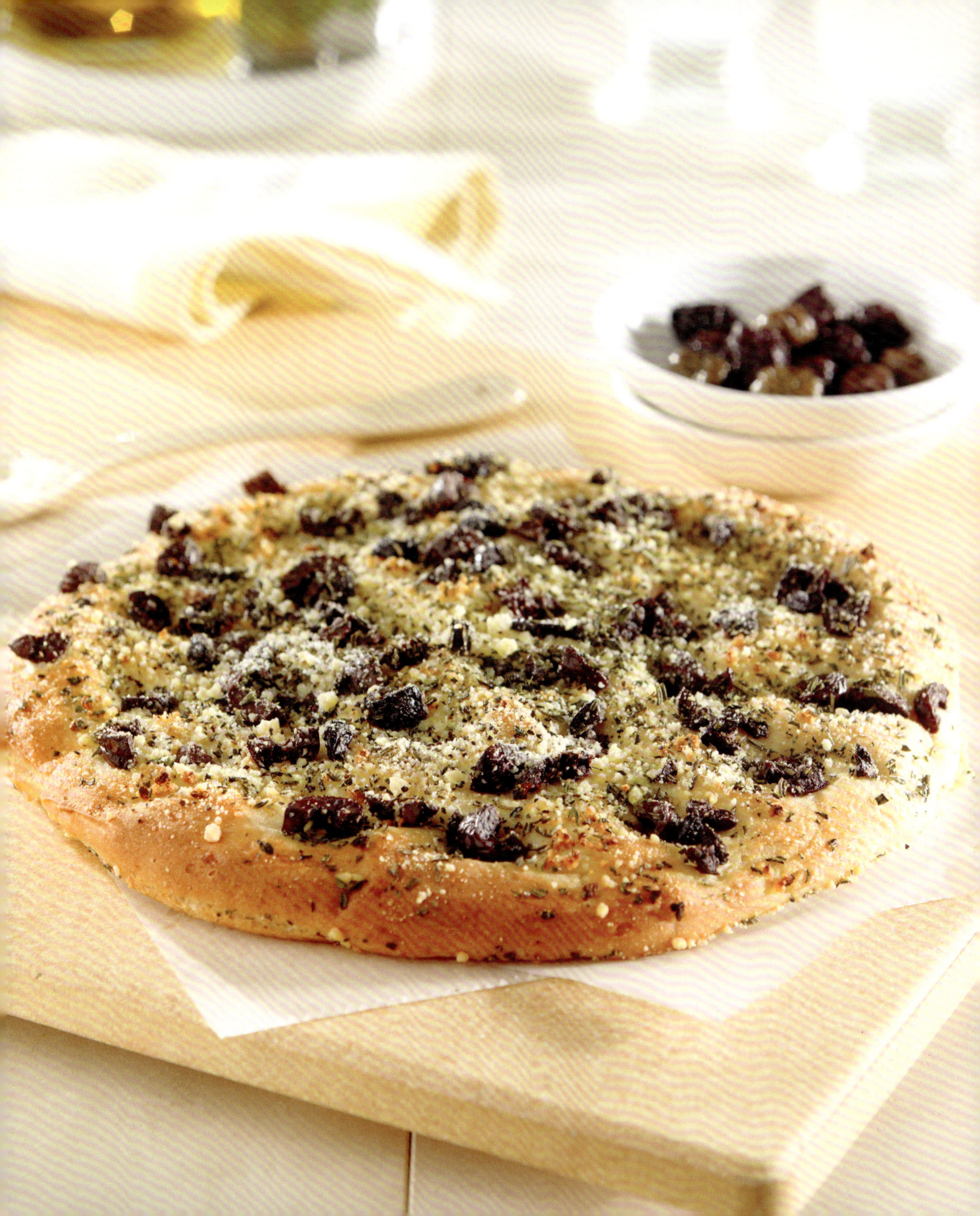

Pepperoni Pizza
MAKES 4 SERVINGS (1 PIZZA)

- 1 package (¼ ounce) active dry yeast
- ½ teaspoon sugar
- ⅔ cup warm water (105° to 115°F)
- 2 to 2¼ cups all-purpose flour
- 2 tablespoons olive oil
- ½ teaspoon salt
- 1 tablespoon cornmeal
- ½ cup pizza sauce
- 2 cups (8 ounces) shredded mozzarella cheese
- 18 to 20 slices pepperoni

1. Dissolve yeast and sugar in warm water in large bowl of stand mixer; let stand 5 minutes or until bubbly.

2. Add 2 cups flour, oil and salt; mix with dough hook at low speed 2 minutes or until soft dough forms, adding additional flour, 1 tablespoon at a time, if necessary to clean side of bowl. Mix at low speed 5 minutes.

3. Shape dough into a ball. Place dough in large greased bowl; turn to grease top. Cover and let rise in warm place 1 hour or until doubled in size.

4. Preheat oven to 500°F; place rack in lower third of oven. Sprinkle pizza pan or baking sheet with cornmeal.

5. Gently punch down dough; turn out onto lightly floured surface. Roll out dough into 12-inch circle about ¼ inch thick; transfer to prepared pizza pan. Spread sauce over dough, leaving ½-inch border. Top with cheese and pepperoni.

6. Bake 10 minutes or until crust is golden brown and cheese is melted and browning in spots. Remove to wire rack to cool 5 minutes.

> **TIP** For additional flavor, sprinkle the pizza with dried oregano and black pepper before baking.

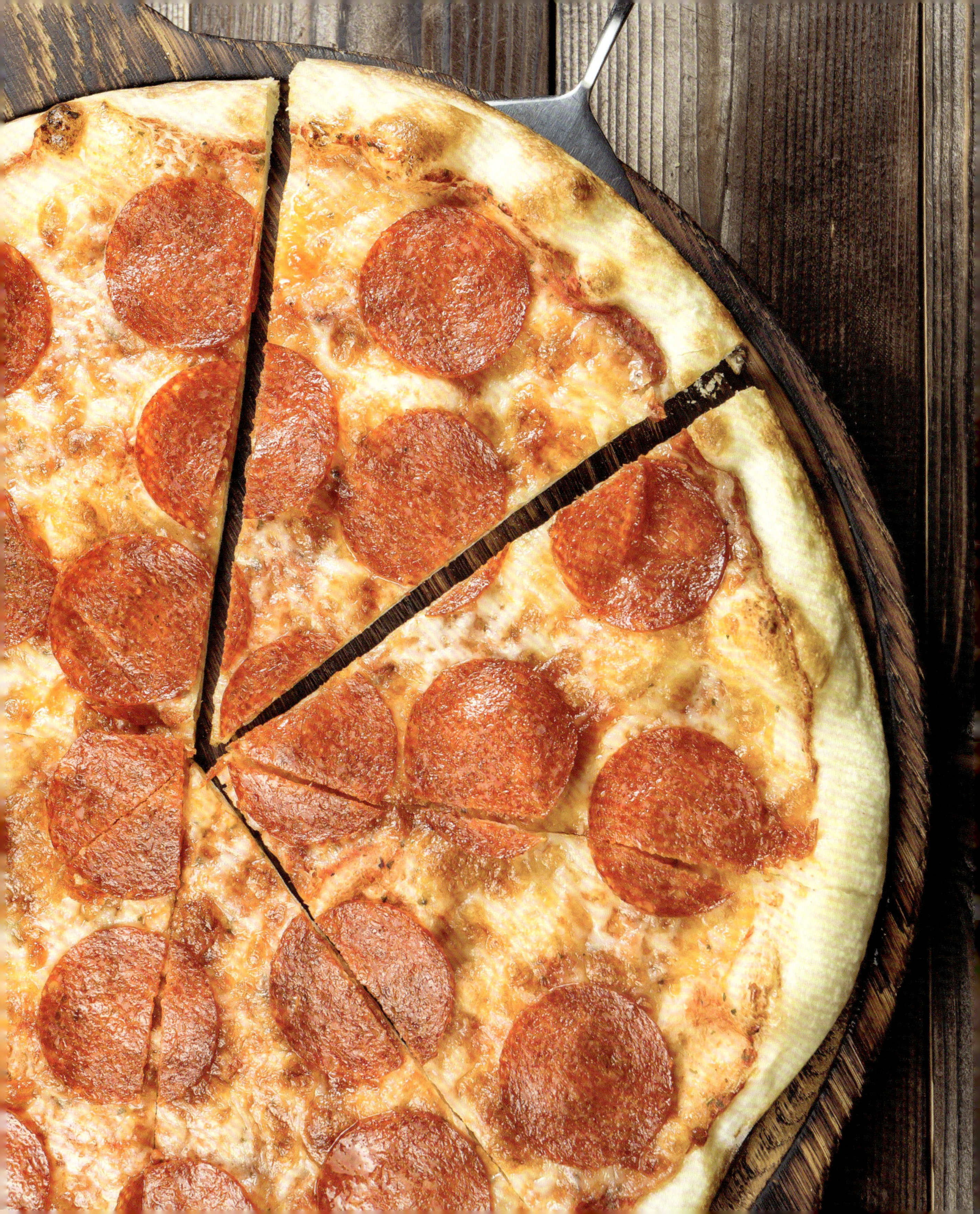

Khachapuri (Georgian Cheese Bread)

MAKES 2 SERVINGS

- 1 loaf (16 ounces) frozen bread dough, thawed according to package directions
- 1½ cups (6 ounces) shredded mozzarella cheese
- 1½ cups (6 ounces) crumbled feta cheese
- 1 teaspoon olive oil
- 1 teaspoon everything bagel seasoning (optional)
- 2 eggs
- Black pepper

1. Line baking sheet with parchment paper. Divide dough in half. Roll out one half into 11×8½-inch oval on lightly floured surface; transfer to prepared baking sheet.

2. Combine mozzarella and feta in medium bowl; mix well. Sprinkle ½ cup cheese mixture over dough, spreading almost to edge. Starting with long sides of oval, roll up dough and cheese towards center, curving into boat shape and leaving about 3 inches open in center. Press ends to seal. Fill center with 1 cup cheese mixture. Repeat rolling and filling steps with remaining half of dough and cheese mixture.

3. Cover loosely with plastic wrap; let rise 20 to 30 minutes or until puffy. Preheat oven to 400°F. Just before baking, brush edges of dough with oil; sprinkle with everything bagel seasoning, if desired.

4. Bake 12 minutes. Remove baking sheet from oven; use back of spoon to create indentations for eggs in center of cheese. Crack egg into each indentation;* sprinkle with pepper.

5. Bake 8 minutes for soft eggs or 10 minutes for firm eggs. Serve immediately.

*For more control, crack egg into small bowl and slide egg from bowl into cheese mixture.

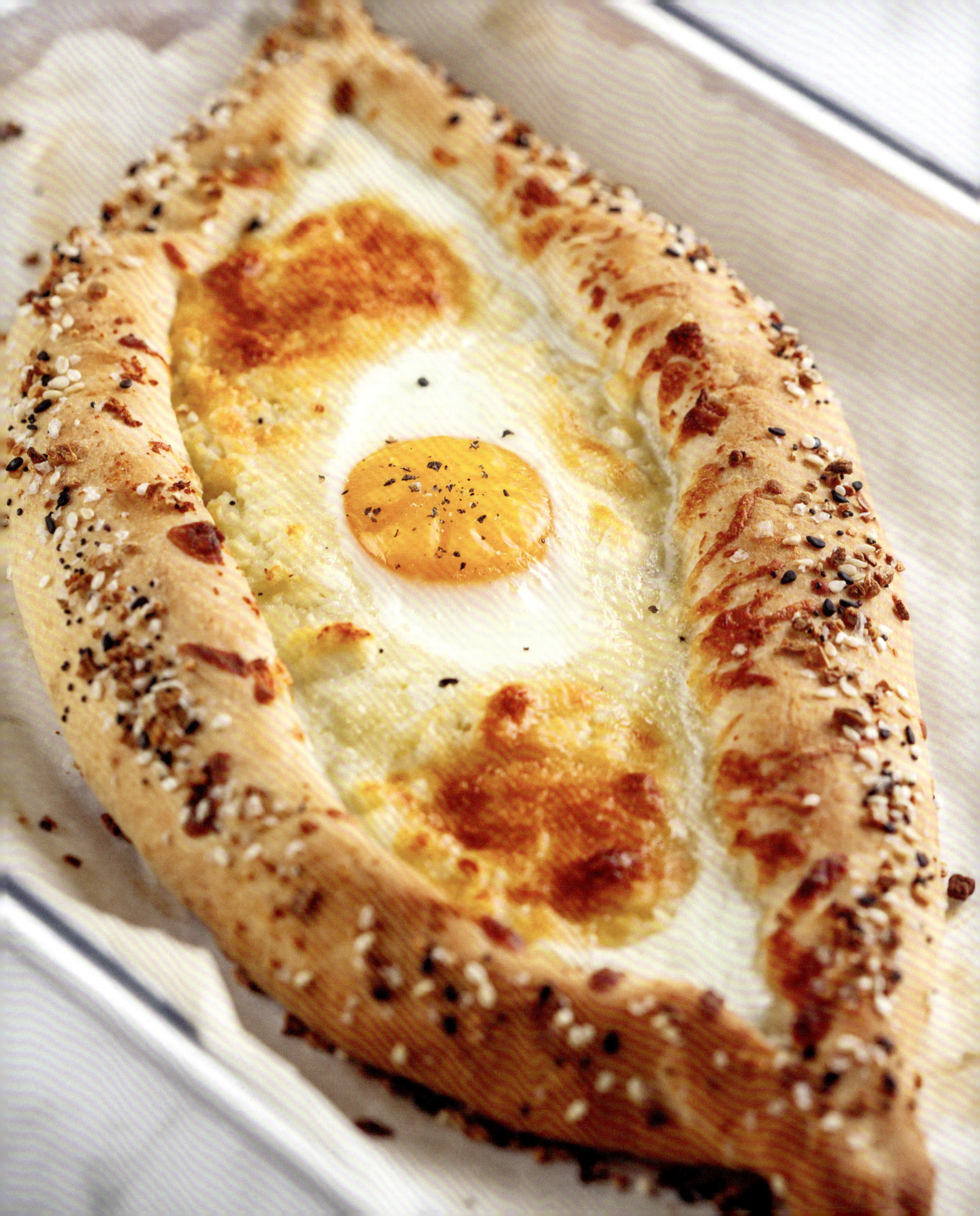

Wild Mushroom Flatbread

MAKES ABOUT 8 SERVINGS

- 1 can (about 14 ounces) refrigerated pizza dough
- 1 tablespoon olive oil
- 1 package (4 ounces) sliced cremini mushrooms
- 1 package (4 ounces) sliced shiitake mushrooms
- 1 shallot, thinly sliced
- 2 cloves garlic, minced
- ½ teaspoon salt
- ¾ cup (3 ounces) grated Gruyère cheese
- 2 teaspoons chopped fresh thyme

1. Preheat oven to 400°F. Line baking sheet with parchment paper. Spray with nonstick cooking spray.

2. Roll out dough into 15×10-inch rectangle on lightly floured surface; place on prepared baking sheet. Bake 10 minutes.

3. Meanwhile, heat oil in large skillet over medium-high heat. Add mushrooms; cook and stir 5 minutes. Add shallot and garlic; cook and stir 5 minutes or until vegetables are tender. Season with salt.

4. Spread mushroom mixture evenly over crust; top with cheese and thyme.

5. Bake 8 minutes or until cheese is melted. Cut into squares.

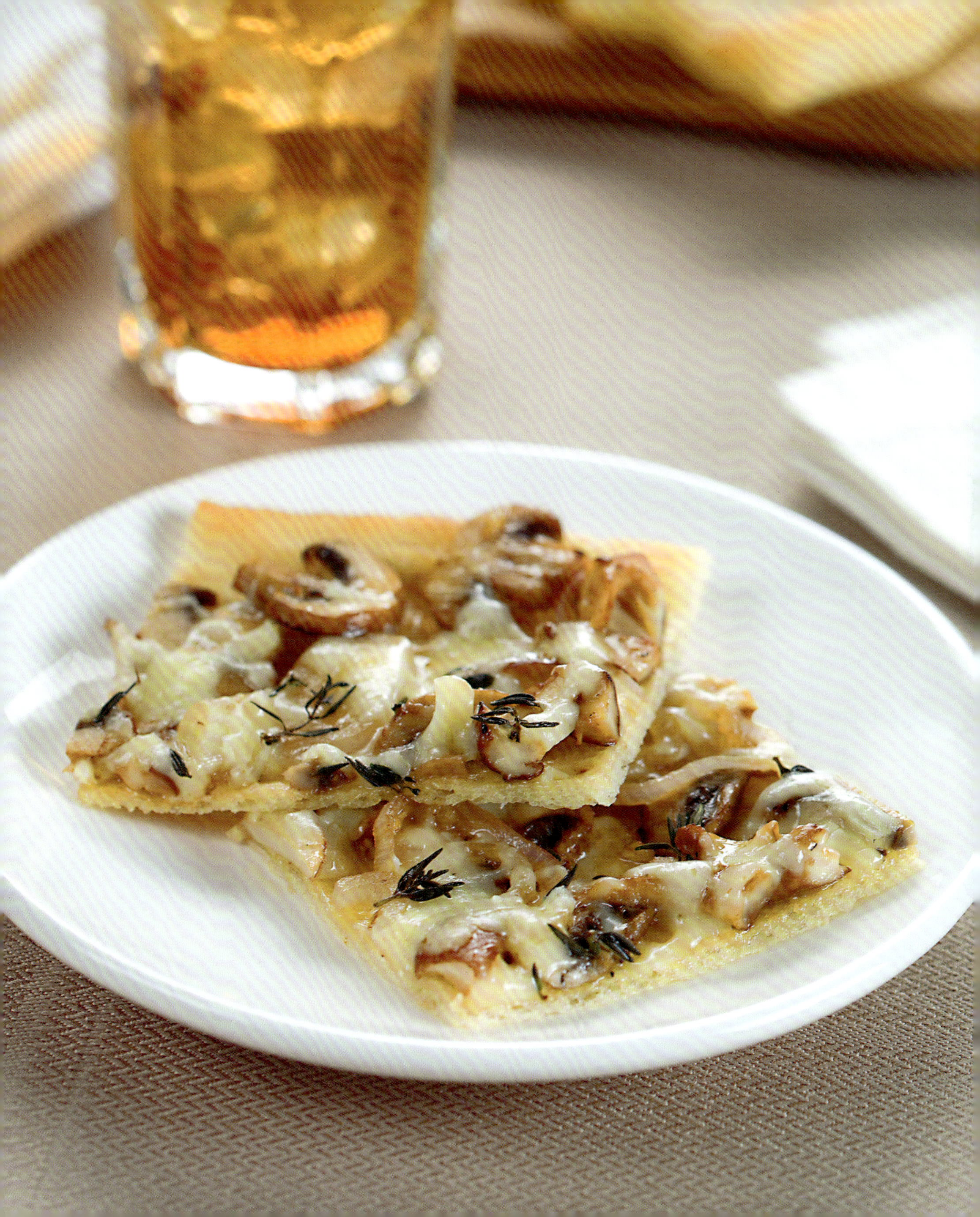

Deep Dish Sausage and Spinach Pizza

MAKES 4 TO 6 SERVINGS

- 1 loaf (16 ounces) frozen bread dough, thawed according to package directions
- 8 ounces bulk Italian sausage
- ⅔ cup pizza sauce
- 1½ cups (6 ounces) shredded mozzarella cheese
- 1 package (10 ounces) frozen chopped spinach, thawed and squeezed dry
- ½ cup grated Parmesan cheese

1. Spray work surface with nonstick cooking spray; roll out dough into 12-inch circle. Cover with plastic wrap; let rest 30 minutes.

2. Meanwhile, cook sausage in medium skillet over medium-high heat 10 minutes or until browned, stirring to break up meat. Drain fat. Stir in pizza sauce.

3. Preheat oven to 450°F. Position oven rack near bottom of oven. Spray 9-inch cake pan with cooking spray.

4. Place dough in prepared pan, pressing into bottom and 1 to 1½ inches up side of pan. Sprinkle half of mozzarella over dough; layer with half of sausage mixture, half of spinach, half of Parmesan, remaining half of sausage mixture and spinach. Top with remaining mozzarella and Parmesan.

5. Bake 15 to 18 minutes or until crust is golden brown and cheese is melted and beginning to brown in spots. Cool in pan on wire rack 5 minutes before cutting into wedges.

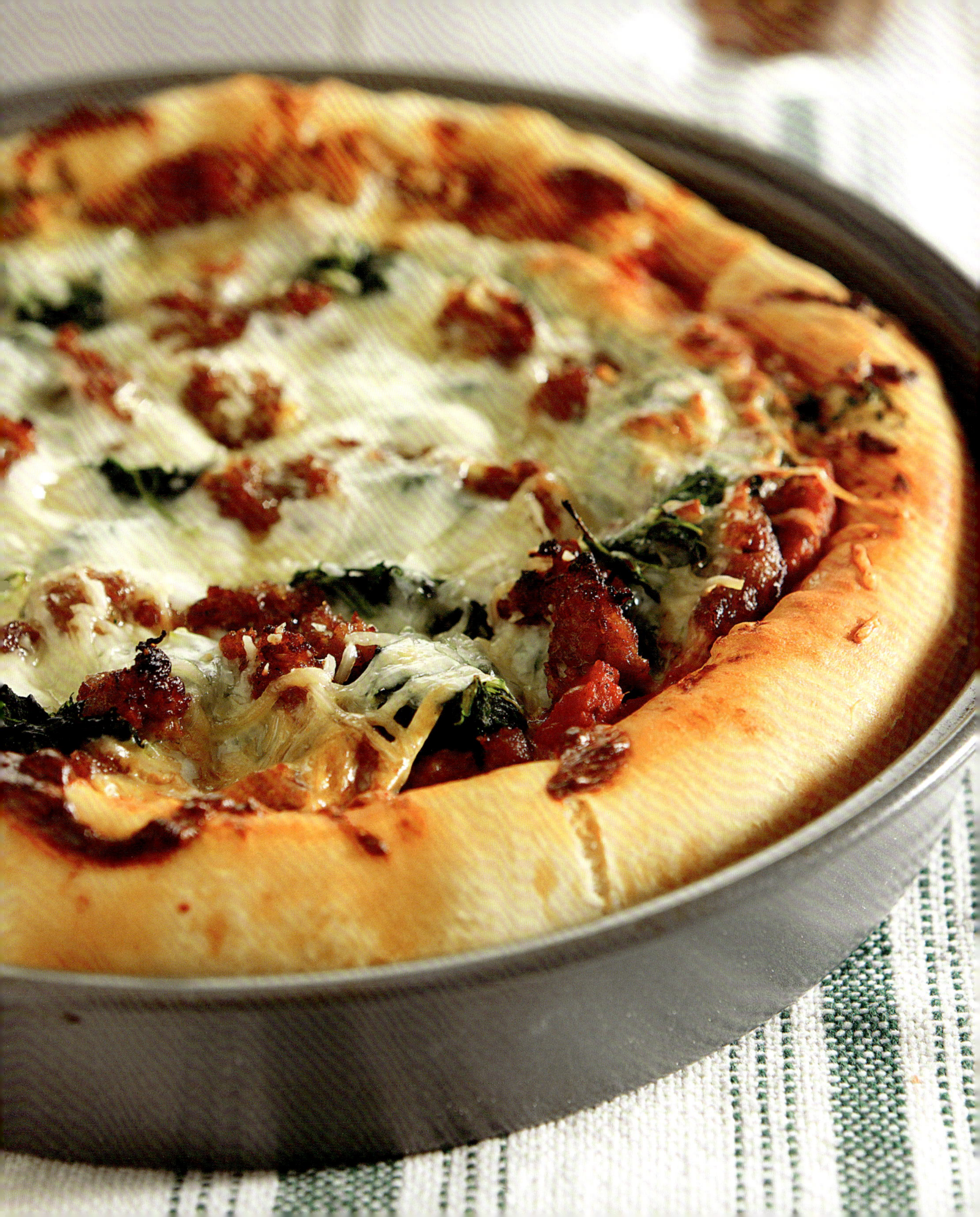

Roasted Pepper and Olive Focaccia

MAKES 12 SERVINGS

1 package (¼ ounce) active dry yeast
1 teaspoon sugar
1½ cups warm water (105° to 115°F)
4 cups all-purpose flour, divided
7 tablespoons olive oil, divided
1 teaspoon salt
¼ cup roasted red peppers, drained and cut into strips
¼ cup pitted black olives

1. Dissolve yeast and sugar in warm water in large bowl of stand mixer; let stand 5 minutes or until bubbly. Add 3½ cups flour, 3 tablespoons oil and salt; mix with dough hook at low speed until soft dough forms. Add remaining flour, 1 tablespoon at a time, if necessary to prevent sticking. Mix 5 minutes or until dough is smooth and elastic.

2. Shape dough into a ball. Place dough in large greased bowl; turn to grease top. Cover and let rise in warm place 1 hour or until doubled in size.

3. Brush 15×10-inch baking pan with 1 tablespoon oil. Punch down dough; turn out onto lightly floured surface. Flatten dough into rectangle; roll out almost to size of pan. Place dough in pan; gently press dough to edges.

4. Make indentations in top of dough every 1 or 2 inches with fingertips or handle of wooden spoon. Brush with remaining 3 tablespoons oil. Gently press roasted peppers and olives into dough. Cover and let rise in warm place 30 minutes or until doubled in size. Preheat oven to 450°F.

5. Bake 12 to 18 minutes or until golden brown. Cut into squares or rectangles. Serve warm.

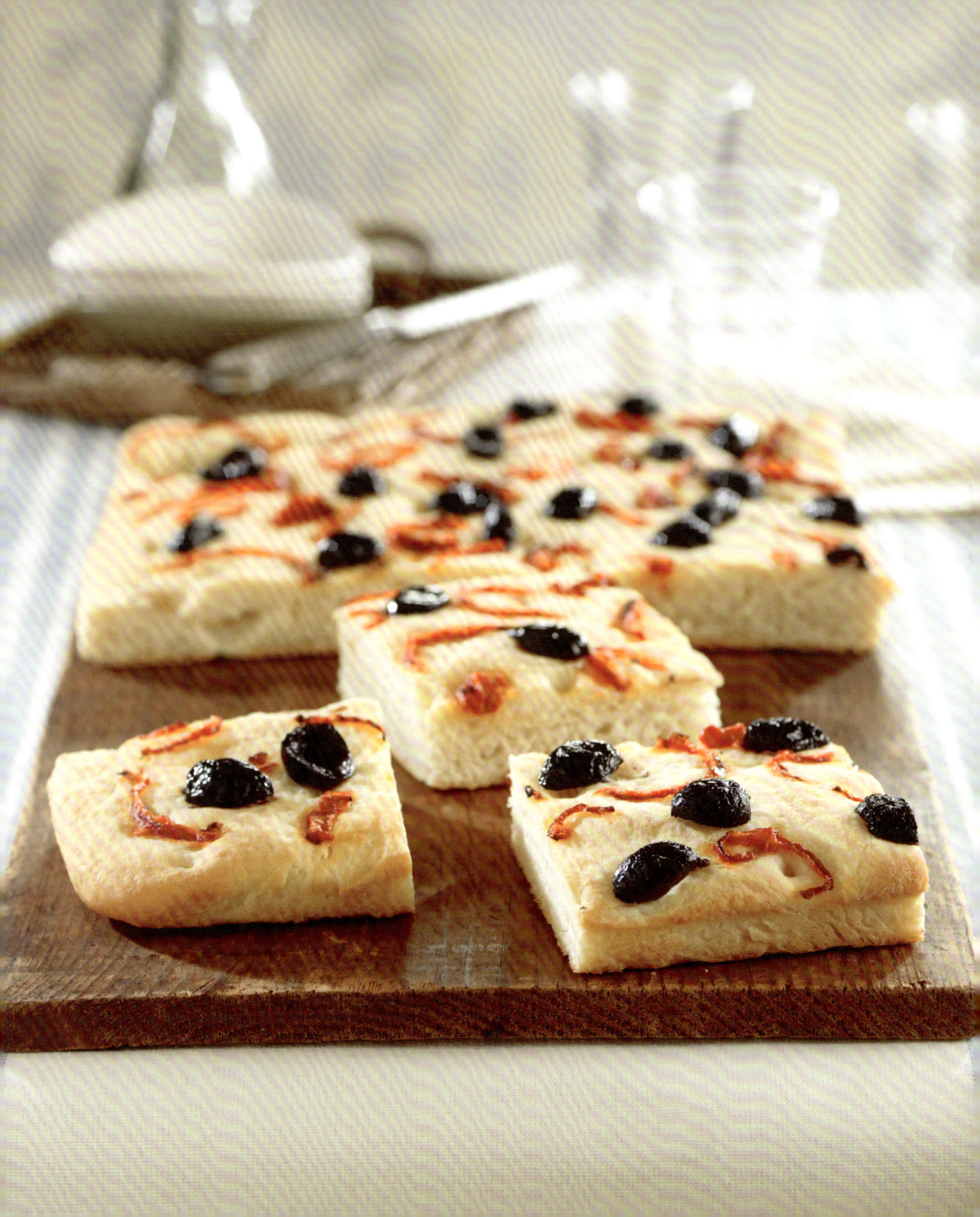

Taco Pizza

MAKES 4 SERVINGS

- 1 can (about 14 ounces) refrigerated pizza dough
- 12 ounces ground beef or ground turkey
- ½ cup chopped onion
- 1 can (8 ounces) tomato sauce
- 1 package (about 1 ounce) taco seasoning mix
- 2 medium plum tomatoes, thinly sliced, or 1 cup chopped tomato
- 1 cup (4 ounces) shredded Cheddar cheese
- 1½ cups shredded lettuce

1. Preheat oven to 425°F. Spray 12-inch pizza pan with nonstick cooking spray.

2. Unroll dough; press into prepared pan, building up edges slightly. Prick dough with fork. Bake 7 to 10 minutes or until lightly browned.

3. Meanwhile, cook ground beef and onion in large skillet over medium-high heat about 6 minutes or until browned, stirring to break up meat. Drain fat.

4. Stir in tomato sauce and taco seasoning mix; bring to a boil. Reduce heat to medium-low; cook 3 minutes. Spread beef mixture over warm crust. Bake 5 minutes.

5. Top pizza with tomatoes and cheese; bake 2 to 3 minutes or until cheese is melted. Top with lettuce. Cut into wedges.

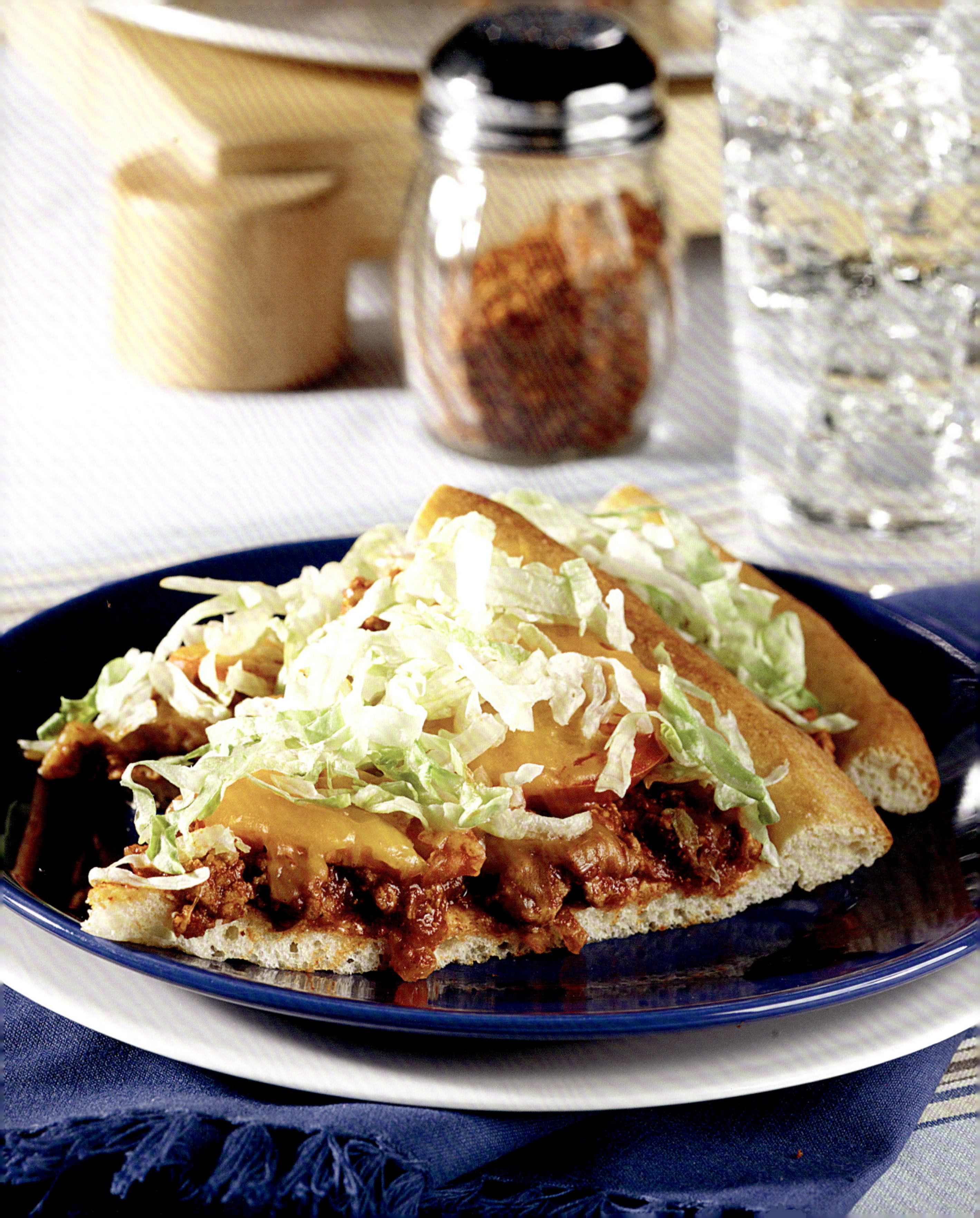

Fast Pesto Focaccia

MAKES 16 SERVINGS

1 can (about 14 ounces) refrigerated pizza dough
2 tablespoons pesto sauce
4 oil-packed sun-dried tomatoes, drained

1. Preheat oven to 425°F. Spray 8-inch square baking pan with nonstick cooking spray.

2. Unroll dough on work surface. Fold in half; press gently into prepared pan.

3. Spread pesto evenly over dough. Coarsely chop sun-dried tomatoes or snip with kitchen scissors. Sprinkle over pesto, pressing pieces lightly into dough. Use handle of wooden spoon to make indentations in dough every 2 inches.

4. Bake 10 to 12 minutes or until golden brown. Cut into squares; serve warm or at room temperature.

Breakfast Pizza

MAKES 6 SERVINGS

- 1 can (about 14 ounces) refrigerated pizza dough
- 1 package (7 ounces) frozen fully cooked sausage patties, thawed
- 3 eggs
- ½ cup milk
- 1 teaspoon Italian seasoning
- Salt and black pepper
- 2 cups (8 ounces) shredded Italian blend cheese

1. Preheat oven to 425°F. Spray 12-inch pizza pan with nonstick cooking spray.

2. Unroll dough; pat onto bottom and up side of prepared pan. Bake 5 minutes or until set but not browned.

3. Meanwhile, cut sausage into ½-inch pieces. Whisk eggs, milk and Italian seasoning in medium bowl until well blended. Season with salt and pepper. Spoon sausages over partially baked crust; sprinkle with cheese. Carefully pour egg mixture over sausage and cheese.

4. Bake 15 to 20 minutes or until eggs are set and crust is golden.

Caprese Pizza

MAKES 6 SERVINGS

- 1 package (16 ounces) frozen pizza dough or 1 loaf (16 ounces) frozen bread dough, thawed according to package directions
- 1 container (12 ounces) bruschetta sauce (see Note)
- 1 container (8 ounces) pearl-size fresh mozzarella cheese (perlini), drained*
- Chopped fresh basil (optional)

*If pearl-size mozzarella is not available, use one (8-ounce) ball of fresh mozzarella and chop into ¼-inch pieces.

1. Preheat oven to 400°F. Spray baking sheet with nonstick cooking spray.

2. Roll out dough into 15×10-inch rectangle on lightly floured surface. Transfer to prepared baking sheet. Cover loosely with plastic wrap; let rest 10 minutes. Meanwhile, place bruschetta sauce in colander; let drain 10 minutes.

3. Prick surface of dough several times with fork. Bake 10 minutes.

4. Spread drained bruschetta sauce over crust; top with cheese. Bake 10 minutes or until cheese is melted and crust is golden brown. Serve warm; sprinkle with basil, if desired.

> **NOTE** Bruschetta sauce is a mixture of diced fresh tomatoes, garlic, basil and olive oil. It is typically found in the refrigerated section of the supermarket with other prepared dips such as hummus.

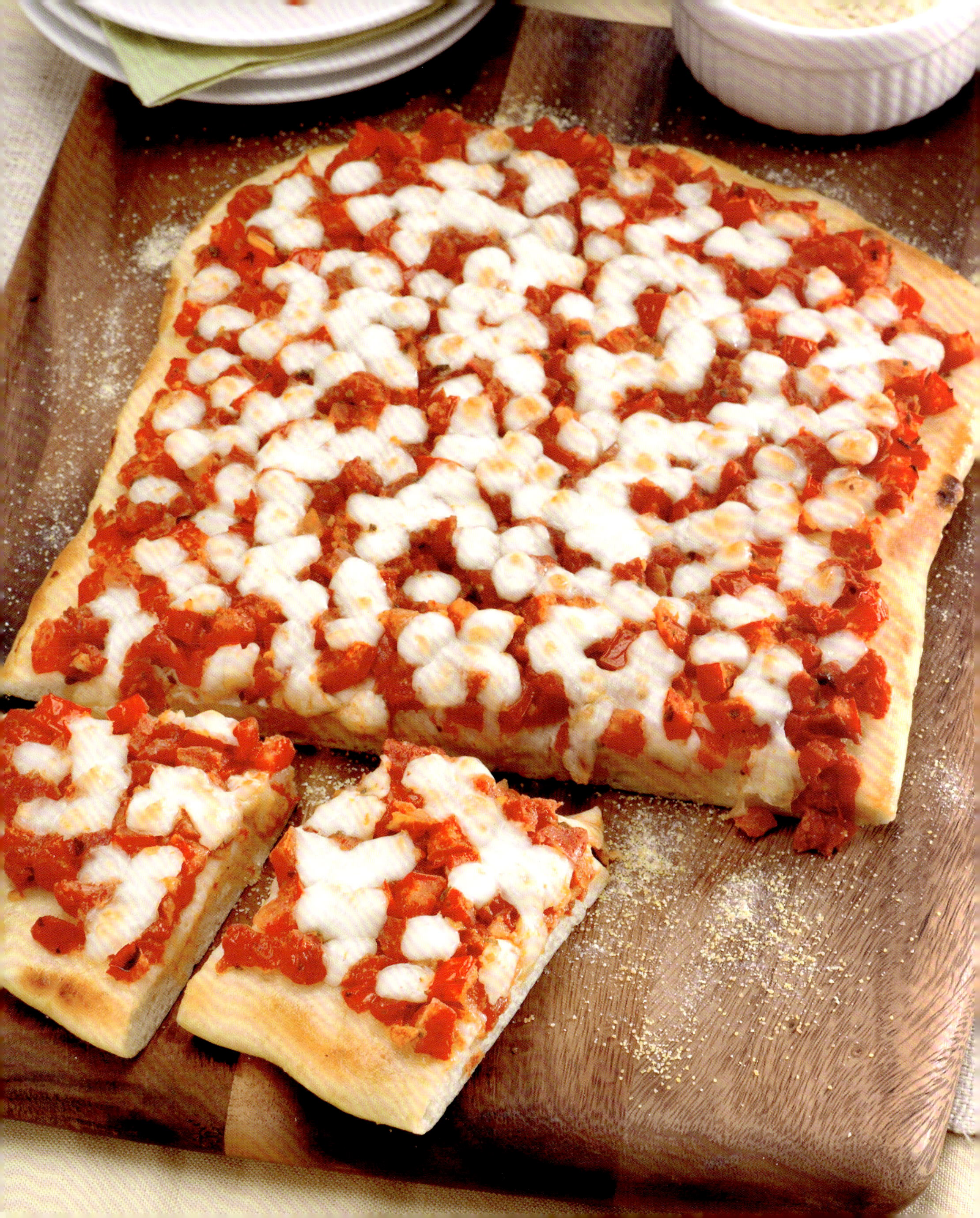

Caramelized Onion and Shrimp Flatbread

MAKES 6 SERVINGS

- 2 tablespoons olive oil, divided
- 3 large onions, thinly sliced
- ¼ teaspoon salt
- 1 can (about 14 ounces) refrigerated pizza dough
- 8 ounces small raw shrimp, peeled
- ⅛ cup chopped fresh chives
- 3 ounces goat cheese, crumbled
- ¼ teaspoon black pepper

1. Heat 1 tablespoon oil in large skillet over medium heat. Add onions; cook and stir 8 minutes. Stir in salt. Reduce heat to medium-low; cook 25 minutes or until onions are soft and deep golden brown, stirring occasionally. If onions are cooking too quickly, reduce heat to low.

2. Meanwhile, preheat oven to 425°F. Unroll dough on 15×10-inch baking pan; press dough evenly to edges of pan. Bake 8 to 10 minutes or until crust is golden brown.

3. Turn off oven. Spread caramelized onions over crust.

4. Heat remaining 1 tablespoon oil in same skillet over medium heat. Add shrimp; cook and stir 2 minutes or until pink and opaque.

5. Arrange shrimp over onions on pizza; sprinkle with chives, goat cheese and pepper. Place pizza in warm oven 1 to 2 minutes or until cheese is soft. Cut into squares.

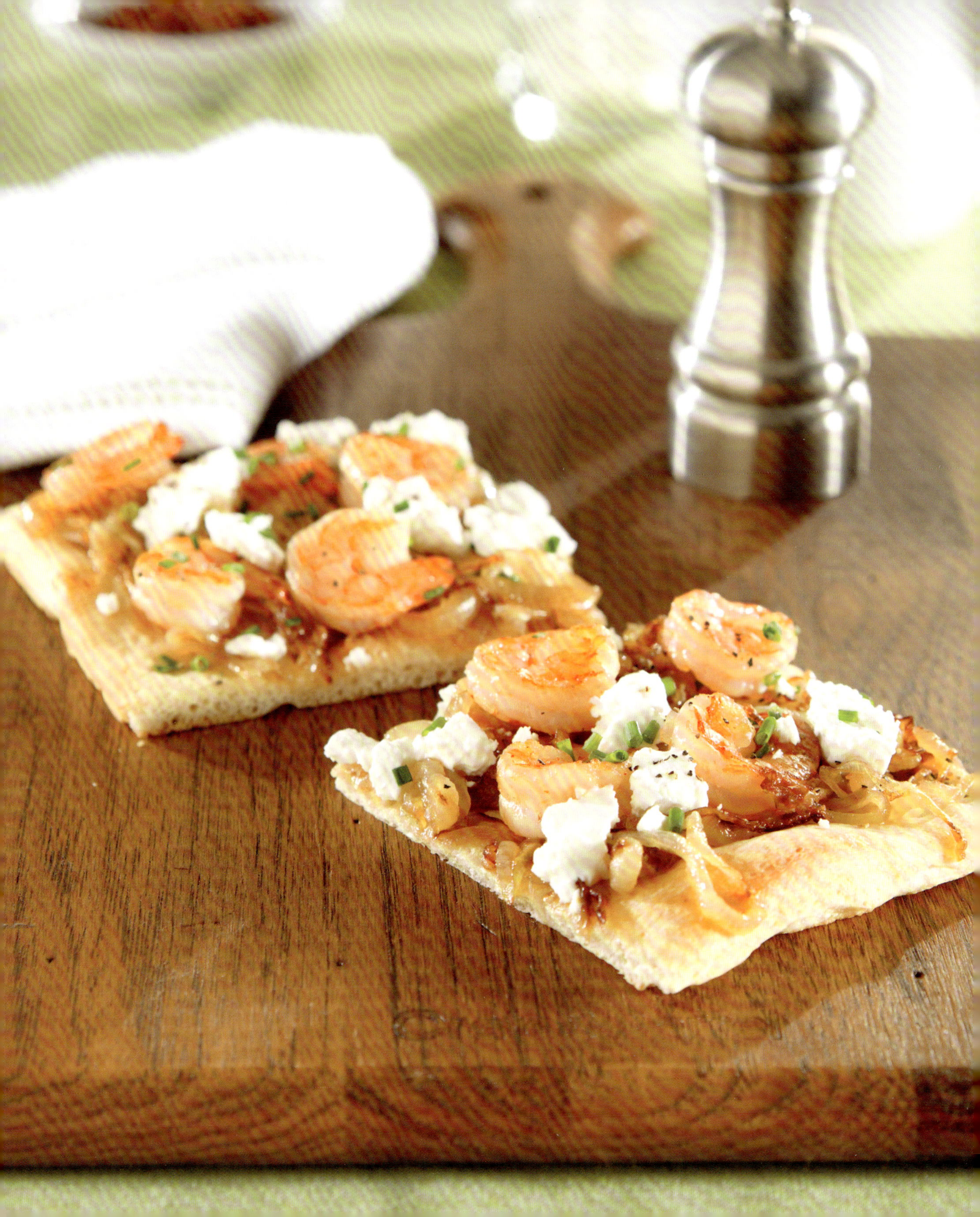

BBQ Chicken Skillet Pizza

MAKES 4 TO 6 SERVINGS

- 1 loaf (16 ounces) frozen bread dough, thawed according to package directions
- 1 tablespoon olive oil
- 2 cups shredded cooked chicken*
- ¾ cup barbecue sauce, divided
- ¼ cup (1 ounce) shredded mozzarella cheese
- ¼ cup thinly sliced red onion
- ½ cup (2 ounces) shredded smoked Gouda cheese
- Chopped fresh cilantro (optional)

*Use a rotisserie chicken for best flavor and convenience.

1. Preheat oven to 425°F. Roll out dough into 15-inch circle on lightly floured surface. Brush oil over bottom and side of large (12-inch) cast iron skillet; place in oven 5 minutes to preheat.

2. Combine chicken and ½ cup barbecue sauce in medium bowl; toss to coat. Remove hot skillet from oven; press dough into bottom and about 1 inch up side of skillet.

3. Spread remaining ¼ cup barbecue sauce over dough. Sprinkle with mozzarella; top with chicken mixture. Sprinkle with half of onion and Gouda; top with remaining onion.

4. Bake 25 minutes or until crust is golden brown. Garnish with cilantro.

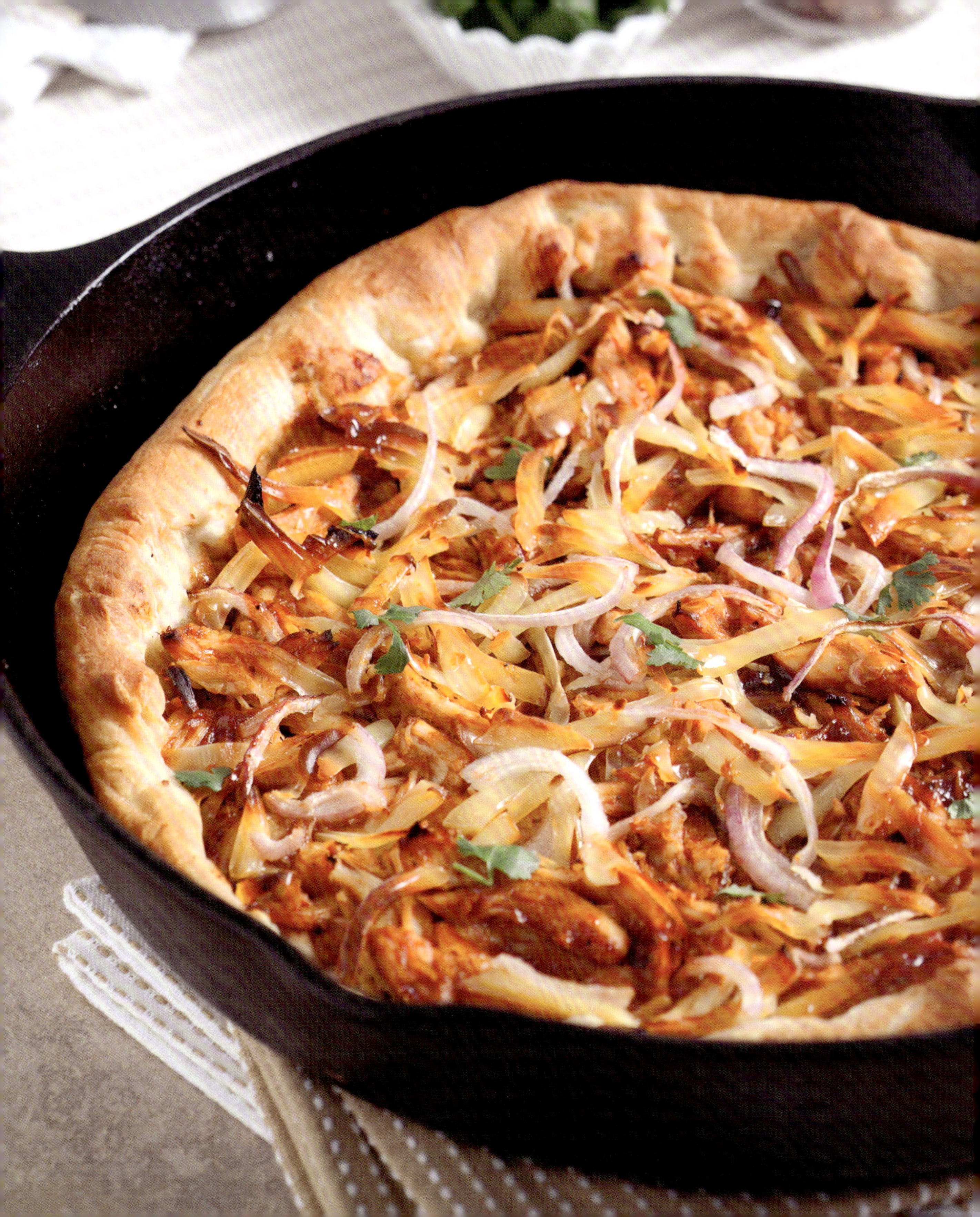

Tomato Cheese Focaccia

MAKES ABOUT 6 SERVINGS

- 1 package (¼ ounce) active dry yeast
- ¾ cup warm water (105° to 115°F)
- 2 cups all-purpose flour
- ½ teaspoon salt
- 4½ tablespoons olive oil, divided
- 1 teaspoon Italian seasoning
- 8 oil-packed sun-dried tomatoes, well drained
- ½ cup (2 ounces) shredded provolone cheese
- ¼ cup grated Parmesan cheese

1. Dissolve yeast in warm water in small bowl; let stand 5 minutes or until bubbly. Combine flour and salt in food processor. Add yeast mixture and 3 tablespoons oil; process until dough forms a ball. Process 1 minute.

2. Turn dough out onto lightly floured surface. Knead about 2 minutes or until dough is smooth and elastic. Shape dough into a ball. Place dough in large greased bowl; turn to grease top. Cover and let rise in warm place about 30 minutes or until doubled in size.

3. Brush 10-inch round cake pan, deep-dish pizza pan or springform pan with ½ tablespoon oil. Punch down dough; let rest 5 minutes.

4. Press dough into prepared pan. Brush with remaining 1 tablespoon oil; sprinkle with Italian seasoning. Press sun-dried tomatoes into top of dough; sprinkle with provolone and Parmesan. Cover and let rise in warm place 15 minutes. Preheat oven to 425°F.

5. Bake 20 to 25 minutes or until golden brown. Cut into wedges.

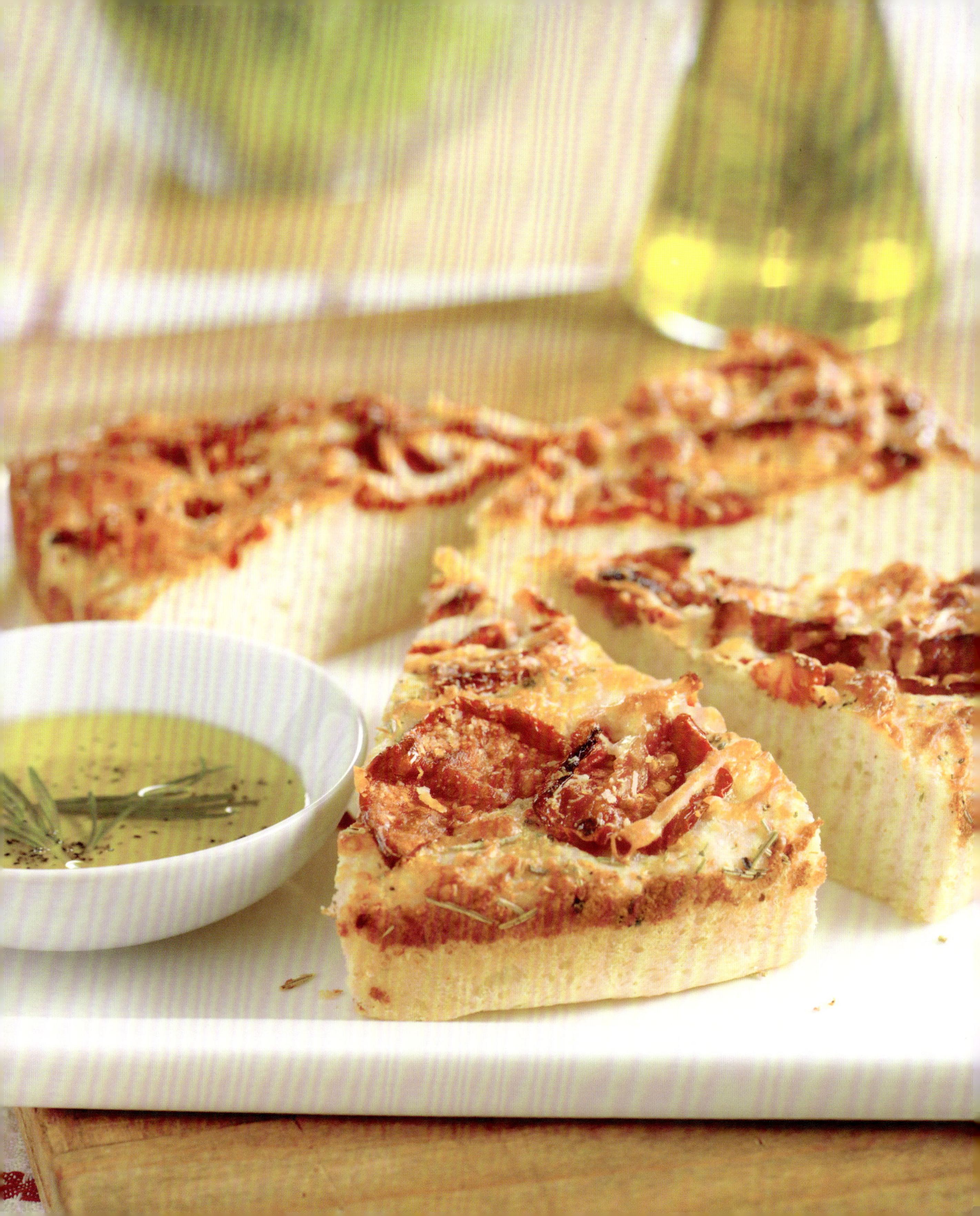

Easy Mushroom Pizza
MAKES 8 SERVINGS (2 PIZZAS)

3 to 3½ cups all-purpose flour
1¼ cups warm water (120°F)
3 tablespoons olive oil, divided
1 package (¼ ounce) instant yeast
1¼ teaspoons salt, divided
8 to 10 medium mushrooms, cut into ⅛-inch-thick slices
⅛ teaspoon black pepper
1 cup pizza sauce, divided
3 cups (12 ounces) shredded mozzarella cheese, divided
Pinch dried oregano and red pepper flakes
Fresh thyme or chopped fresh basil (optional)

1. Combine 3 cups flour, water, 2 tablespoons oil, yeast and 1 teaspoon salt in large bowl of stand mixer. Mix with dough hook at low speed about 2 minutes or until soft dough forms, adding additional flour, 1 tablespoon at a time, if necessary to clean side of bowl. Mix at medium-low speed 5 minutes.

2. Shape dough into a ball. Place dough in large greased bowl; turn to grease top. Cover and let rise in warm place about 1 hour or until doubled in size.

3. Preheat oven to 500°F. Combine mushrooms, 1 teaspoon oil, remaining ¼ teaspoon salt and pepper in small bowl; toss to coat.

4. Gently punch down dough; turn out onto lightly floured surface. Divide dough in half; keep one half covered to prevent drying out. Roll out remaining half of dough into 12-inch circle; transfer to pizza pan or baking sheet.

5. Brush edge of dough with 1 teaspoon oil. Spread ½ cup pizza sauce over dough, leaving ¼-inch border. Sprinkle with 1½ cups cheese; top with half of mushrooms. Sprinkle with oregano and red pepper flakes.

6. Bake about 10 minutes or until crust is golden brown and cheese is melted. Sprinkle with fresh herbs, if desired; remove to wire rack to cool 5 minutes. While pizza is baking, roll out and top remaining half of dough with remaining oil, pizza sauce, cheese and mushrooms.

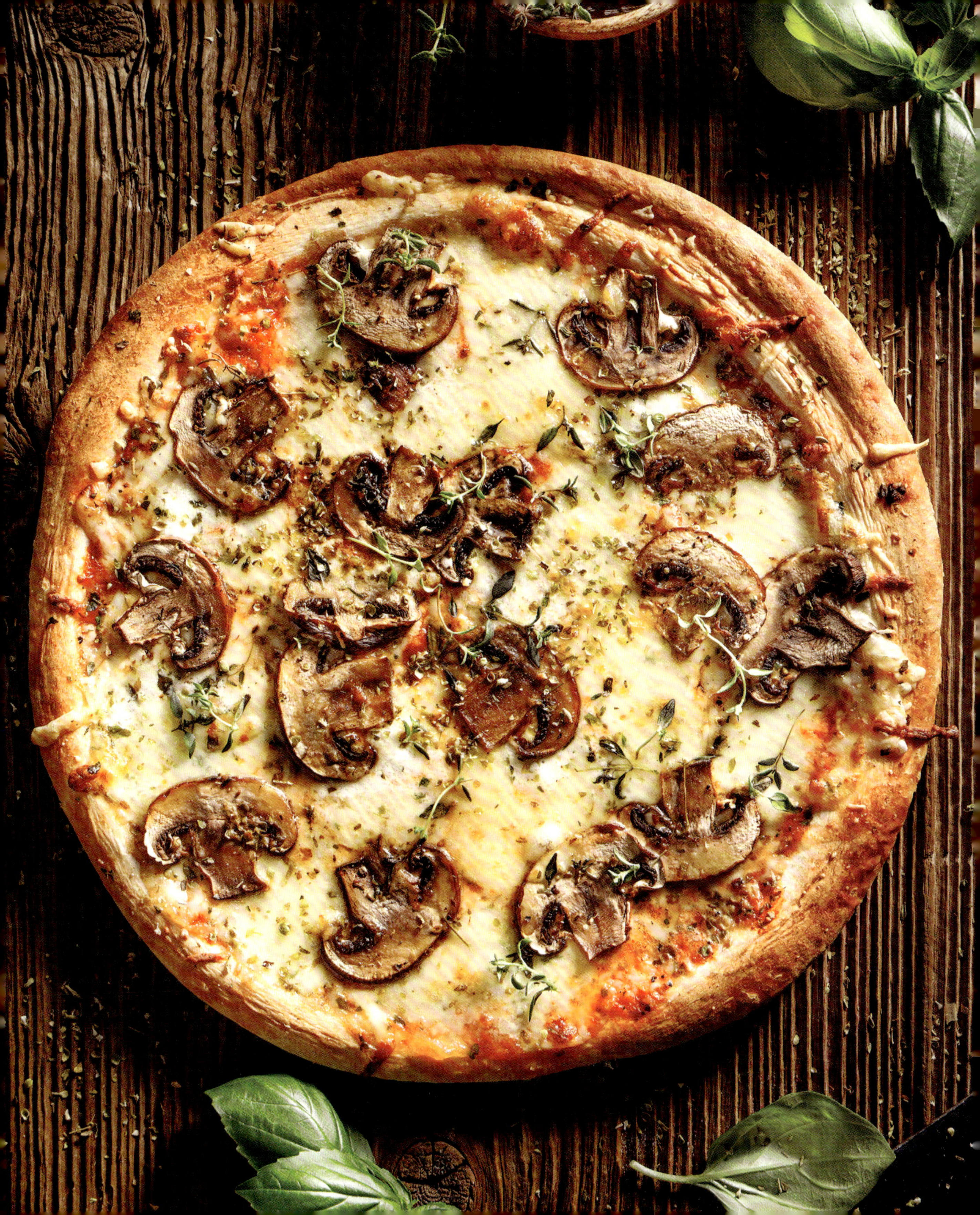

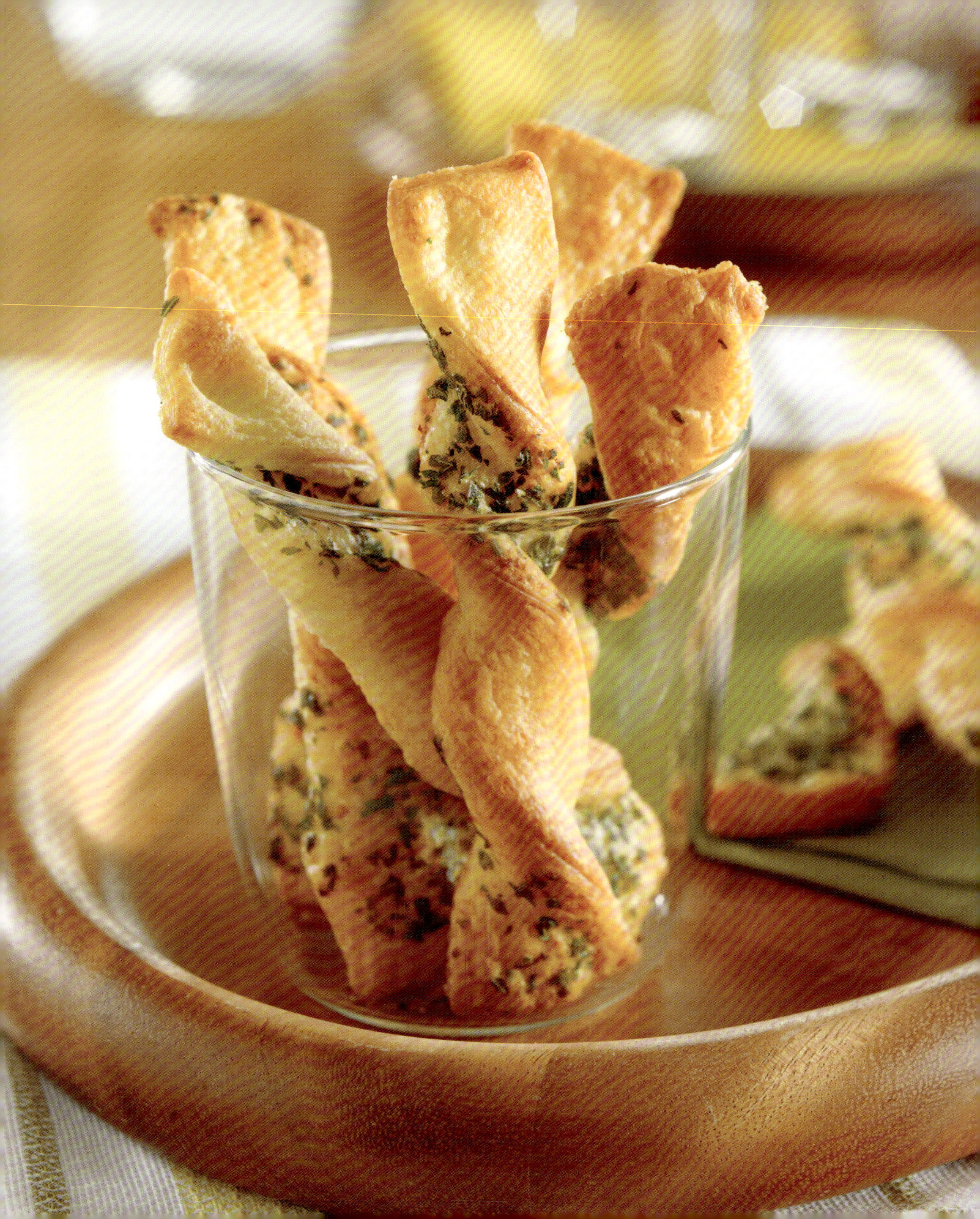

SHORTCUT BREADS

Herb Cheese Twists
MAKES 10 BREADSTICKS

- 2 tablespoons butter
- ¼ cup grated Parmesan cheese
- 1 teaspoon dried parsley flakes
- 1 teaspoon dried basil
- 1 can (about 6 ounces) refrigerated buttermilk biscuits (5 biscuits)

1. Preheat oven to 400°F. Line baking sheet with parchment paper or spray with nonstick cooking spray.

2. Place butter in small microwavable bowl; microwave on MEDIUM (50%) 1 minute or just until melted. Cool slightly; stir in cheese, parsley flakes and basil.

3. Separate biscuits; stretch each biscuit into 5×2-inch rectangle. Spread 1 teaspoon butter mixture on each rectangle. Cut in half lengthwise; twist three or four times. Place on prepared baking sheet.

4. Bake 8 to 10 minutes or until golden brown.

Salad-Topped Focaccia Rounds

MAKES 4 SERVINGS

1 can (11 ounces) refrigerated French bread dough
½ cup thinly sliced red onion, divided
¼ teaspoon dried rosemary (optional)
4 cups spring greens
3 tablespoons olive oil vinaigrette
½ cup crumbled feta cheese

1. Preheat oven to 350°F. Lightly spray baking sheet with nonstick cooking spray.

2. Unroll dough on lightly floured surface; sprinkle with ¼ cup onion and rosemary, if desired. Press onion gently into dough. Cut dough into four squares; shape each into rough circle about 4 inches in diameter. Place on prepared baking sheet.

3. Bake 12 to 14 minutes or until bottoms are lightly browned. Cool on wire rack 5 minutes.

4. Combine greens, remaining ¼ cup onion and vinaigrette in medium bowl; toss gently to coat. Top each focaccia with 1 cup salad; sprinkle with 2 tablespoons cheese.

Quick Pull-Aparts

MAKES 12 ROLLS

- 1 can (about 11 ounces) refrigerated French bread dough
- 1 tablespoon olive oil
- ½ teaspoon dried basil
- 1 tablespoon grated Parmesan cheese

1. Preheat oven to 350°F. Spray 9-inch round cake pan with nonstick cooking spray.

2. Place dough on cutting board; cut into 12 pieces with serrated knife. Brush dough lightly with oil; arrange pieces smooth side up almost touching in prepared pan. Sprinkle with basil.

3. Bake 22 to 24 minutes or until golden brown and rolls sound hollow when gently tapped. Remove to wire rack.

4. Lightly spray tops of rolls with cooking spray. Sprinkle with cheese; serve warm.

Cheesy Pizza Bread
MAKES 1 LOAF

- 1 loaf (16 ounces) frozen bread dough, thawed according to package directions
- ⅓ cup plus 2 tablespoons pizza sauce, divided
- 1 cup (4 ounces) shredded mozzarella cheese
- ½ cup shredded Parmesan cheese
- 1 egg, beaten

1. Preheat oven to 350°F. Line 9×5-inch loaf pan with parchment paper or spray with nonstick cooking spray.

2. Roll out dough into 20×10-inch rectangle on lightly floured surface. Spread ⅓ cup pizza sauce evenly over dough, leaving ½-inch borders. Sprinkle with mozzarella and Parmesan. Starting with long side, roll up dough jelly-roll style; pinch seam to seal. Cut roll in half lengthwise; turn halves cut sides up. Twist halves together, keeping filling facing up as much as possible.

3. Arrange dough in prepared pan, winding twisted dough back and forth in pan. Brush top of dough with beaten egg. Fill in crevices and folds of dough with spoonfuls of remaining pizza sauce.

4. Bake about 40 minutes or until bread is golden brown and cooked through. (Cover loosely with foil if dough browns too quickly.) Cool in pan on wire rack 10 minutes. Serve warm.

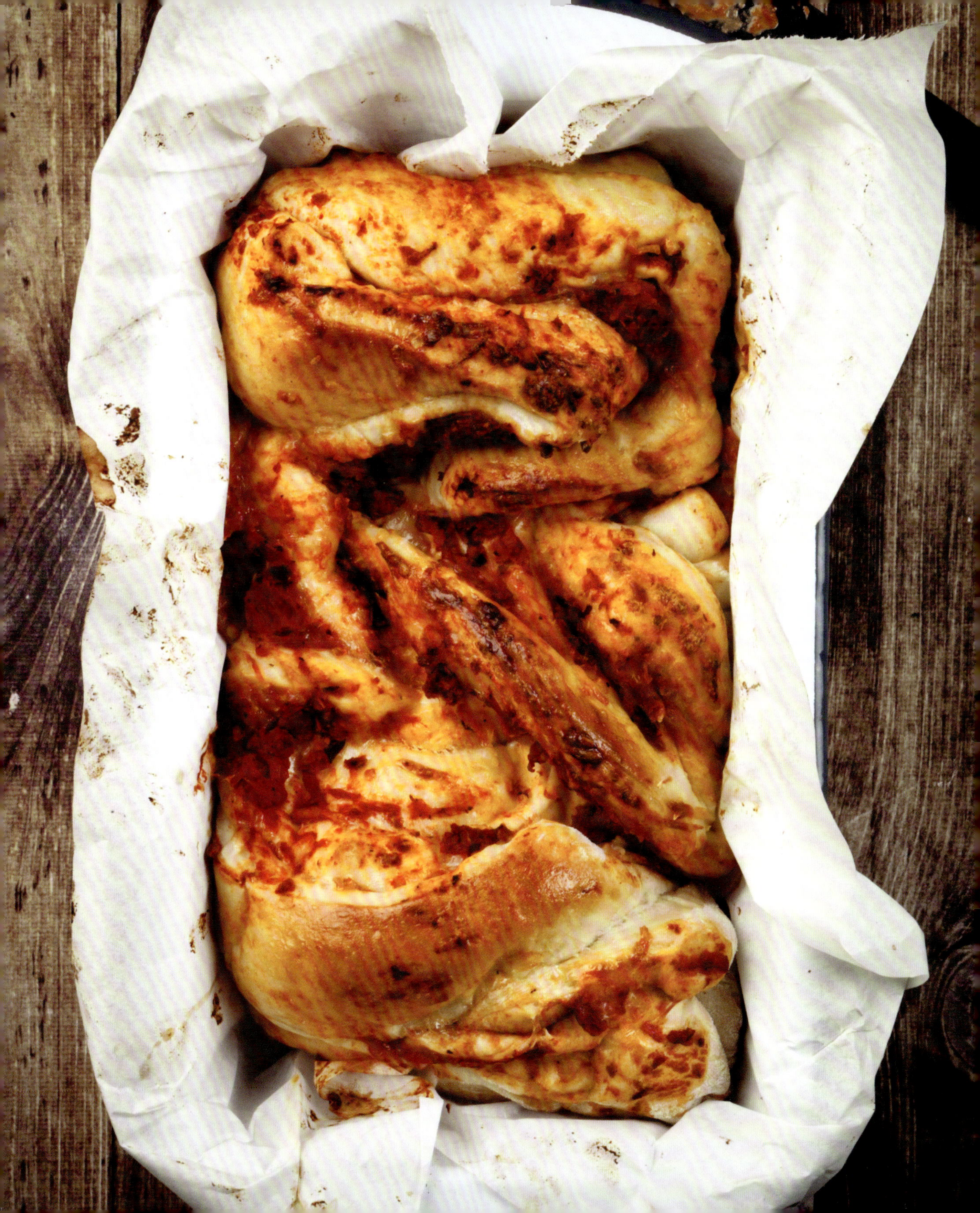

Fruit-Filled Biscuits

MAKES 16 BISCUITS

1¼ cups finely chopped apple (1 small apple)

⅓ cup dried mixed fruit bits

2 tablespoons packed brown sugar

½ teaspoon ground cinnamon

1 can (about 16 ounces) refrigerated jumbo buttermilk biscuits (8 biscuits)

1 cup sifted powdered sugar

4 to 5 teaspoons orange juice

1. Preheat oven to 350°F. Line baking sheet with parchment paper or spray with nonstick cooking spray.

2. Combine apple, dried fruit, brown sugar and cinnamon in small bowl; mix well.

3. Separate biscuits; cut each biscuit in half horizontally to create 16 rounds. Roll each round into 3½-inch circle. Spoon 1 rounded tablespoon apple mixture in center of each circle. Moisten edges of dough with water. Pull dough up and around filling, completely enclosing filling. Pinch edges to seal. Place seam side down on prepared baking sheet.

4. Bake 16 to 18 minutes or until golden brown. Cool on wire rack 10 minutes.

5. Meanwhile, combine powdered sugar and 4 teaspoons orange juice in small bowl; whisk until smooth. Add additional orange juice, if necessary, to reach drizzling consistency. Spoon glaze over rolls. Serve warm.

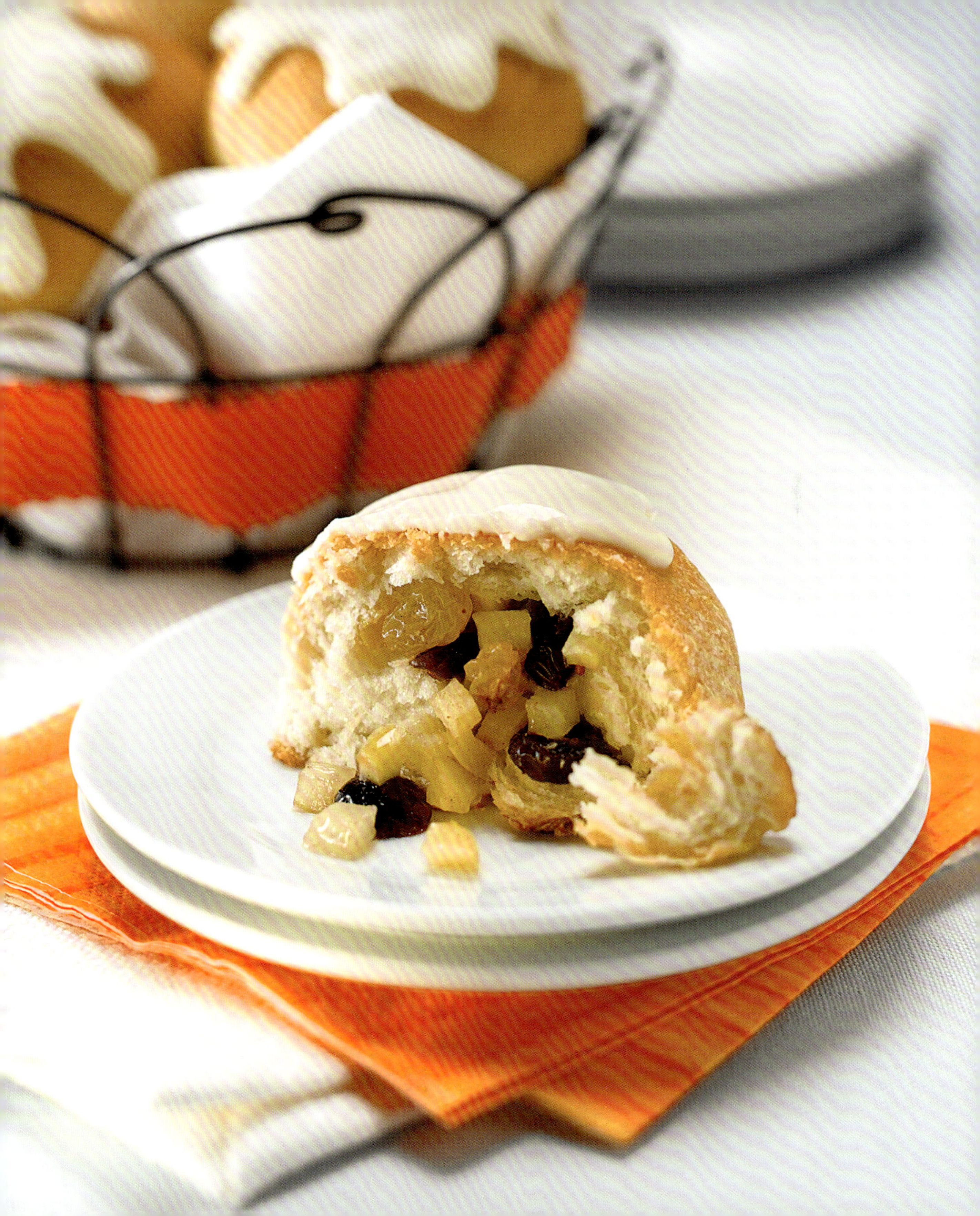

Olive Herb Pull-Aparts

MAKES 10 SERVINGS

- 2½ tablespoons olive oil, divided
- 4 cloves garlic, minced
- 1 can (12 ounces) refrigerated buttermilk biscuits (10 biscuits)
- ¼ teaspoon red pepper flakes
- 1 small red onion, thinly sliced
- ½ cup shredded or chopped fresh basil
- ½ (2¼-ounce) can sliced black olives, drained
- 2 teaspoons chopped fresh rosemary
- ¼ cup (1 ounce) crumbled feta cheese

1. Preheat oven to 400°F. Line baking sheet with parchment paper or spray with nonstick cooking spray.

2. Combine 1½ tablespoons oil and garlic in small bowl. Separate biscuits; arrange on prepared baking sheet about ½ inch apart. Lightly spray with olive oil cooking spray; let stand 10 minutes.

3. Flatten biscuits. Sprinkle with red pepper flakes, gently pressing into biscuits. Brush with garlic oil; top with onion. Combine basil, olives, rosemary and remaining 1 tablespoon oil in small bowl; mix well. Spread mixture over biscuits; sprinkle with cheese.

4. Bake 10 minutes or until golden brown. Serve warm or at room temperature.

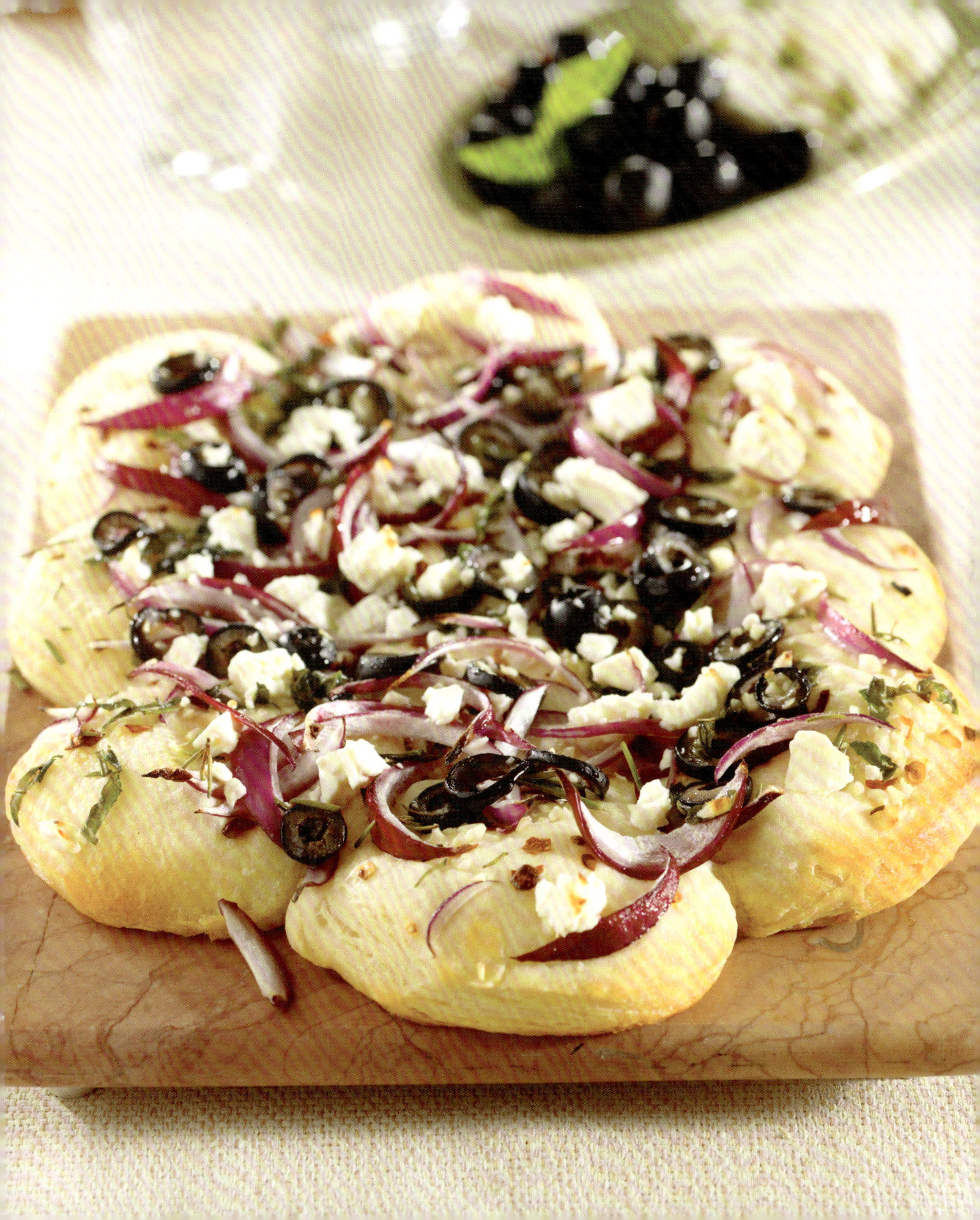

Super Simple Cheesy Bubble Loaf

MAKES 1 LOAF

- 2 cans (12 ounces each) refrigerated buttermilk biscuits (10 biscuits per can)
- 2 tablespoons butter, melted
- 1½ cups (6 ounces) shredded Italian cheese blend

1. Preheat oven to 350°F. Spray 9×5-inch loaf pan with nonstick cooking spray.
2. Separate biscuits; cut each biscuit into four pieces with scissors. Layer half of biscuit pieces in prepared pan.
3. Drizzle with 1 tablespoon butter; sprinkle with 1 cup cheese. Top with remaining biscuit pieces, 1 tablespoon butter and ½ cup cheese.
4. Bake 25 minutes or until golden brown. Serve warm.

TIP It's easy to change up the flavors in this simple bread. Try Mexican cheese blend instead of Italian, and add taco seasoning mix and/or hot pepper sauce to the melted butter before drizzling it over the dough. Or, sprinkle ¼ cup chopped ham, salami or crumbled crisp-cooked bacon between the layers of dough.

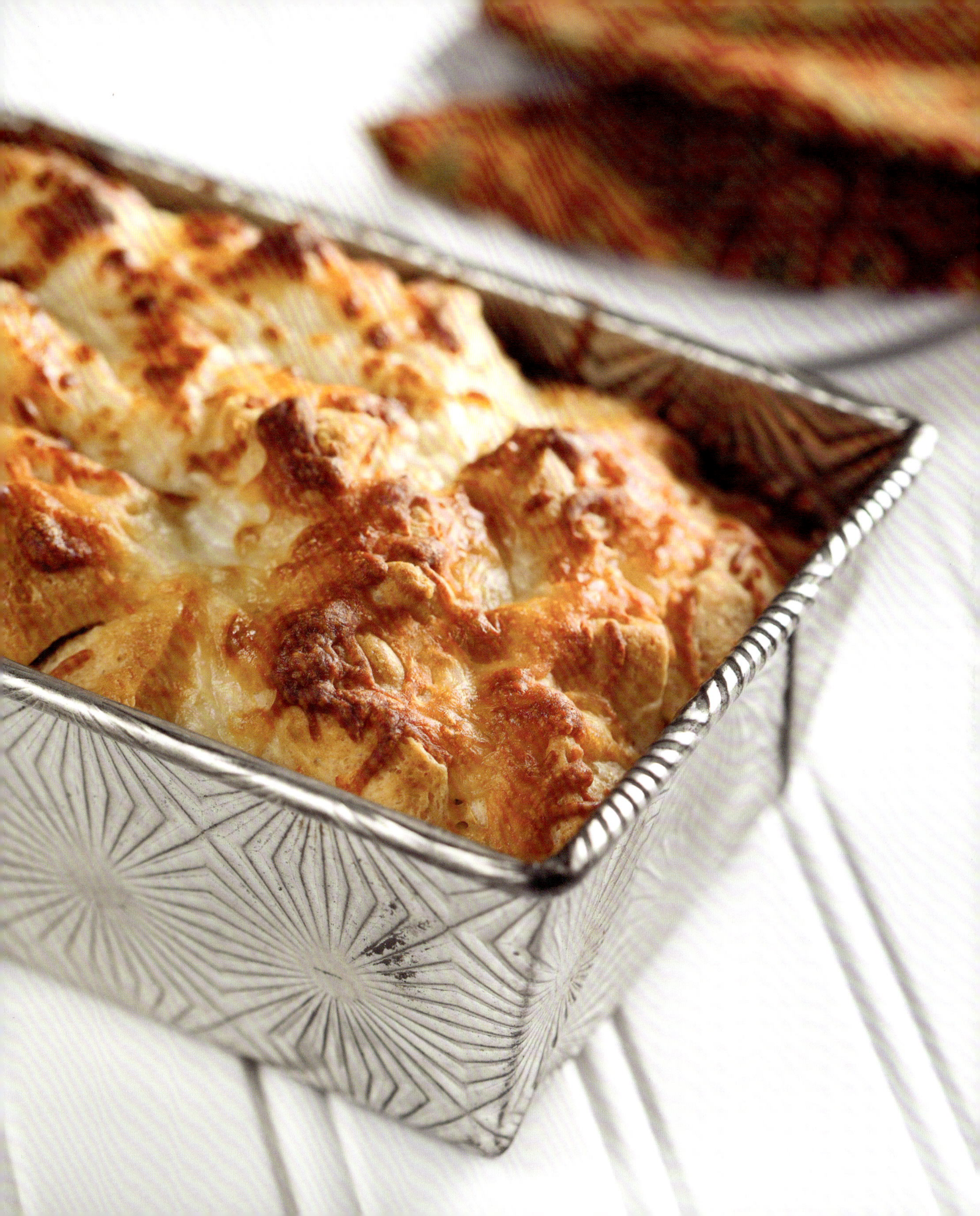

Spicy Pizza Biscuits

MAKES 20 BISCUITS

- 1 can (12 ounces) refrigerated flaky buttermilk biscuits (10 biscuits)
- 80 mini pepperoni slices or 20 small pepperoni slices
- 8 to 10 pickled jalapeño pepper slices, chopped
- 1 teaspoon dried basil
- ½ cup pizza sauce
- 1½ cups (6 ounces) shredded mozzarella cheese
- Shredded Parmesan cheese (optional)

1. Preheat oven to 400°F. Spray 20 standard (2½-inch) nonstick muffin cups with nonstick cooking spray.

2. Separate biscuits; split each biscuit in half horizontally to create 20 rounds. Place in prepared muffin cups.

3. Press four mini pepperoni slices into center of each round; sprinkle with jalapeños and basil. Spread pizza sauce over pepperoni; sprinkle with mozzarella.

4. Bake 8 to 9 minutes or until bottoms of biscuits are golden brown. Sprinkle with Parmesan, if desired. Cool in pan 2 minutes; remove to wire racks. Serve warm.

Savory Olive Twists

MAKES 12 BREADSTICKS

1 can (about 11 ounces) refrigerated breadstick dough
1 egg white, beaten
12 pimiento-stuffed green olives, chopped
  Paprika

1. Preheat oven to 375°F. Line baking sheet with parchment paper.

2. Unroll breadstick dough; separate into 12 pieces along perforations. Brush dough lightly with egg white; sprinkle with olives and paprika. Twist each stick three or four times; place on prepared baking sheet.

3. Bake 11 to 13 minutes or until golden brown.

SHORTCUT BREADS

A

Apple
- Apple Butter Spice Muffins, 56
- Apple Date Nut Muffins, 82
- Applesauce Spice Bread, 14
- Carrot Oat Muffins, 60
- Cheddar Apple Muffins, 66
- Fruit-Filled Biscuits, 180

Apple Butter Spice Muffins, 56
Apple Date Nut Muffins, 82
Applesauce Spice Bread, 14

B

Banana
- Banana Chocolate Chip Muffins, 76
- Loaded Banana Bread, 28

Banana Chocolate Chip Muffins, 76
Barbecue Chicken Flatbread, 146
BBQ Chicken Skillet Pizza, 168

Beef
- Reuben Rolls, 128
- Taco Pizza, 160

Berry Buckwheat Scones, 96

Biscuits
- Cheddar Biscuits, 35
- Corn and Sunflower Seed Biscuits, 38
- Country Buttermilk Biscuits, 36
- Drop Biscuits, 36
- Easy Cheese Biscuits, 52
- Fruit-Filled Biscuits, 180
- Ham and Swiss Cheese Biscuits, 42
- Mustard Pepper Biscuits, 49
- Oatmeal Drop Biscuits, 50
- Sour Cream Dill Biscuits, 36
- Spicy Pizza Biscuits, 186
- Sweet Cherry Biscuits, 48
- Sweet Potato Biscuits, 40
- Wheaty Cranberry Buttermilk Biscuits, 44
- Yogurt Chive Biscuits, 46

Blueberry
- Blueberry Hill Bread, 5
- Blueberry Muffins, 64

Blueberry Hill Bread, 5
Blueberry Muffins, 64
Boston Black Coffee Bread, 16

Breadsticks
- Herb Cheese Twists, 175
- Savory Olive Twists, 187

Breakfast Pizza, 163
Brown Soda Bread, 10

C

Caprese Pizza, 164
Caramelized Onion and Shrimp Flatbread, 166

Carrot
- Carrot Oat Muffins, 60
- Garden Vegetable Muffins, 77

Carrot Oat Muffins, 60
Casserole Cheese Bread, 108
Cheddar Apple Muffins, 66
Cheddar Biscuits, 35
Cheddar Quick Bread, 26

Cheese
- Barbecue Chicken Flatbread, 146
- BBQ Chicken Skillet Pizza, 168
- Breakfast Pizza, 163
- Caprese Pizza, 164
- Caramelized Onion and Shrimp Flatbread, 166
- Casserole Cheese Bread, 108
- Cheddar Apple Muffins, 66
- Cheddar Biscuits, 35
- Cheddar Quick Bread, 26
- Cheesy Pizza Bread, 178
- Chili Cheese Bread, 120
- Deep Dish Sausage and Spinach Pizza, 156
- Easy Cheese Biscuits, 52
- Easy Mushroom Pizza, 172
- Fiesta Bread, 30
- French Cheese Bread, 104
- Garden Vegetable Muffins, 77
- Greek Spinach Cheese Rolls, 134

Cheese (continued)
- Ham and Swiss Cheese Biscuits, 42
- Hawaiian Pizza Rolls, 140
- Herb Cheese Twists, 175
- Khachapuri (Georgian Cheese Bread), 152
- Mexican Pizza, 143
- Olive and Herb Focaccia, 148
- Olive Herb Pull-Aparts, 182
- Pepperoni Cheese Bread, 114
- Pepperoni Pizza, 150
- Pepperoni Pizza Rolls, 130
- Quattro Formaggio Focaccia, 144
- Quick Pull-Aparts, 177
- Red Pepper Bread, 100
- Reuben Rolls, 128
- Salad-Topped Focaccia Rounds, 176
- Spicy Pizza Biscuits, 186
- Sun-Dried Tomato Basil Muffins, 62
- Super Simple Cheesy Bubble Loaf, 184
- Taco Pizza, 160
- Tomato Cheese Focaccia, 170
- Wild Mushroom Flatbread, 154

Cheesy Pizza Bread, 178

Cherry
- Cherry Lemon Poppy Seed Muffins, 58
- Sweet Cherry Biscuits, 48

Cherry Lemon Poppy Seed Muffins, 58

Chicken
- Barbecue Chicken Flatbread, 146
- BBQ Chicken Skillet Pizza, 168

Chili Cheese Bread, 120

Chocolate
- Banana Chocolate Chip Muffins, 76
- Chocolate Peanut Oatmeal Muffins, 68

Chocolate *(continued)*
   Loaded Banana Bread, 28
   Peanut Butter Chocolate Chip Bread, 8
   Quick Chocolate Chip Sticky Buns, 136
Chocolate Peanut Oatmeal Muffins, 68
Cinnamon-Date Scones, 88
Cinnamon Pecan Rolls, 126
Corn
   Corn and Sunflower Seed Biscuits, 38
   Mexican Pizza, 143
Corn and Sunflower Seed Biscuits, 38
Corn Bread Muffins, 70
Cornmeal
   Boston Black Coffee Bread, 16
   Corn Bread Muffins, 70
   Fiesta Bread, 30
   Pepperoni Pizza, 150
   Raspberry Corn Muffins, 55
   Simple Golden Corn Bread, 6
   Three-Grain Bread, 122
Country Buttermilk Biscuits, 36
Cranberry
   Cranberry Oatmeal Mini Muffins, 80
   Cranberry Scones, 94
   Harvest Quick Bread, 32
   Wheaty Cranberry Buttermilk Biscuits, 44
Cranberry Oatmeal Mini Muffins, 80
Cranberry Scones, 94
Crunchy Whole Grain Bread, 112

D
Date Nut Bread, 12
Dates
   Apple Date Nut Muffins, 82
   Cinnamon-Date Scones, 88
   Date Nut Bread, 12
   English-Style Scones, 92
Deep Dish Sausage and Spinach Pizza, 156

Dough, Frozen
   BBQ Chicken Skillet Pizza, 168
   Caprese Pizza, 164
   Cheesy Pizza Bread, 178
   Cinnamon Pecan Rolls, 126
   Deep Dish Sausage and Spinach Pizza, 156
   Easy Rosemary Rolls, 138
   Greek Spinach Cheese Rolls, 134
   Khachapuri (Georgian Cheese Bread), 152
   Pepperoni Pizza Rolls, 130
   Quick Honey Butter Rolls, 125
   Super Simple Cheesy Bubble Loaf, 184
Dough, Refrigerated
   Barbecue Chicken Flatbread, 146
   Breakfast Pizza, 163
   Caramelized Onion and Shrimp Flatbread, 166
   Fast Pesto Focaccia, 162
   Fruit-Filled Biscuits, 180
   Hawaiian Pizza Rolls, 140
   Herb Cheese Twists, 175
   Mexican Pizza, 143
   Olive Herb Pull-Aparts, 182
   Quick Chocolate Chip Sticky Buns, 136
   Quick Pull-Aparts, 177
   Reuben Rolls, 128
   Salad-Topped Focaccia Rounds, 176
   Savory Olive Twists, 187
   Spicy Pizza Biscuits, 186
   Taco Pizza, 160
   Wild Mushroom Flatbread, 154
Drop Biscuits, 36

E
Easy Cheese Biscuits, 52
Easy Mushroom Pizza, 172
Easy Rosemary Rolls, 138
English-Style Scones, 92

F
Fast Pesto Focaccia, 162
Fiesta Bread, 30
Flatbread
   Barbecue Chicken Flatbread, 146
   Caramelized Onion and Shrimp Flatbread, 166
   Wild Mushroom Flatbread, 154
Focaccia
   Fast Pesto Focaccia, 162
   Olive and Herb Focaccia, 148
   Quattro Formaggio Focaccia, 144
   Roasted Pepper and Olive Focaccia, 158
   Salad-Topped Focaccia Rounds, 176
   Tomato Cheese Focaccia, 170
French Cheese Bread, 104
Fruit and Nut Oat Bread, 18
Fruit-Filled Biscuits, 180

G
Garden Vegetable Muffins, 77
Greek Spinach Cheese Rolls, 134

H
Ham and Swiss Cheese Biscuits, 42
Harvest Quick Bread, 32
Hawaiian Pizza Rolls, 140
Herb Cheese Twists, 175
Honey Butter, 6
Honey Whole Wheat Casserole Bread, 108

I
Irish Soda Bread, 25

K
Khachapuri (Georgian Cheese Bread), 152

INDEX | **189**

L

Lemon
- Cherry Lemon Poppy Seed Muffins, 58
- Lemon Poppy Seed Muffins, 78

Lemon Poppy Seed Muffins, 78
Loaded Banana Bread, 28

M

Maple Magic Muffins, 72
Mexican Pizza, 143

Muffins
- Apple Butter Spice Muffins, 56
- Apple Date Nut Muffins, 82
- Banana Chocolate Chip Muffins, 76
- Blueberry Muffins, 64
- Carrot Oat Muffins, 60
- Cheddar Apple Muffins, 66
- Cherry Lemon Poppy Seed Muffins, 58
- Chocolate Peanut Oatmeal Muffins, 68
- Corn Bread Muffins, 70
- Cranberry Oatmeal Mini Muffins, 80
- Garden Vegetable Muffins, 77
- Lemon Poppy Seed Muffins, 78
- Maple Magic Muffins, 72
- Peanut Butter Bran Muffins, 74
- Raspberry Corn Muffins, 55
- Sun-Dried Tomato Basil Muffins, 62

Mushrooms
- Easy Mushroom Pizza, 172
- Wild Mushroom Flatbread, 154

Mustard Pepper Biscuits, 49

O

Oatmeal Drop Biscuits, 50
Oatmeal Honey Bread, 102

Oats
- Apple Date Nut Muffins, 82
- Carrot Oat Muffins, 60
- Chocolate Peanut Oatmeal Muffins, 68
- Cranberry Oatmeal Mini Muffins, 80
- Crunchy Whole Grain Bread, 112
- Fruit and Nut Oat Bread, 18
- Oatmeal Drop Biscuits, 50
- Oatmeal Honey Bread, 102
- Three-Grain Bread, 122

Olive and Herb Focaccia, 148
Olive Herb Pull-Aparts, 182

Orange
- Fruit-Filled Biscuits, 180
- Orange Current Scones, 85
- Orange Walnut Bread, 22

Orange Current Scones, 85
Orange Walnut Bread, 22

P

Peanut Butter
- Peanut Butter Bran Muffins, 74
- Peanut Butter Chocolate Chip Bread, 8

Peanut Butter Bran Muffins, 74
Peanut Butter Chocolate Chip Bread, 8

Peanuts
- Chocolate Peanut Oatmeal Muffins, 68
- Peanut Butter Chocolate Chip Bread, 8

Pecans
- Apple Butter Spice Muffins, 56
- Cherry Lemon Poppy Seed Muffins, 58
- Cinnamon Pecan Rolls, 126
- Cranberry Scones, 94
- Quick Chocolate Chip Sticky Buns, 136
- Sweet Potato Biscuits, 40

Pepperoni Cheese Bread, 114
Pepperoni Pizza, 150
Pepperoni Pizza Rolls, 130

Pizza
- BBQ Chicken Skillet Pizza, 168
- Breakfast Pizza, 163
- Caprese Pizza, 164
- Cheesy Pizza Bread, 178
- Deep Dish Sausage and Spinach Pizza, 156
- Easy Mushroom Pizza, 172
- Hawaiian Pizza Rolls, 140
- Mexican Pizza, 143
- Pepperoni Pizza, 150
- Pepperoni Pizza Rolls, 130
- Spicy Pizza Biscuits, 186
- Taco Pizza, 160

Pull-Apart Rye Rolls, 132

Pumpkin
- Pumpkin Bread, 20
- Pumpkin Ginger Scones, 90

Pumpkin Bread, 20
Pumpkin Ginger Scones, 90

Q

Quattro Formaggio Focaccia, 144

Quick Breads
- Applesauce Spice Bread, 14
- Blueberry Hill Bread, 5
- Boston Black Coffee Bread, 16
- Brown Soda Bread, 10
- Cheddar Quick Bread, 26
- Date Nut Bread, 12
- Fiesta Bread, 30
- Fruit and Nut Oat Bread, 18
- Harvest Quick Bread, 32
- Irish Soda Bread, 25
- Loaded Banana Bread, 28
- Orange Walnut Bread, 22
- Peanut Butter Chocolate Chip Bread, 8
- Pumpkin Bread, 20
- Simple Golden Corn Bread, 6
- Zucchini Bread, 24

Quick Casserole Bread, 108
Quick Chocolate Chip Sticky Buns, 136

Quick Honey Butter Rolls, 125
Quick Pull-Aparts, 177

R
Raspberry
    Berry Buckwheat Scones, 96
    Raspberry Corn Muffins, 55
Raspberry Corn Muffins, 55
Red Pepper Bread, 100
Reuben Rolls, 128
Roasted Pepper and Olive Focaccia, 158
Rolls & Buns
    Cinnamon Pecan Rolls, 126
    Easy Rosemary Rolls, 138
    Greek Spinach Cheese Rolls, 134
    Hawaiian Pizza Rolls, 140
    Olive Herb Pull-Aparts, 182
    Pepperoni Pizza Rolls, 130
    Pull-Apart Rye Rolls, 132
    Quick Chocolate Chip Sticky Buns, 136
    Quick Honey Butter Rolls, 125
    Quick Pull-Aparts, 177
    Reuben Rolls, 128
Rustic Sour Cream Bread, 116

S
Salad-Topped Focaccia Rounds, 176
Sandwich Bread, 99
Sausage
    Breakfast Pizza, 163
    Deep Dish Sausage and Spinach Pizza, 156
    Fiesta Bread, 30
    Pepperoni Cheese Bread, 114
    Pepperoni Pizza, 150
    Pepperoni Pizza Rolls, 130
Savory Olive Twists, 187
Scones
    Berry Buckwheat Scones, 96
    Cinnamon-Date Scones, 88
    Cranberry Scones, 94
    English-Style Scones, 92

Scones (continued)
    Orange Current Scones, 85
    Pumpkin Ginger Scones, 90
    Walnut Ginger Scones, 86
Simple Golden Corn Bread, 6
Sour Cream Dill Biscuits, 36
Spicy Pizza Biscuits, 186
Spinach
    Deep Dish Sausage and Spinach Pizza, 156
    Greek Spinach Cheese Rolls, 134
Sugar and Spice Bread, 110
Sun-Dried Tomato Basil Muffins, 62
Super Simple Cheesy Bubble Loaf, 184
Sweet Cherry Biscuits, 48
Sweet Potato Biscuits, 40

T
Taco Pizza, 160
Three-Grain Bread, 122
Tomato Cheese Focaccia, 170

W
Walnut Fig Bread, 106
Walnut Ginger Scones, 86
Walnuts
    Applesauce Spice Bread, 14
    Date Nut Bread, 12
    Fruit and Nut Oat Bread, 18
    Harvest Quick Bread, 32
    Maple Magic Muffins, 72
    Orange Walnut Bread, 22
    Walnut Fig Bread, 106
    Walnut Ginger Scones, 86
Wheaty Cranberry Buttermilk Biscuits, 44
Whole Wheat
    Boston Black Coffee Bread, 16
    Brown Soda Bread, 10
    Carrot Oat Muffins, 60
    Crunchy Whole Grain Bread, 112
    Harvest Quick Bread, 32
    Honey Whole Wheat Casserole Bread, 108

Whole Wheat (continued)
    Irish Soda Bread, 25
    Oatmeal Honey Bread, 102
    Red Pepper Bread, 100
    Three-Grain Bread, 122
    Walnut Fig Bread, 106
    Walnut Ginger Scones, 86
    Wheaty Cranberry Buttermilk Biscuits, 44
    Whole Wheat Herb Bread, 118
Whole Wheat Herb Bread, 118
Wild Mushroom Flatbread, 154

Y
Yeast Breads
    Casserole Cheese Bread, 108
    Chili Cheese Bread, 120
    Crunchy Whole Grain Bread, 112
    Easy Mushroom Pizza, 172
    French Cheese Bread, 104
    Honey Whole Wheat Casserole Bread, 108
    Oatmeal Honey Bread, 102
    Olive and Herb Focaccia, 148
    Pepperoni Cheese Bread, 114
    Pepperoni Pizza, 150
    Pull-Apart Rye Rolls, 132
    Quattro Formaggio Focaccia, 144
    Quick Casserole Bread, 108
    Red Pepper Bread, 100
    Roasted Pepper and Olive Focaccia, 158
    Rustic Sour Cream Bread, 116
    Sandwich Bread, 99
    Sugar and Spice Bread, 110
    Three-Grain Bread, 122
    Tomato Cheese Focaccia, 170
    Walnut Fig Bread, 106
    Whole Wheat Herb Bread, 118
Yogurt Chive Biscuits, 46

Z
Zucchini Bread, 24

Metric Conversion Chart

VOLUME MEASUREMENTS (dry)

⅛ teaspoon = 0.5 mL
¼ teaspoon = 1 mL
½ teaspoon = 2 mL
¾ teaspoon = 4 mL
1 teaspoon = 5 mL
1 tablespoon = 15 mL
2 tablespoons = 30 mL
¼ cup = 60 mL
⅓ cup = 75 mL
½ cup = 125 mL
⅔ cup = 150 mL
¾ cup = 175 mL
1 cup = 250 mL
2 cups = 1 pint = 500 mL
3 cups = 750 mL
4 cups = 1 quart = 1 L

VOLUME MEASUREMENTS (fluid)

1 fluid ounce (2 tablespoons) = 30 mL
4 fluid ounces (½ cup) = 125 mL
8 fluid ounces (1 cup) = 250 mL
12 fluid ounces (1½ cups) = 375 mL
16 fluid ounces (2 cups) = 500 mL

WEIGHTS (mass)

½ ounce = 15 g
1 ounce = 30 g
3 ounces = 90 g
4 ounces = 120 g
8 ounces = 225 g
10 ounces = 285 g
12 ounces = 360 g
16 ounces = 1 pound = 450 g

DIMENSIONS

1/16 inch = 2 mm
⅛ inch = 3 mm
¼ inch = 6 mm
½ inch = 1.5 cm
¾ inch = 2 cm
1 inch = 2.5 cm

OVEN TEMPERATURES

250°F = 120°C
275°F = 140°C
300°F = 150°C
325°F = 160°C
350°F = 180°C
375°F = 190°C
400°F = 200°C
425°F = 220°C
450°F = 230°C

BAKING PAN SIZES

Utensil	Size in Inches/Quarts	Metric Volume	Size in Centimeters
Baking or Cake Pan (square or rectangular)	8×8×2	2 L	20×20×5
	9×9×2	2.5 L	23×23×5
	12×8×2	3 L	30×20×5
	13×9×2	3.5 L	33×23×5
Loaf Pan	8×4×3	1.5 L	20×10×7
	9×5×3	2 L	23×13×7
Round Layer Cake Pan	8×1½	1.2 L	20×4
	9×1½	1.5 L	23×4
Pie Plate	8×1¼	750 mL	20×3
	9×1¼	1 L	23×3
Baking Dish or Casserole	1 quart	1 L	—
	1½ quart	1.5 L	—
	2 quart	2 L	—